EDUCATION FOR
THE INNER CITY

Education for the Inner City

compiled and edited by
MICHAEL MARLAND
Headmaster, North Westminster Area Community School,
London

with papers by

TESSA BLACKSTONE
NICHOLAS DEAKIN
MAURICE KOGAN
DAVID QUINTON
MICHAEL RUTTER
MARTEN SHIPMAN
PAT WHITE
PAUL WIDLAKE

HEINEMANN EDUCATIONAL BOOKS
LONDON

Heinemann Educational Books Ltd
22 Bedford Square, London WC1B 3HH

LONDON EDINBURGH MELBOURNE AUCKLAND
HONG KONG SINGAPORE KUALA LUMPUR NEW DELHI
IBADAN NAIROBI JOHANNESBURG
EXETER (NH) KINGSTON PORT OF SPAIN

First published 1980

British Library Cataloguing in Publication Data
Education for the inner city. – (Organization in schools).
1. Education, Urban – Great Britain – Congresses
I. Marland, Michael   II. Series
370.19'348'0941   LC5136.G7

ISBN 0-435-80588-6

Printed in Great Britain by
Richard Clay (The Chaucer Press) Ltd,
Bungay, Suffolk

Contents

Preface

This book is a collaboration in a great variety of ways, and thus reflects one of the overwhelming lessons that a teacher learns from working in the inner city: collaboration is all. The text is based on a conference held at Churchill College, Cambridge, in 1979, directed by the editor, and generously sponsored by IBM (UK) Ltd. The conference itself was a response to the expressed need to bring together the work of various specialisms which contribute to an understanding of educational problems and possibilities, and to do so in a positive spirit of showing what could be, and is, achieved. The following two quotations from the conference programme set the scene:

> The problems of the inner city are receiving attention from central and local government and from voluntary organizations. It is appropriate too for business, with its interest in and concern for the stability and health of our society, to make a major contribution.
>
> IBM is already contributing to a number of programmes aimed at the regeneration of inner cities. In 1977, for example, we sponsored jointly with the Urban and Economic Development Group a seminar on 'Creating Work through Small Enterprise'. Out of this came a project, to which we have seconded an employee, to encourage investment and employment in Southwark.
>
> The schools have a key role to play in shaping our society and never more so than in the inner city. We are therefore pleased to be co-sponsors of a conference whose purpose is to emphasize the type of education suited to the special social problems of inner-city life. (L. H. Peach, IBM (UK) Ltd)

And my own introduction:

> If the inner city is to flourish, the education that serves its people must also flourish. We have seen the ever-present but mounting problems of the inner-city life gradually increase the difficulties of the education of its young people almost to a point when parents, teachers, the public – and possibly the pupils themselves – have come to regard schooling in the real inner-city areas as virtually hopeless.
>
> Most analyses of the situation have concentrated on the effect of the inner

city on the schools. This conference turns the focus the other way round, and asks what the schools can do for the inner city. It accepts that education is not only affected by its environment, but markedly affects that environment: for every teacher bewailing the impossibility of teaching inner-city children, there is a parent bewailing the impossibility of sending a child to an inner-city school; for every teacher who leaves the inner city to teach in 'easier' schools, there may be a family which leaves to send their children to 'easier' schools. Many aspects of the inner-city malaise are affected by the effectiveness of its schooling.

We intend to consider the latest facts on the inner city, the findings of the most recent research, and the relationship between the different aspects. I hope the conference will then move towards analysing the courses of action that could strengthen inner-city education – action at all levels: governmental, LEA, district, school, teacher team, and individual teacher, as well as intra-professional.

Considerable thanks are due to IBM for sponsoring the conference and giving it such strong support, both in terms of encouragement and practical help. I should like especially to thank Len Peach, Director of Personnel and Corporate Affairs; John Lewis, Manager of Community Programmes; Brian Kington, Manager of Education and Scientific Programmes; and Norman Longworth, Education and Scientific Programmes Adviser. The conference itself was ably administered by Folly Perry, Ian Leslie, Linda Parsons, and Ben Marland.

I should like to thank the conference members for their keen interest, strong commitment, and sharp questioning. Of particular value were the eight specially invited discussants: John Bazalgette, Senior Consultant, Grubb Institute; Dr Ann Brown, Child Health Physician, City and East London Health Authority; Henderson Clarke, Project Co-ordinator, Lambeth Whole-School Development Project; Martin Lightfoot, Director, Schools Council Industry Project; Sylvester Munroe, Education Correspondent, *Newsweek*, Chicago; Robert Thornbury, Warden, Sherbrooke Teachers' Centre; Roger Watkins, Deputy Director, Centre of Educational Disadvantage, Manchester; and Professor Stephen Winter, Chairman of Department of Education, Tufts University, Massachusetts, USA.

I had the privilege of spending thirteen weeks studying inner-city education in the United States of America. During that time I visited eighteen cities and one hundred schools, and met scores of interested people: parents, pupils, teachers, librarians, administrators and journalists. I am grateful to the Inner London Education Authority for granting leave of absence; the English Speaking Union for awarding me the Senior Walter Hines Page Scholarship; to my colleagues at Woodberry Down, and especially the Deputy Head-mistress, Shirley Hase, for their work at school during my absence; above all I remember warmly the hospitality, interest and knowledge of my English Speaking Union hosts and the professionals I met in the United States.

Although written by British authors, and addressing itself pre-dominantly to the British inner city, the book makes considerable reference to the USA, just as the conference from which it derives was illuminated by the participant observers from the USA, Professor Stephen Winter and Sylvester Munroe.

I also wish to express my personal and professional indebtedness to the Inner London Education Authority, for whom I have taught since 1961. There is probably no other education authority in the world that gives its teachers such support and such freedom, and faces the problems of education for the inner city with such conviction and ingenuity.

Finally, I wish to thank the colleagues with whom I have taught and from whom I have learnt; the parents, who have taught me so much; and the pupils, who reward so warmly.

M.M.

1 Introduction

Michael Marland

Like many who will read this book, I work in the middle of a true inner-city area, an extremely difficult one. Perhaps we all reckon that whichever area we happen to work in is the worst, and I realize that despite the multitudinous educational and social problems of Hackney, where I was when I prepared this book, there are even more difficult inner-city areas in Britain and the USA.

The first characteristic that strikes me about working in the kind of schools this book is about is that rarely a day goes by when you do not at the end of the day feel depressed because so many things have gone wrong or so many things have gone undone that needed doing. On the other hand probably most teachers feel like I do that hardly a day goes by when you do not come out thinking 'Well, I have done something really worthwhile; somebody has benefited today from this.' I have an awful feeling, however, that the world does not know fully what the difficulties are. The Borough of Hackney, where I worked for many years, has the most remarkable statistics. If it is good to be low, it is high; if it is good to be high, it is low. Whether it is infant mortality or psychiatric referral, reading rates or staying-on at school, Hackney manages to be whichever extremity one would not wish to be.[1] And I get the feeling that the world belabours us all for not doing what it expects us to do, but yet does not really know the state of the corridors, playgrounds, and classrooms of the schools in which we have to try to educate our children. This feeling of alienation is shared by teachers on both sides of the Atlantic.

[1] E.g. it consistently has the lowest proportion of eleven-year-old children in the highest achievement band: 13 per cent as compared with an Inner London Education Authority norm of 25 per cent; similarly, that age group's behaviour, as judged by the Rutter scale for disturbed behaviour, is one of the two worst for ILEA – indeed whereas eight divisions fall near or below the mean of 21 per cent, Hackney registers 29 per cent. Demographic figures are equally striking: in the 1971 census it had the highest proportions of one-person and very large (six or more persons) households in Greater London, and the smallest proportion of medium-sized households; the same census showed a high and increasing illegitimacy rate: 19·1 illegitimate births per 100 live births, as compared with only 8·4 nationally.

The problems in social, behavioural and attainment terms are massive. London pupils include twice as many pupils of disturbed behaviour; they include three times the national norm for one-parent families; they contain twice as many pupils with reading quotients below 80. And other inner-city areas could repeat these statistics. Yet inner cities differ one from each other, and section from section. There is no single problem faced in an inner-city school which is unique. Can there, then, be said to be a characteristic inner-city education problem? Perhaps David Quinton gives the clearest answer on pages 54 and 55. He shows that in families a single disability is not in itself a great pull-back. However, when the factors are doubled or tripled there is a sudden, indeed a dramatic, increase in the effect of the difficulties. This intensity of problems becomes, as it were, a change in quality, not merely quantity, and creates a pattern of problems that can fairly be called 'inner-city', and which require addressing with a unified approach.

In both Britain and America, though, there do seem to be signs of hope. In Britain there is rehabilitation especially under 'urban partnership'.[1] In America there are Federal funds going into these difficult areas. There are signs of people moving back, signs of self-help and community movements of various sorts, and signs of teacher stability, although not in many of the subjects that our schools are so dependent on. The public seem to think that the teaching profession is now full and stable, but forget that many of the kinds of subject teachers that are required, especially in inner-city schools, are the ones who are still in short supply.

Perhaps most interesting is the beginning of a movement that is replacing the view of bringing up children which stressed their need for suburban quiet. Movement out of the city, as Nicholas Deakin makes clear, was heavily child-orientated: 'a better life for the children'. That attitude is being reversed here and there. Admittedly most of those returning to inner Chicago, London, or Liverpool have been those whose children have grown up, the childless, or the single. However, now a few are even arguing that the city has something to offer the growing child that is denied him in the suburbs. Here, for instance, is a popular columnist writing about bringing up children:

> Suburbs may be a good place for children to 'be', but a lousy place for them to grow up . . . For the past several weeks I've talked with suburban families from Boston to Kentucky. I keep hearing parents complain that the suburb is a homeland where their children have nothing to do except be children. They are worrying whether their communities are better at preserving childhood than preparing for adulthood.[2]

[1] A scheme devised under the Labour Government in 1977 for central government to fund environmental improvements in severely depressed inner-city areas, the scheme to be administered by a partnership committee of local and central governmental interests.

[2] Ellen Goodman, in *The Boston Globe*, 31 October 1978, p. 21.

This looks like the start of a substantial change in popular attitudes, and one that will have real implication for schooling in the inner city. Thus, many of the contributors follow Tessa Blackstone and ask 'Are there not positive aspects of inner-city life on which to try to build?' If education will analyse its context, clarify its needs, work with its related professions, develop proper planning at all levels, and maintain its sensitive heart, there is plenty to build on.

The second general point, one that is also common in cities on both sides of the Atlantic, is that ordinary people have a very deep and very widespread wish for what they call 'good schooling'. There may be grounds for challenging this: their motives for wanting it, their care in defining what they mean, the very concept 'good schooling', or the practicality of what they want. There are certainly grounds for challenging the frequently held corollary of that wish, which is that there was once a golden age of schooling in the inner city just around the corner before last. But I think there are no grounds for challenging the existence in everyone one talks to in the inner city of this very strong feeling that they want something called 'a good schooling' in their cities. This seems to me a good thing, something that should be fostered, and something that should be used. Too often we in education have, in effect, conspired with politicians to use that public concern, almost to exploit it, by promising wider effects, more rapid success, and easier success than an actual professional analysis regards as reasonable. Does not this, in a way, contribute to the lack of public confidence? It is true that the British inner-city schools have not lost public confidence completely. Indeed we seem to be gaining it somewhat at the moment. However, there is an almost total lack of public confidence in all inner cities of America. Every single person one stops to talk to, a taxi driver, a person in the shops, anybody, and asks 'What do you think of the schools?', always replies: 'Hopeless; we are getting out as soon as we can', or 'We have got out already'. Whether they are right in their judgement is another matter, but the lack of public confidence is really frightening, because it is so upsetting for the pupils, the parents and the teachers. The flight to private schools which that leads to is also frightening. In the land of the 'common, public, free schools' a sixth of the population in one inner city, or a fifth, or a quarter in other cities, are actually in private schools. Without public confidence we cannot do our work. One of the themes of this book is to ask what the right way is to gain true public confidence.

The problems that the schools face if they are going to achieve this confidence are very weighty indeed. If one reads that 143 students were arrested in Los Angeles for selling drugs on the high school campus, and that although one of the boys of 15 doing this was able to buy a water bed, colour television and stereo for his bedroom, his parents had not noticed anything strange, one is reminded that these kinds of problems are not problems the schools can tackle alone. A

boy I saw in a school who came for disciplining to the deputy
principal, who I felt was such a nice, polite, well behaved, clean
looking lad, turned out to have been very properly behaved indeed:
he had asked for permission to be absent from school – so he could
go and hold up the bank with a shotgun. Unfortunately he left his
'leave of absence' chit in the bank and they caught up with him.
These kinds of problems are obviously reminders that many matters
which upset schooling and require action by schools must be seen as
wider problems requiring multi-disciplinary approaches. Thus one
of the keynotes of this book is the need for a multi-disciplinary
approach – none of us, in whichever profession we are, can go it
alone. Matters like inadequate housing, poverty, general inability to
cope with the complexities of life, cannot be faced by the schools
alone, but there is a need to define ways in which the schools can
react to them.

We cannot ignore legal and fiscal issues. For instance, until the
1979 Education Act very large authorities in Britain were unable to
alter the size of entry of their schools unless they did it across the
area as a whole. This was a legal problem which severely inhibited
professional educational approaches for planned reduction in school
size. The kind of financial situation that exists in America, whereby
the suburbs are affluent, and yet cities like Cleveland can actually
go bankrupt, poses a financial problem and a legal problem which
have to be faced together. Similarly there are population shifts which
change education. Housing patterns, after all, create a kind of segregated education which most of us try to get away from. We know
from work such as that which Nicholas Deakin writes about that the
pull of the new towns in Britain did little to improve the housing
situation in the old inner-city areas. We also know that what it did do
was take out the most firmly rooted people, those who had the
greatest loyalty to the inner-city area, and those who had the greatest
skills. Similar kinds of problems are shown in, for instance, real
estate advertisements in America. One from a suburban estate agent
in America starts: 'The buyers who want the best schools for their
children, swimming pool, large lot, warmth and charm, four bed-
rooms, two baths . . .' Interestingly, it is the attraction of the 'best
schools' which is put first. There is clearly a relationship between
housing policies and schooling which we do not seem to have begun
to work at.

I feel that many, even in the profession, have never really accepted
the urban school. Most British towns built after the war placed their
new schools on the edge of town. It seemed common sense, but in a
way that was a denial of urban-ness as a school characteristic. It is
even noticeable in many cities that the schools have very rural names.
It is only a small bit of symbolism, but I have noticed that most
schools in London have a forest, a wood or a bit of green in their
title. It seems to me that we have almost never faced up to the fact of

urban-ness and we have a kind of rural nostalgia that has gone to
the roots of all our schooling.

Finally, there is a public belief, much fostered by conservative
politicians of all political parties, that inner-city schools today have
broken from a past that was golden. Listening to parents in Britain
especially one constantly hears that the challenge is to get schools
back to how they used to be – when they were, it is claimed in
Manchester, London and Birmingham – successful for the inner-city
child.

I have come to be extremely doubtful whether, if you put like pupil
against like pupil, our schools are actually succeeding any less well
than they did in the past; indeed there is clear evidence that they are
doing better. Recent educational historians in America have begun to
be very critical of what one calls 'the by-now longstanding conventional wisdom that holds tightly to the efficacy of the American
Dream and the past glory of its sandman – the public school.'[1] 'The
sandman of the American dream' is a good description of both parts
of the legend: the social mobility of waves of immigrants and the
power of the schools to help that. The magic of the sandman never
worked. These historians[2] have doubted how much that kind of
school in the middle of the American cities at the time of immigration
was actually able to educate the immigrant masses, as legend has said
it did, into socially powerful occupations, and to contribute
substantially to population mobility. British educational sociologists
have long attacked the schooling pattern of city schools. What they
attacked has been seen as separate schooling, and they regarded the
separate selective grammar school and those euphemistically called
non-selective schools as doing little for any but the sons and
daughters of those who were already on the move upwards, or
already had some kind of well-placed establishment in the socio-
economic scale. Clearly both countries actually had comparatively
little social mobility, and clearly education has played only a small
part in it. Would it be unduly critical of the past to doubt whether
either the US or the British urban education systems actually did
much more than amplify what was already happening? Is it very
heretical to suggest that it was incredibly difficult to give more than a
minority of the large number of immigrants into American cities in
the early years of this century, or the large number of poor people in
the cities of Britain, the kind of skills that legend has suggested very
many were given? Colin Greer says the rate of school failure among
the urban poor in the US has been consistently and remarkably high

[1] Colin Greer, *The Great School Legend* (Harmondsworth: Penguin Books, 1976), p. 38.

[2] For example, David B. Tyack, *The One Best System: A History of American Urban Education* (Cambridge, Mass.: Harvard University Press, 1974); Michael Katy, *The Irony of Early School Reform: Educational Innovation in Mid-nineteenth Century Massachusetts* (Cambridge, Mass.: Harvard University Press, 1968).

since before 1900: 'United States census data for 1910, 1920, and 1930 reveal that assumptions of school success preceding social progress where it occurred are as ill-informed as most popular assumptions about the inevitability of mobility itself.'[1] Indeed, Herbert J. Gans in his foreword to Greer's book goes as far as to declare:

> The public schools of the late nineteenth and early twentieth centuries did not help poor children, but instead failed them in large numbers and forced them out of school. Indeed, the actual function of the public school was just the reverse of the legendary function; it certified the children of the poor as socially inferior at an early age, and thus initiated the process that made them economically inferior in adulthood and kept them poor.[2]

It seems pretty clear that it was the availability of various kinds of unskilled jobs that acted as a catch-all to make up where the schools of the past failed. Indeed, it seems that in the USA a considerable part of the 'Americanization' of immigrants was by means of the education of employment rather than of school. Further, this education of employment, with its associated 'night school' can claim credit for a part, probably a large one, of the educational achievement of all but the professional classes. It is not that schools make no difference: as Michael Rutter shows in Chapter 8, they clearly do; but it is the case that they have not had the effect that myth claims for them, and that, as Pat White argues in Chapter 6, the removal of an immense range of semi-skilled jobs has revealed the problems of schools.

It is asking for trouble for practising teachers such as me to say this, for the frequent reply is that one is using the argument only as a way of slipping out of the accusation of failure. However, it is a point that needs making firmly, because if we believe in the legend of the urban success of schools in the past, it puts us on the wrong track for the future. Such belief suggests that we have merely to go back to something or other – back to standards, back to basics, or back to old patterns of school organization. If, on the other hand, we accept that we have grounds for doubting the success of urban schooling in the past, the question that we face is even more serious, because we are searching not merely for a way of reverting, but for a way of creating. Schools have got to find a way of teaching the children of poor inner-city families, otherwise those children will have even less chance than they had in the days gone by.

For those of us on both sides of the Atlantic who are teachers in inner-city schools there is a task of living with constant criticism. Certainly many of us, much of the time, have our faults, but I would suggest that the jobs teachers are asked to do at the moment, particularly in inner-city secondary schools, in terms of intellectual,

[1] Colin Greer, op cit., p. 85.
[2] ibid., p. vii.

emotional, physical and organizational talents, compare with very few. If we say we have got to get better teachers, I would want to consider where are we going to get them from. In Brecht's play, *Mother Courage*, the chief character, Mother Courage herself, criticizes the commander, and when asked why she thinks he is a *bad* commander, replies: 'Because he needs *brave* soldiers, that's why. If his plan of campaign was any good, why would he need *brave* soldiers? Wouldn't plain, ordinary soldiers do? Wherever there are great virtues, it's a sure sign something's wrong.'[1] Cynical maybe, but there is a relevant truth in her point that: 'In a good country virtues wouldn't be necessary. Everybody could be quite ordinary, middling.'[2] For what is worrying to me as a head teacher is that I fear I am called upon to provide the kind of leadership in which teachers have to be willing to go not only beyond the call of duty, but beyond the call of reasonable exhaustion. I do not believe that is good leadership, and I consider that an education system in which there is no mercy for the teacher who is anything less than perfect the whole time is an education system that cannot actually work, because we are never going to get an army of soldiers willing to die for their commander; nor should we. Therefore I believe we should consider what training we require, what kind of support we require, what kind of organization we require. Possible ways forward are likely to be the result of a new synthesis, and not result merely from 'better teaching', 'more resources', 'a relevant curriculum', 'good pastoral care', etc. All these components are likely to be important, but the need is for an over-all system within which the individual teacher, team of teachers, school and community of schools, can work to help the pupils.

I would like to put the challenge in historic terms. Educators, parents, those associated professions, elected local government members have had to face various daunting challenges: the beginning of compulsory education, the creation of intellectual standards in the selective schools in the early part of this century, seeing schooling through the Second World War, the post-Newsom interest in the average and below-average child, comprehensive reorganization. These have been the great challenges and the great crusades of our predecessors. Our generation, it seems to me, faces a task just as important and just as daunting as any of those crusades of the past; a task that is every bit as difficult as the tasks of the past, every bit as difficult as the beginning of compulsory education. That is the task of ensuring that education in the inner city is effective for its pupils, and that it is at the same time education *for* the inner city. This is the challenge that our generation of people in education will be judged by in the future, and it is a more important challenge than

[1] Bertolt Brecht, *Mother Courage and her Children*, trans. Eric Bentley (London: Methuen, 1962), p. 17.
[2] ibid.

some of the ones that surface in the Press and in the educational forums. I would suggest, however, that if we are going to meet it, we have got to bring together all those who care about the health of the inner city. That is, those who care about the health of the families, the children, and the environment, the work, the education and all the other web of services, to use the phrase that Maurice Kogan coins in Chapter 9; and see how we can work together. So this book is dedicated to the question 'What can education do *for* the inner city?'

PART ONE

The Context

2   The Challenge of the Inner City

Tessa Blackstone

Introduction

Drunkenness and dirt and bad language prevailed, and violence was common reaching at times even to murder. Fifteen rooms out of twenty were filthy to the last degree, and the furniture in none of these would be worth 10 shillings, in some cases not 5 shillings. Not a room would be free from vermin, and in many life at night was unbearable. Several occupants have said that in hot weather they don't go to bed, but sit in their clothes in the least infested part of the room. What good is it they said, to go to bed when you can't get a wink of sleep for bugs and fleas? A visitor in these rooms was fortunate indeed if he carried nothing of the kind away with him . . . The little yard at the back was only sufficient for a dustbin and closet and water tap serving for six or seven families. The water would be drawn from cisterns which were receptacles for refuse, and perhaps occasionally a dead cat . . . The houses looked ready to fall, many of them being out of the perpendicular.

This quote is taken from Charles Booth's *Life and Labour of the People of London*,[1] describing London in the late nineteenth century. The general picture he gives of the poorer parts of the city are of streets strewn with garbage and houses with broken windows, and of filthy children, of hunger, cold and degradation. A similar picture is painted of Chicago in the 1920s by the early urban sociologists, whose classic descriptions of city life are still relevant today.

In a great city where the population is unstable, where parents and children are employed out of the house and often in distant parts of the city, where thousands of people live side by side for years without so much as a bowing acquaintance, these intimate relationships of the primary group are weakened and the moral order which rested upon them is gradually dissolved. Under the disintegrating influences of city life most of our traditional institutions, the church, the school, and the family have been quietly modified . . . It is around the public school and its solicitude

[1] (London, 1902–1903.)

for the moral and physical welfare of the children that something like a
new neighbourhood and community spirit tends to get itself organized.[1]

A decade later, Lewis Mumford wrote:

First the back gardens and the breathing spaces disappear ... then the
original residential areas are eaten into from within as if by termites, as the
original inhabitants move out and are replaced by lower economic strata:
then these overcrowded quarters serving as an area of transition between
the commercial centre and the better dormitory areas become in their
disorder and their misery, special breeding points for disease and crime.[2]

Writing at about the same time, Louis Wirth analysed the problem
of city life in terms of anomie and social void. 'The contacts of the
city may indeed be face to face but they are nevertheless impersonal,
superficial, transitory and segmental. The reserve, the indifference,
and the blasé outlook which urbanites manifest in their relationships may thus be regarded as devices for immunizing themselves
against the personal claims and expectations of others.' He went on
to say 'The close living together and working together of individuals
who have no sentimental and emotional ties fosters a spirit of
competition, aggrandizement and mutual exploitation.'[3] The picture
he paints is a bleak one of personal disorganization, mental break-
down, suicide, delinquency, crime, corruption and disorder.

The city has been seen as an area of deprivation and disorder by
many commentators for more than a century. This tradition
continues today. The inner city is seen as problem-ridden. Need we see
it in such stark terms? Are there not also positive aspects of inner-city
life on which to try to build? For example, it is much easier to
provide a wide range of public facilities than in less densely
populated areas. It is easier to make these facilities local and therefore easily accessible and to provide specialized services and a wide
range of choice. This is true of social services such as health and of
recreational facilities such as sport or the arts. Secondly, the multi-
cultural nature of the inner city could provide welcome variety, for
example, through different kinds of shops and different kinds of
restaurants. And most important of all it may be easier to counteract
the segmented roles described by the early urban sociologists than
they suggested. Many urban communities are stable, except when
disrupted by certain housing and planning policies, and allow for
community identification and community activities.

The characteristics of inner cities

In spite of the fact that it would be wrong to perceive inner-city areas
in an entirely negative way, there is little doubt that in contemporary

[1] R. Park and E. Burgess, *The City* (Chicago: University of Chicago Press, 1925).

[2] L. Mumford, *The Culture of Cities* (New York: Harcourt Brace, 1938).

[3] L. Wirth, 'Urbanism as a way of life', *A.J.S.*, vol. 44 (July 1938).

Britain these areas suffer from various kinds of deprivation. I wish here only to highlight some of the indices of this deprivation. Perhaps the most recent and the fullest account has been given in the inner-area studies sponsored by the Department of the Environment which were carried out in three small areas of inner London, Birmingham and Liverpool.[1]

There are certain respects in which the dimensions of the problem have changed in recent years. The most important of these is that the population has declined in many inner-city areas. Thus between 1966 and 1976 Glasgow lost 205 000 (21 per cent), Liverpool lost 150 000 (22 per cent), Manchester lost 110 000 (18 per cent), Inner London lost 500 000 (16 per cent), Birmingham lost 85 000 (8 per cent). Among the smaller cities, only Newcastle with more than 40 000 population loss (over 12 per cent) and Nottingham with 25 000 (8 per cent) loss experienced such a fall in population.[2] It might be argued that population decline in the crowded central areas of big cities is to be welcomed rather than lamented. Indeed during the 1950s and 1960s this was probably the prevalent view, but as one of the Chicago sociologists of the 1920s argued, 'when a community starts to decline in population due to a weakening of the economic base, dis-organization and social unrest follow'.[3] While not wishing to go as far as this claim, the nature of the population decline that has taken place is disturbing. A much greater proportion of those leaving have come from skilled and professional occupations leaving behind in the inner city a growing proportion of semi-skilled and unskilled people. Figures in the White Paper show that in 1971 unskilled and semi-skilled men accounted for 38 per cent of the labour force in inner Birmingham, 35 per cent in inner Manchester and 34 per cent in inner Glasgow, compared with 23 per cent nationally. Between 1966 and 1971 only 15 per cent of migrants from Birmingham, and 16 per cent from Manchester, were semi-skilled or unskilled workers.

Unemployment in many of the inner-city areas is high. There has been a substantial loss of jobs as part of the over-all economic decline of large sections of the central areas of cities. In Liverpool, for example, unemployment has risen from 4·5 per cent to 12·3 per cent in ten years while that for all Britain has risen from 3·1 per cent to 6·7 per cent. The loss of jobs in the Port and Railways on Merseyside has hit the unskilled hard. Although regional policy since the last war has brought 100 000 new manufacturing jobs to Mersey-side to offset this, they have been located on the edge of the conurbation and not in the inner city, where there has been a loss of manufacturing jobs as well which has accelerated in the last five years. The inner-area study found that approximately one in three men living in the worst areas of Liverpool was unemployed in 1975. It also

[1] Department of Environment, *Inner Area Studies, Liverpool, Birmingham and Lambeth*, Summaries of Consultants' Final Reports (London: HMSO, 1977).

[2] White Paper, *Policy for the Inner Cities* (London: HMSO, June 1977).

[3] R. D. McKenzie, in R. Park and E. Burgess, *The City*, op. cit.

found that more than half the unemployed had been out of work for more than two years during the previous five. Moreover many of these men were in their twenties and thirties, at a period in their lives when their responsibilities involving young children were likely to be greatest. The prospects for an improvement in job opportunities and a decline in unemployment are small as long as public and private investment in these areas remains low. The low level of investment is of course in part a function of past policies which advocated removing industry from the centre of cities.

The White Paper argued that 'the most characteristic single feature of the inner city is the age of its housing. Despite the extensive redevelopment and clearance of slum property since the war, there still remains a great deal of poor quality housing lacking basic amenities, not in good repair and set in a drab environment.' Even where old housing has been replaced by new, the quality of the environment of the local inhabitants may not have improved. Indeed, as everyone is now painfully aware, it may have worsened. Again past policies of planners, architects and others responsible for housing allocation have exacerbated some problems. The main indices used to measure housing problems are overcrowding, the lack of bath, inside W.C. or hot water, the sharing of dwellings and the lack of exclusive use of basic amenities. In the UK as a whole since the war there has been a substantial improvement in the quality of housing, so that we now compare favourably with many European countries. This is particularly true with regard to the amount of space in British housing. However, 20 per cent of households still lack exclusive use of basic amenities. In the worst one per cent of enumeration districts this rises to 55 per cent.[1]

In addition to the hard facts of unemployment and poor housing, researchers have identified a sense of helplessness among the population of the inner cities. The Birmingham area study found:

There is widespread lack of confidence in the area and in its government. The opinion that the area is going downhill in general . . .
There is a lack of community cohesion and in some parts of the area high level of tension between neighbours.
There is poor provision in relation to needs of such services as child care and education.
Small Heath has an unfavourable public image: this is a bad address to give when seeking a job or mortgage.

The sense of helplessness is, of course, enhanced by poverty caused by both unemployment and low wages. It is further compounded by high concentrations of ethnic minority groups, who become scapegoats for many of the problems the general population face. In turn prejudice and discrimination means that the aspirations of the

[1] S. Holterman, 'Areas of urban deprivation in Great Britain: an analysis of 1971 census data', in E. Thompson (ed.), *Social Trends* (London: HMSO, 1975).

minority group population are not met. Racial tension is heightened so that a potentially dangerous situation exists.

Although all this undoubtedly adds up to a bleak picture of inner-city conditions, it may not be the case that deprivation is as concentrated in these areas as it suggests. Using census data, Holterman asked three questions:

1. Where are the worst areas?
2. To what extent are deprived people spatially concentrated in the worst areas?
3. To what extent do areas with a high proportion of people with one kind of deprivation tend to contain people with other sorts of deprivation? That is to what extent do the worst areas overlap?.

Her analysis of enumeration districts indicated that those with high levels of deprivation are mainly in the conurbations and that those local authorities in the centre of these conurbations contain proportionately more of them than other parts of the conurbation. She also found that there is severe deprivation on the periphery of the big cities, presumably in the large post-war housing estates. Clydeside emerged as an area of particularly high deprivation. She found, however, that on single indicators the degree of spatial concentration is relatively low. Thus, to take overcrowding as an example, it would be necessary to give priority area treatment to as many as 15 per cent of enumeration districts in order to bring into the net 61 per cent of households suffering from overcrowding. When examining multiple deprivation, taking two or more indicators, she found that there are many areas where both housing deprivation and unemployment coincide but 'the spatial coincidence of these problems is far from complete'.

Past policies

This then is the challenge that has faced governments for some time. It first began to be recognized in the mid-1960s. Surprisingly perhaps one of the first official attempts to develop a response to it derived from the recommendations of an inquiry into primary education. The Plowden Report[1] published in 1967 emphasized the need to improve housing and other social services as well as proposing ways of positive discrimination in education. It suggested the identification of educational priority areas. Teachers were to be paid a special supplement to their salaries to encourage them to stay longer in schools in deprived areas, and priority was to be given in building programmes in these areas.

[1] Central Advisory Council for Education (England), *Children and their Primary Schools* (London: HMSO, 1967).

This first attempt at an area approach to deprivation was followed by the setting up of Community Development Projects (CDPs). These were announced in 1969. They involved the provision of central government resources to carry out action research in certain designated poor urban areas. They were not, however, confined to the inner city. The twelve areas included, for example, mining districts in South Wales. They were designed as neighbourhood-based experiments which were to try to involve local communities in solving the problems of deprivation and decay. At about the same time the government announced a new urban programme which was designed to channel extra resources for specific projects in the urban areas for special social need. Projects could be initiated by local authorities and voluntary bodies. They were virtually confined to social policy and included things like new day nurseries or nursery centres. The urban programme was run, perhaps surprisingly, by the Home Office as were the CDPs. The reason for this may have been the importance of race in influencing the development of an area approach. Events in the United States in the mid- and late-1960s led commentators here in Britain to raise the possibility of a similar spectacle of race riots in our big cities. Slightly before the advent of CDPs and the urban programe, Section 11 of the 1966 Local Government Act provided for special help to immigrant areas. Other schemes included programmes developed by the Department of Employment such as the Community Industry Scheme. This was set up in 1971 basically as a self-help programme aimed particularly at young blacks in certain special areas. A little later the Department of the Environment, through the 1974 Housing Act, encouraged local authorities to designate housing action areas in priority neighbourhoods to supplement the general improvement areas which the 1969 Housing Act introduced. More recently the government introduced the concept of comprehensive community programmes (CCPs) and tried this out in Gateshead. The concept involved the collaboration of central and local government, in some cases on an authority-wide basis. As such it differed from the CDPs, which involved smaller areas and outside areas and outside teams of researchers and community workers.

The amount of resources involved in these area-based policies or programmes has been small. The urban programme which is the most general and the largest, involved expenditure of less than £30 million in 1976–77 in England and Wales. Compared with total expenditure on any of the main social services which amount to several thousand millions each year, this is trivial. As such, it does not represent a very substantial commitment on the part of the government to solving deprivation through area-based policies.

Present policy

More recently in 1977, the government introduced a new initiative in the form of Inner City Partnership Schemes. These schemes involved expenditure of some £120 million a year. This is still small, although considerably greater than anything done before. The Partnership Schemes are based on a review of policy towards the inner cities which was described in the White Paper already quoted, *Policy for the Inner Cities*. The new policy rests on a number of assumptions. First, that the main policies and programmes of government must be reorientated to improve the quality of life in cities. Secondly, that more attention must be given to the economic base of the inner city. Thirdly, that better co-ordination is required in central and local government's approaches to inner-city problems. Fourthly, that resources should be concentrated on a number of key areas where the problems are particularly severe, rather than spread more thinly around a larger number of areas. These assumptions represent a departure from previous area-based policies, in particular in the importance they attach to economic questions. This is partly a reflection of the growing problem of unemployment brought about by world-wide recession, as well as the specific problems of British inner cities, and partly due to the strong emphasis placed on economic and employment questions by the reports produced by the CDPs.

The method devised to put these proposals into practice has been to set up seven Partnership Schemes in the following areas:

Manchester and Salford
Newcastle and Gateshead
Birmingham
Liverpool
Hackney and Islington
Lambeth
Docklands.

The Partnership Programmes are to last for three years in the first instance but are likely to be continued for a further period. They are run by joint committees of central and local government, chaired by a Minister from the Department of the Environment, but with representation of local industry and voluntary bodies. The aim is to develop comprehensive programmes to deal with all aspects of deprivation. However, each area will be free to develop its own unique package of proposals. In addition to the Partnership Schemes, a number of Programme Authorities[1] have been selected to

[1] North Tyneside, South Tyneside, Sunderland, Middlesbrough, Bolton, Oldham, Wirral, Bradford, Hull, Leeds, Sheffield, Wolverhampton, Leicester, Nottingham, Hammersmith.

receive extra resources. These authorities were thought to merit
special attention although they did not justify Partnership treatment. Each of them will receive between £1 and £2 million a year
from the expanded urban programme but, unlike the Partnership
arrangements, Ministers and government departments will not be
directly involved in the preparation of the programmes. The
Programme Authorities are also not being specifically invited to
make the case for increased allocation through main spending
programmes. The government admitted that the success of the
new policy depends on the main expenditure programmes, whether
in housing, education, transport or health, being adequately adapted
to give them an inner-city bias. In a period of severe public
expenditure constraint, how much scope there is for doing this is
debatable. However, the old Department of Education and Science
argument that the money left over from the school building
programme for special projects in the inner city is likely to be small
because of the commitment to provide 'roofs over heads' now carries
less weight. Moreover the decline in the school population in the
inner city should free educational buildings for community use. To
use them in this way will involve imagination and ingenuity as well as
a more tolerant attitude and better co-ordination than has existed in
the past. But in other areas such as health, attempts to redistribute
resources from richer regions to poorer regions may make it more
difficult to help pockets of inner-city deprivation within richer
regions, such as in the metropolitan area.

The last government produced a long list of possible fields for
additional expenditure. Under industry these include the provision
of sites for industrial development, making available suitable shop
premises for small businesses, including those requiring to be
reallocated, and the development of industrial improvement areas.
Under employment they include help for the Training Services
Agency in the field of adult education, assistance to the Employment
Services Agency in job creation, for example, and improvement in
the Careers Services, especially for young people. The environmental possibilities put forward are the provision of open space and
recreation areas, environmental work in connection with industrial
sites, and the purchase of boarded-up shops for conversion to other
uses. They also include remedial suggestions such as clearing up 'eye-
sores', improving street-naming, removing waste and clutter, and
measures to reduce noise. Proposals for housing include mortgage
advances to assist with house improvement (this might be a way of
helping and encouraging some skilled and white-collar workers to
stay in the inner cities), the employment of residential caretakers on
Council estates (an important way of reducing vandalism), the
provision of hostels and dwellings for single people and two-person
families, and help with alternative tenure schemes such as co-
operatives. In the social services area possible fields for extra

expenditure include additional social workers for child-care and care of the elderly, more provision of day-care for the elderly including transport to day centres, and the provision of hostels or reception centres for people without a settled way of life (such provision is desperately needed to help keep such people out of short stays in prison). Suggestions for education cover minor capital works such as the refurbishing of schools and the extension of playgrounds. They also cover the appointment of additional teachers and special literacy and numeracy programmes designed to improve educational attainment. Provision of play facilities and play leadership, and facilities for the care of the very young, including child-minding, are included. Some changes are also suggested in further education. Lastly, transport proposals include traffic management schemes to remove through traffic from residential streets, the provision of special journey to work facilities, better local access roads for industrial sites, and the improvement of street lighting, pavements and walk-ways.

If all these suggestions were followed up in Partnership and in Programme Authorities, there seems little doubt that the quality of life of the residents in these areas would be improved. However, how far it would be fundamentally changed rests on the economic circumstances of the area. If jobs continue to be scarce and incomes low, many will continue to experience a standard of living and quality of life lower than the rest of the population. In a recent paper Malcolm Wicks[1] argued that in the areas of policy covered by the Department of the Environment there was more likely to be an improvement than in health, social services or education. The Annex to the 1977 White Paper contains examples of how policies in these areas already take account of the particular needs of the deprived. For example: 'H.M. Inspectors will continue to pay special attention to inner-city schools in their local work and more generally they will give special attention to the monitoring of activities relevant to inner-city problems.'[2] Wicks rightly notes that these 'are all good sentiments but the gap between fine prose and a White Paper and a substantial impact on policies that leads to real improvement in people's lives is a large one.'

The 1977 White Paper represents a complete turn-around in policy. For many years there has been a strongly-held belief that industry should be removed from the inner city and that large sections of its population should also be accommodated elsewhere. The new towns are the most manifest representation of this approach. The large estates built on the outskirts of cities such as Liverpool. Manchester and Glasgow represent another less successful example of it. Attempting to reverse policies which have been

---

[1] M. Wicks, 'Social Policy and the Inner Cities', in M. Brown and S. Baldwin (eds), *Year Book of Social Policy in Britain*, 1977 (London: Routledge and Kegan Paul, 1978).

[2] White Paper, op. cit.

accepted for twenty or more years will not be easy. The biggest test of all will be whether industry can be attracted back into the inner city. It is, of course, debatable whether some kinds of industry should be sited close to densely populated residential areas. While meeting the goal of providing jobs, it may defeat the goal of improving the environment. The argument that it is not possible to reverse long-term economic change by the kind of intervention and encouragement proposed in the new policies certainly carries some weight. The government's industrial strategy which is concerned to increase productivity and enhance efficiency so that the UK can become more competitive may not always be consistent with bringing industry back into the centre of cities.

Research and monitoring

The last government committed itself to monitoring the Partnership Schemes. They have also instituted a large research programme covering various aspects of inner-city problems. There are some sixty-five research projects being undertaken by universities and research institutes sponsored by government departments including the Department of the Environment, the Home Office, the Manpower Services Commission, the Scottish Office, the Department of Education and Science and the Department of Health and Social Security. The projects cover a wide range of subjects, including such problems as the effects of migration on the inner city, employment problems and the education and training of school leavers. In addition to these projects financed by departments, the Social Science Research Council is considering undertaking a major research programme in this area. The importance of trying to evaluate and monitor the new policy cannot be overestimated. Some of the government sponsored research already under way which is relevant to inner cities will be of more direct use to policy-makers than others. As well as this research, projects attempting to monitor directly the effects of different types of programme are needed. We shall need to know which groups are benefiting most and how far people's behaviour is being affected. Are fewer skilled people leaving for example? Are more firms investing?

Education in the inner cities

One of the things that strikes an educationalist in reading current discussions about inner-city policy is the relatively little attention given to education. The White Paper for example makes little reference to it. The only reference in the section on 'What needs to be done', is to the wider use of school buildings. In the discussion on the 'Need to improve skills' there is no reference to education. In the section in the Annex on 'Main programmes' there is no mention of educational expansion except for nursery education. There is nothing on the curriculum at all other than the reference to HMIs quoted earlier.

Halsey[1] has lamented the failure to introduce and develop large schemes of positive discrimination. The money available has been small and it has probably been spread too diffusely. The Educational Priority Area Research findings on inner London are now well known. In those schools selected for special help, only a minority of the children could be considered seriously deprived and there are more children outside these schools who are deprived than inside them. The problem of spreading resources is partly a consequence of helping institutions rather than individuals. In the US, under federal government schemes known as Title 1, extra resources are provided for individual children whose eligibility is determined by various need criteria, rather than to institutions. Thus extra provision may be made available to a particular school but only those children who are eligible on these criteria are allowed to benefit from it. This system also has disadvantages in that it may involve separating out some children and labelling or stigmatizing them.

The methods of positive discrimination used in education perhaps need to be varied rather than relying on a single approach. It may be advisable to provide some money on an institutional basis. For example, schools with serious problems in terms of difficulties associated with their intake, problems of retaining staff, and poor buildings, may need additional resources to boost morale and improve facilities. Alternatively, it may be appropriate to provide extra resources for a particular group such as immigrants or ethnic minorities or single parents. Such money would normally be tied up in a particular programme which would then be evaluated. Again, extra resources might be provided for a particular service – for example, careers advice, where until now there has been very little attempt at positive discrimination. Lastly, there may be some advantage in providing small amounts of extra money which are unlinked to any particular institution, social group or service, but which are available for teachers and others who have a good idea which they wish to promote and try out.

Other contributors make more specific suggestions about the role of education in the inner city. They also say a great deal about the relationship between education and employment, and the transition between school and work, which is an issue of great importance. I want to raise a few more general questions about the way we might respond to the problems of the inner city and to point to the particular contribution education might make in this wider context.

---

[1] A. H. Halsey, 'Whatever happened to positive discrimination?' *Times Educational Supplement*, 21 January 1977.

Some policy problems

It has sometimes been asked whether it is right to place so much emphasis on the inner city in meeting concerns about deprivation. Many rural areas, such as parts of East Anglia, are also deprived. Similarly, the problems of the outer city are sometimes as severe as those of the centre. Some of the post-war developments on the out-skirts of big cities suffer more from lack of recreational facilities, poor transport and inadequate social services than inner areas. While recognizing this, it is nevertheless the case that in order to achieve anything politically, it is necessary to simplify somewhat. For this reason the emphasis on the inner city seems to me to have been justified. It does pose a major challenge. The inner city need not be a bad place in which to live. We have only to look at inner Paris, for example, to become aware of this. On the whole it is probably fair to say that people are not poor because they live in inner cities but live in inner cities because they are poor. As the White Paper points out 'The innermost areas, in and around the city centre itself, tend to serve as a refuge for those least able to cope in society.'

Social mix

It is vital to avoid the creation of one-class communities whether at one end of the social system, predominantly unskilled and unem-ployed, or at the other end, wealthy and middle class. If at all possible the population of local communities and their schools should approximate to that of the population nationally. Housing policy is crucial. In future we should try to avoid the mistakes of the past in which vast public housing ghettos were created. This limits choice for those living in these areas, encourages migration out of them for those who want some other form of tenure, and discourages migration into them by young people wanting to buy their homes. The new policies of rehabilitation and renovation of old housing will help, so will active housing associations, generous local authority mortgage schemes and a more progressive approach from building societies. Improvements in inner-city transport, including the reduction of transport subsidies to commuters, would help bring back skilled and middle-class people who work in the centre of cities. If all new universities had been built in the inner city instead of on sites in the country like public schools, this would have helped to provide some inner-city areas with a more socially mixed population.

Population decline

The decline of inner-city populations through migration has already been mentioned but migration is, of course, not the only cause of decline. There has been a dramatic drop in the birth-rate in the UK as a whole. In 1965 approximately 980 000 children were born; by 1975 this number had fallen to approximately 690 000. On some assumptions, the projections suggest that this figure could continue to fall to about 570 000 by the end of the 1970s. (Although 1978 has turned out to be the first year since 1965 that the birth-rate has not fallen.)

When the child population falls as dramatically as this, the government is unlikely to accept that resources can continue to be provided at the same level as during earlier periods with larger child populations. This is well illustrated by a report produced by the Central Policy Review Staff[1] which said 'rising numbers generate demands of proportionately more expenditure; static (or relatively declining numbers) do not yield proportionate savings. This asymmetry is suspect.' They go on to say that it is important that 'resources are not misallocated by default, i.e. they should not "automatically" accrue to the improvement of a particular service as a result of the accident of its having fewer clients unless this is consistent with over-all priorities.'

There are three possible responses to this situation:

1. To continue as at present, with the same number of primary and secondary schools, the same organizational patterns and the same curricula, but with the schools and the classes within them becoming smaller.
2. To undertake some marginal changes by, for example, closing a few schools, reducing the number of teachers by making redundant those who work part-time, and providing a little training on the special needs of minority-group children for teachers either at the initial training stage or through in-service training.
3. To take the decline in numbers as the rationale for major re-thinking about current resource use and how to meet needs in inner-city education.

The third of these would seem the most constructive response. To do the first would be unlikely to bring much benefit to the children concerned, although it is the least disruptive. Research evidence suggests that somewhat smaller classes are unlikely to bring substantial benefits in the form of improved pupil performance (though dramatic reductions in class size have not been adequately tested). It would mean, because of the attitude of the government to public expenditure in an area of declining population, that many new or existing needs which are of high priority outside the compulsory school sectors would not be met because primary and secondary schools would take such a high share of the reduced resources. This is the main reason why any possible benefits from smaller size are likely to

[1] Central Policy Review Staff, *Population and the Social Services* (London: HMSO, 1977).

be cancelled out by more serious disbenefits. The second policy response, while making some adjustments to new circumstances, would not be sufficient to meet the major educational needs of inner-city children in the most cost-effective way.

If the third approach is accepted, what does it entail? To give one or two examples:

1. Nursery education and day care for children under 5 might be combined in school premises, to provide a much-needed service for working mothers and others in need. The amount of capital required to meet much of this need would be small.

2. In the UK, at least, new patterns of education for those aged between 16 and 18 could be explored. Those who remain in full-time education after the end of compulsory schooling at 16 have, in the last few years, been deciding in greater numbers to prepare for their school-leaving examinations not in the schools but in the further education sector. One consequence is that, as the numbers in the age-group fall, the specialized courses provided in schools at this stage of British education become less and less viable on economic and educational grounds because the numbers following them in the different sectors are too small. Consequently it will be necessary to make some difficult decisions about whether to end secondary education at 16 in some areas, and concentrate full-time 16 to 18 education in the post-school sector. Alternatively, it might be necessary to deny young people the choice of going into full-time further education and insist that they remain at school to take courses that have traditionally been provided there.

3. The possible use of schools for adults might be explored. The idea of older secondary-school pupils and those aged over 18 working together is not a new one. It has been introduced with some success in Sweden. For example, some adults who did not complete secondary education may wish at a later age to acquire school-leaving examinations which are needed to secure higher education. Declining numbers in schools make it easier for them to be accommodated. Other adults may wish to follow non-examination courses of one kind or another in secondary schools.

4. New types of school buildings which are portable and use prefabricated materials should also be developed in order to maximize flexibility. The use of rented accommodation which can later be disposed of should also be considered, particularly at the post-secondary stage.

To achieve all this could require moving some children out of existing half-used schools into other half-used schools, thus vacating accommodation for new purposes, such as provision for the under 5-year-olds, or 16 to 19-year-olds. However, closing schools is difficult to carry out because of opposition from their staffs and the unions to which they belong, and of parents and local community groups. There are, however, bad schools which population decline could provide a useful opportunity to abolish. There are, moreover, problems in defining the appropriate criteria for closure. These need to be discussed. They should probably include the relationship between a given school and the local community and the parents, and the quality of the school's extracurricular activities, as well as more conventional criteria such as how steeply rolls are falling, the quality of the buildings, and the educational standards measured by, for example, examination results.

Non-statutory provision

Compared with other areas of social policy such as personal social services, education has made relatively little use of voluntary or non-statutory organizations to provide additional services to those provided by central and local government.

Community participation

The educational system, as with other services, has become more professionalized. While there are certain advantages in the professionalization of teachers, there are also disadvantages. There is a danger that the clients of the educational system, pupils, students and parents, will be badly served because of the growth of professional self-interest. In the inner cities, where parents and others using the services are less likely to be well-informed about their rights, and less likely to be competent enough and confident enough to challenge the professionals, this problem may be greater than elsewhere.

The more critical the public becomes of the professions, the more governments will feel the need to resist the ever-growing recruitment of vast armies of teachers, social workers, auxiliaries, etc., and the greater the likelihood that there will be a wish to make greater use of various forms of non-statutory provision. Such provision may be important. In a number of ways it may provide more choice for the consumer. It may provide services for those with special needs which cannot be easily made available by a large, bureaucratically-controlled system. (An example are the free schools which, in one or two inner cities in the UK, have been able to provide some education for children who have refused to attend ordinary schools.) In certain circumstances, non-statutory bodies may find it easier to experiment and to innovate. Voluntary provision through various organizations may also allow self-help to operate in a way that is more effective than through a professional and bureaucratic statutory system.

One of the difficulties that those seeking to make greater use of non-statutory provision face in inner-city areas is that the number of people willing to undertake unpaid, purely voluntary, community

activity is smaller in such areas than elsewhere. Many men are likely
to be manual workers doing extensive overtime, and many women
will wish to undertake paid employment to supplement their family's
income as soon as their family commitments allow them. As a
consequence neither men nor women will have the time to involve
themselves in such activities. However, high levels of unemployment
and earlier retirement should free some people to participate in part-
time voluntary work, but it requires energy and organization to tap
resources of this kind. It may be necessary for quite substantial public
funds to be diverted for this. Existing voluntary organizations might
be provided with extra funds from public sources to develop various
kinds of projects to help inner-city schools. Examples might be the
provision of additional recreational facilities, some of which would
have a strong educational element, or facilities to take school pupils
on visits outside the school, etc. The formation of new groups might
be encouraged, to develop and implement imaginative ideas both
within the schools and elsewhere in the community.

In the upper level of inner-city secondary schools, where pupils are
beginning to consider their future careers, there may be a case for
extending contacts with local industry. Local firms might be used as a
possible source of careers guidance or, more importantly, of
vocational education and work experience. Where contacts of this
kind cannot be arranged for pupils, it may be advantageous for
teachers to be in closer contact with industry in the locality of their
schools. A scheme which links Woodberry Down School in London
with IBM is an example of this. (See p. 181.) In the US a number of
interesting experiments have taken place involving private industry in
schools. Some firms have adopted particular schools and provided
them with additional resources, as well as making available employment opportunities for pupils leaving school. Many pupils in inner-
city schools will work not for the private sector but in public services
such as transport or in local authority clerical and manual jobs.
Similar contacts to those suggested above regarding the private sector
might be made in the public sector.

Even in the poor areas of inner cities many schools have valuable
facilities which lie idle for large parts of the year. The need to develop
the multiple use of schools facilities applies generally, but particularly strongly in the inner city where access to such facilities may
be difficult for large sections of the population. Opening up of
schools' facilities, particularly in such areas as arts and crafts and
sport, might in some places be associated with support being given to
the school by the local community in terms of, for example,
advertising and displays of school-children's work in local shops.
Because of problems of sharing facilities between different groups it
may be easier to close some schools and hand over the building to
the community than to provide for community use in all schools,
although this is a somewhat defeatist solution.

Ethnic minorities

Ethnic minority group children are an increasing proportion of inner-city school populations and it is vital that we put more effort into meeting their needs. There are three areas where action is required:

1. *Language policies*. Not enough has been done to provide instruction in the language of the minority group
2. *Multi-cultural education*. More provision of textbooks and other materials which recognize the cultural diversity of pupils in inner-city schools is required
3. *Teacher training*. This has often failed to take into account the multi-cultural multi-ethnic character of inner-city schools.

It is important not only to provide for minority group needs but also to consider what steps should be taken to maintain and develop racial tolerance in the indigenous population. Our minority groups are the source of desirable rather than undesirable diversity. This is the message that has to be communicated to young people. In many ways our politicians have failed and our schools must, therefore, try to make up for this failure.

I have tried to outline some of the problems that inner cities face, to describe some of the policies that have been introduced in recent years, and to point to a few things that we should be considering for the future. I have at one point been critical of the professions; at the same time I am well aware of the demands placed on those who work in inner cities, especially in their schools. We need, however, continually to encourage those who are lagging behind to reach the standards of the most dedicated and the most committed in order to meet the challenge that the inner city provides.

3   Inner-city Problems in Perspective: the London case

Nicholas Deakin

There is one feature of the city in general, and London in particular, which has been true since its Victorian heyday: it has always been a place of hope. And within the city, the inner areas have performed a crucial function in providing the opportunity for newcomers to establish themselves, and acquire the money and skills that will enable them to make their way. This function is reflected in a whole shelf-full of plays and novels: the provincial coming to London to seek his future has been a standard plot since the Elizabethans. In saying, as some critics frequently do, that people are now 'voting with their feet' against the inner city and all that it stands for is to neglect the large number of in-migrants who continue to come to London and to other major cities. While that inward migration continues (and in the case of London, in the last year for which fully reliable gross migration figures are available (1970) just under a quarter of a million people moved into the conurbation) there are reasonable grounds for believing that the inner areas will retain their vitality. But both the continued arrival of newcomers on any scale, and the willingness of existing inhabitants to stay put, depends crucially on their attitudes towards the city and the assets and disadvantages that it is seen as conferring.

Viewed from the broad national perspective, the picture seemed fairly straightforward. The National Movers' Survey, conducted in 1970/71,[1] showed (unsurprisingly) that people saw housing and employment as the most important reason for moving. But in the case of London, in-migrants differed strikingly from those moving out: the former saw jobs as the most important reason, while the

---

[1] Cited by E. K. Gilje, *Migration Patterns in and around London*, Greater London Council Research Memorandum 470 (London: Greater London Council, 1976).

latter stressed housing. (The proportions were: moving *out* of London, 48 per cent mentioned housing and 19 per cent, jobs; moving *into* London, 17 per cent gave housing and 56 per cent jobs.) In general terms, the availability of housing seems to have been a particularly significant factor in promoting departure in the decade from the early 1960s to the early 1970s, which saw such a steep rise in house prices in London and tipped the balance of economic advantage in favour of searching for housing outside London with its higher wage rates. Those entering London since this period have had to contend not only with high house prices in the owner-occupied sector and with the rapid decline in the quantity of cheap housing to rent in the private sector, but also with a rapid rise in fares, which has cut the commuters' advantage over inner-Londoners.

These are general impressions. A more detailed systematic analysis of the reason behind movement out of London is possible from the results of two social surveys – one conducted by Clare Ungerson and myself in North Islington[1] and the other by Peter Willmott and colleagues in Lambeth.[2]

The Islington study was conducted in an area of substantial housing stress. Compared with the borough as a whole, the area possessed a very low proportion of professional workers and employers or managers (3 per cent compared with 20 per cent), and twice as many unskilled or semi-skilled workers. Half the inhabitants were born in London, and half of these in Islington itself; but a quarter came from outside the UK altogether (predominantly from Eire, the West Indies and Cyprus, in that order). Though the proportion of owner-occupiers was more than twice the borough average, these were not the middle-class newcomers who have transformed other areas of Islington – the Barnsburies and Canon-buries – beyond recognition. Overcrowding and poor access to facilities underlined the problems facing the purchasers of the worn-out Edwardian villas and workman's cottages that made up the bulk of the owner-occupied stock. Half the residents of the area, how-ever, still lived in privately rented accommodation. The other major difference between the area and the borough as a whole was the higher proportion of the elderly in its population (38 per cent of residents were over 55). In sum, a typical inner-London stress neighbourhood, with a fairly standard population mix.

This makes it particularly interesting that, when asked about their attitudes to the area, 60 per cent of respondents expressed general satisfaction with it. Factors like the availability of shopping, proximity to relatives, good access through public transport and varied facilities for entertainment were singled out, in that order, as

---

[1] Nicholas Deakin and Clare Ungerson, *Leaving London* (London: Heinemann Educational Books, 1977).

[2] Graeme Shankland, Peter Willmott and David Jordan, *Inner London: Policies for Dispersal and Balance* (London: HMSO, 1977).

being particularly satisfactory. On the debit side, mention was made of a generally 'depressing and dirty' environment, the presence of foreigners (or coloured people) in large numbers, disadvantages of the area for bringing up children, and high levels of traffic (poor schools were mentioned by only 1 per cent of the sample). Asked about their accommodation, 47 per cent professed satisfaction, despite the poor over-all standards, especially in the private sector; those who objected referred to poor (or non-existent) amenities, lack of space, and damp.

Looking now at leavers, of those who had actually decided to move, 63 per cent gave housing as one of their reasons for leaving, about half of the sample specifying this as the most important of all their grounds for departure. Other reasons cited included the wish to be in country surroundings (22 per cent), to be near other relatives who had moved (22 per cent), and other reasons connected with the family (space to play, better schools) (18 per cent). Fifteen per cent mentioned job opportunities, but only 6 per cent gave it as the most important reason. Among the movers, the vast majority (two-thirds) came from the private rented sector (there was not one owner-occupier among them). Even more striking to us, was the fact that 38 per cent of those who went were born in the borough. The 'traditional' skilled working-class residents had clearly ceased to feel the close degree of attachment to their area of residence which sociologists have traditionally credited them with. The over-all conclusion that we reached was that while housing seemed to be the major consideration in reaching the decision to move, environmental factors affecting children and health were also important. And in the case of those moving to a new town, the perceived attractions of the new environment and the opportunities it provided for children seemed to weigh most heavily of all.

The findings of the Lambeth study, conducted in the following year in the Stockwell area in the north of the borough, are along broadly similar lines. Of the same questioned, 26 per cent declared their general intention of leaving the area. The main attraction of the area to those who wished to stay consisted of the access it provided to work, presence of family and friends and a general attachment, either to the area itself or to London generally. Yet, as in the Islington case, long-standing residents, even those with relatives living nearby, were if anything more rather than less likely to move. The black residents of the area – a well-established centre of West Indian settlement – many of whom owned their own homes, were, by contrast, less likely to wish to leave. Similarly, other owner-occupiers and professionals also preferred to stay. Among the working class, there was little difference in intention between those who possessed skills and those who did not.

Asked why they wished to move, most of those who wanted to go mentioned better housing (over a third were looking for a garden and a fifth for better amenities). But dissatisfaction with the local environment and local people was far more important than problems with housing. A third wanted an area which was quieter, more peaceful and with less traffic. One in eight wanted somewhere healthier. A quarter wanted somewhere 'friendlier' or with 'nicer neighbours'; one in eight, an area with fewer blacks. All those with children wanted better play facilities; and four out of ten specified an area with less crime, vandalism or violence. Few, on the other hand, had thought about the possibility of getting other jobs, even if they chose to move. 'It is clear', Willmott and his colleagues conclude, 'that most of these potential migrants wanted a "suburban" environment, in both physical and social senses of the term'.[1]

Taken together, the picture presented by these two pieces of research seems reasonably consistent with what we know from other sources. Discontent with life in the inner city appears to be general, but a good deal of it consists of a wide scatter of not very strongly felt grievances about the environment of inner areas, which are at least partly counterbalanced by a sense of the advantages that are offered by urban life. Those expressing strong dissatisfaction are mainly to be found among the 'traditional' skilled or semi-skilled white working-class ones, especially those with young children, and their concern centres particularly on the housing circumstances of the inner city, the lack of amenities and over-crowding in the private rented sector, and the lack of opportunities for house ownership. They are by far the likeliest to translate discontent into an actual decision to move. By contrast, black residents, in objectively the worst conditions of all despite a relatively high rate of home ownership, are strongly disposed to stay put. Grievances about the delivery of social services, and anxiety about the availability of jobs, neither of which emerged very strongly from the two studies, would probably figure more prominently if either area were re-surveyed now. Concern about crime and vandalism, which featured prominently in the Lambeth study, would also probably come through more strongly. In one respect, at least, the picture conforms to that traditionally found in migration studies: the elderly are less inclined to want to move than those in the early stages of family life. But the desire to move covers virtually the whole spectrum of skills, diminishing only at the top of the range, among the professionals who have elected to live in the inner city.

The last group are, of course, among the main examples of the in-migrants discussed earlier, although (unlike the majority of respondents in the National Movers' Survey) their main motive in moving into an inner borough is likely to be the convenience and accessibility of housing in the squares of Islington or 'oases' (as Willmott terms them) of Lambeth, rather than the job opportunities cited as the

[1] ibid., pp. 117–21.

major reason for the move to London. On the whole, they have had a bad press. Afflicted by the sociologists with the hopelessly mis-leading label of 'gentrifiers', caricatured as 'Camembert colonialists' by young community workers (equally middle-class, but of a different generation) who have followed them into the areas where they have chosen to live, and blamed for a whole variety of heinous sins – making unreasonable demands on the local health service, undermining the professional status of teachers and social workers, manipulating traffic and environmental schemes to the benefit of their property values, even subverting the local Labour party.

In truth, the middle-class residents who have returned to certain neighbourhoods in inner London are a symptom, not a cause of the present state of the inner city. Their presence there represents a stage in the post-war development of the London housing market and illustrates the way in which opportunities for home ownership have reappeared in certain inner boroughs, where the housing had previously been predominantly rented. In part, these opportunities resulted from deliberate acts of policy by successive governments: general encouragement of owner-occupation through changes in the taxation system; the parallel discouragement of letting by private landlords, and the attempts to improve the environment of the inner city through the wide distribution of improvement grants on both an individual and an area basis. At the same time, the fact that the cost of buying houses rose so rapidly and to such a level in these areas under the impact of competition sealed off this opportunity to all but the comparatively wealthy not very long after it first became evident – although the presence of a substantial minority of working-class owner-occupiers in these boroughs, many of them from one or other of London's ethnic minorities, shows that it was not only the mis-called 'gentry' who saw and grasped the opportunity. But the major point to stress is that the return and continued presence of an element of the middle classes demonstrates that, given the right circumstances, inner London remains an attractive place for families to seek homes.

Given these clues to the kind of expectations that people have formed about the inner city, how far is there scope within the existing policies of local and central government for satisfying them?

It has to be conceded straight away that past planning policies have cut sharply against the grain of the kind of preferences expressed in the two surveys cited earlier. In the post-war period, planners have been concerned, in the broadest sense, with rationalizing and tidying up the urban environment. The main problems of conurbations like London were to be solved by decongestion: that is, by lowering the residential densities of the heavily populated areas of inner London, banishing 'non-conforming industry' from these areas, promoting greater freedom of movement for traffic and providing additional open space. The accelerated thinning-out of the population of these areas then thought to be essential in order to achieve these objectives was to be obtained by planned outward migration to new communities outside the Green Belt. In practice, all these objectives have been frustrated. Densities have indeed declined; but the movement of population that has been the major factor in bringing this about was spontaneous and unplanned, and occurred far more rapidly and on a larger scale than anyone could have anticipated when the Abercrombie plans for the future of London were being drawn up at the end of the Second World War.[1] The housing form in which reconstruction mainly took place – the now notorious tower blocks – have mostly proved to be disasters in human terms. London's post-war blocks have not yet reached the stage of being demolished (like Birkenhead's) or sold off for derisory sums (like Liverpool's); but it has been universally accepted that they are unsuitable for family occupation. The space saved by building upwards has not in practice been used to any real advantage, and the prohibitive cost of inner-city land is likely to ensure that this state of affairs continues. Finally, the major road-building programme envisaged in the original Abercrombie plan never took place, despite the steady rise in car ownership in London over the post-war period (the 1971 Census showed that more Londoners drove to work than went by bus or rail). Popular opposition to large road schemes has now reached a pitch sufficient to ensure that they are virtually impossible to construct.

Meanwhile, London's traditionally secure employment base has begun to erode with alarming rapidity – a process arguably accelerated by planners' traditional disapproval of inner-city industry. London has lost a third of its manufacturing jobs over the past fifteen years, a loss only partly compensated for by gains in the office and service sectors. Within the service sector, there is evidence that those industries that are welfare oriented are growing, while profit-oriented commercial services are beginning to decline. Simultaneously, there has been a marked reduction in the number of clerical jobs available within the office sector. The combined effect of these processes has been to diminish sharply the number and range of job opportunities available to the unskilled. At the same time, the advantages that London has always enjoyed in terms of higher income levels have largely disappeared, and the poor, especially in the inner-city areas of the capital, find themselves absolutely as well as relatively disadvantaged.

The London economy has enjoyed one substantial, if unanticipated, bonus in the post-war period: it has been able to draw on new sources of labour – first, the immigrants from the New Commonwealth who entered the country in large numbers in the late 1950s and early 1960s, and settled principally in London; and

[1] Patrick Abercrombie, *Greater London Plan* (London: HMSO, 1945).

secondly, women, who have entered the London labour force in substantially increased numbers over the last decade. But even with this
unexpected assistance, a trinity of largely intractable problems persist:
high rates of unemployment, especially in the inner London employment exchange areas (four of which have had rates persistently
in double figures); a continuing problem of low pay, especially in
the increasingly important service sector, and compounded by
London's higher cost of living; and, most intractable of all, a mis-
match between the jobs remaining in the inner areas and the skills
required to do them, and those possessed by the resident work force.
It is this last problem which accounts for the paradox of large
numbers of unemployed (around 150 000 in London as a whole
throughout the winter of 1978/79) but skilled jobs available and un-
filled, and employers contemplating leaving London as a result.

If post-war planning policies have, by common consent, been little
short of a disaster, housing policies have not been much more successful. However, three substantial achievements must be recorded
on the positive side of the ledger. The slums, in the sense of
the substantial element that remained in London's housing stock at
the end of the war which was beyond the reach of any conceivable
attempt at rehabilitation, have been cleared. Secondly, a very
substantial number of new dwellings have been constructed – half a
million since the end of the war. Coupled with the decline in
population, this has meant that since 1976 there has been a nominal
surplus of dwellings over households in London, in the strictly
arithmetical sense. And thirdly , there has been a steady rise in the
proportion of housing in London in owner-occupation, the tenure
which all studies show the majority of people prefer for themselves.
However, the quality of much of the new housing built for owner-
occupation has been poor, its cost has been high, and very little of it
has been built in the inner areas. This means that the growth there in
the owner-occupied stock has been at the expense of the privately
rented sector, and hence of those who have previously lived in rented
housing.

These successes, partial rather than complete, have been counterbalanced by three crucial failures. First, there is the question of the
basic approach to new housing, through large-scale comprehensive
redevelopment schemes, and building upwards to save space. The
upshot of this approach, as Alice Coleman has recently pointed out,
has been to create 'a paradox of simultaneous high rise, low density
and overcrowding'.[1] Of the high-rise blocks themselves, enough has
probably already been said, not least by architects themselves.
Confronted by the all-too-visible evidence of their profession's
failures, the *Architects Journal*'s Louis Hellman counsels his colleagues
to adopt one of the following alibis:

[1] Alice Coleman, 'Planning and land use', *Chartered Surveyor* (December 1978), pp.
158–63.

(1) point out that you have never designed any yourself;
(2) blame the politicians;
(3) say that they are all right for people with no children, homo-sexuals and Trappist monks;
(4) assert that posterity will prove them to be right.[1]

Judging by the experience of those who have actually lived in them, it seems somewhat unlikely that the final alternative will carry much conviction, when posterity's verdict is delivered.

Secondly, there is the inflexibility of the public housing sector, artificially segregated in London into thirty-four different sub-systems, each operated by the separate authority concerned according to their own rules, and with minimal movement between them. Within each system the style of management is often restrictive to an almost ludicrous degree, as the National Consumer Council's recent study of tenancy agreements demonstrated.[2] More generally, there has been a standard assumption in London housing policy, common to all authorities, that the principal objective is to cater for the standard two-parent family, of the standard size (2·4 children, or whatever the demographers in their not entirely infallible wisdom may prescribe). The public sector has in consequence failed, by and large, to cater for other groups in need who do not fall into this pattern: single people, both young and old, who make up an increasing proportion of the inner-city population; single-parent families, and large families from ethnic minorities.

Nor, thirdly, has enough attention been paid until recently to flexibility within the housing market as a whole – both at the point of entry, where the private rented sector has traditionally provided the first port of call, and subsequently, especially now that the restriction on job opportunities has increasingly come to mean that changing jobs necessarily implies moving home. The erosion of the private rented sector, which has declined from 45 per cent of the London housing stock in 1961 to 27 per cent in 1976, coupled with the steeply rising cost of the remaining housing to rent, has not only knocked out the first rung in the housing ladder but has reinforced a pattern that has steadily established itself over the past fifteen years: if you wish to move up, in terms of housing quality and job opportunities, you will have to reconcile yourself to moving out.

It seems clear from the evidence of the studies already cited, and from other sources, that this is the crux of the issue. Most of the Islington and Lambeth respondents were trading off their expectations of improved housing circumstances against the attractions of the inner city (which still largely retained their force for them), and had come to the more or less reluctant conclusion that they would

---

[1] Louis Hellman, *Architects Journal*, 22 December 1978, p. 1179.
[2] National Consumer Council, *Tenancy Agreements Between Councils and their Tenants* (London: National Consumer Council, 1976).

have to surrender the latter in order to obtain the former. But if they could obtain access to better housing within the inner city, in a more satisfactory environment, the balance might well shift the other way. There are good grounds for supposing that a shorter move, combining the perceived advantages of the city with gains in housing terms (effectively, more space and home ownership) might be seen as the most attractive option of all. For the old attachment to a specific locality seems largely to have lost its force, surviving mainly in the form of sentimental gestures upon appropriate occasions, like the Jubilee street parties, taken up and perpetuated by the newest immigrants to the inner city, the young middle-class squatters, most impermanent of all its residents. The obliteration of the familiar landmarks – and, too often, the original street patterns as well – by comprehensive redevelopment, and the social changes that have resulted from the arrival of a new inner-city population – the ethnic minorities and the almost equally visible (and stigmatized) young – seem together to have snapped the links that held a previous generation to a small cluster of streets which they identified as their own neighbourhood. Now, it is the hard practical advantages of city life that still have the capacity to persuade its inhabitants to consider remaining, not the sentimental or nostalgic associations of any particular area. Hence the importance of the provision of well-paid and accessible jobs, as a major factor in the balance sheet of individual decision-taking. And here, too, lies the importance of the new initiatives that government is taking as part of their inner-city policy, and their likely effectiveness.

The first point that should be made about the policy perspective adopted in the 1977 White Paper[1] is that it is genuinely new, and needs to be recognized as such at the outset. Previous central government statements have treated inner-city issues as residual problems, to be regretted but only to be resolved, if at all, in the context of broader policy priorities. Such measures as have been adopted have been either frankly palliative (like the urban programme) or experimental (like area management, or Community Development Projects – the experiment that got away). As a result, the authors of the White Paper correctly observe, 'too little attention has been paid to the economic well-being and to the community life of the inner areas, and the physical fabric in some parts is badly neglected or decayed' (para 2). The conclusion that Ministers drew from this analysis was that 'the time has now come to give the inner areas an explicit priority in social and economic policy' (para 3). This priority is to be secured by a partnership between all the public agencies concerned: 'at the end of the day', the White Paper states 'both central and local government will be judged by their willingness to implement new priorities, to make funds available, to change policies and to adapt their organizations.'

[1] *Policy for the Inner Cities*, Cmnd 6845 (London: HMSO, 1977).

Ambitious objectives indeed; but in my personal judgement the inner-city programmes so far set in motion do not measure up to them. It can be argued, as Peter Shore, the Secretary of State then responsible, has done, that it is far too early to judge performance over so short a time-span, given the ambitiousness of the goals. 'No responsible person', he said at Harrogate in September 1978, 'can take up a defeatist attitude at this early stage of our efforts to redress the effects of long-standing policies which have only accelerated the decline of inner areas. Our new policies deserve support; they cannot have an impact immediately. It will be a long haul. But they must be given a chance to have an effect.'[1] But eighteen months is long enough to observe (and even judge) the beginnings of a pattern; and, as in the case of all new initiatives which receive rather more than their fair share of publicity, a number of critics are beginning to make themselves heard.

Discarding, for the moment at least, the mere vulgar abuse of the 'inner-city bandwagon' variety, it is possible to identify three strands of criticism. The first concentrates on the efficiency of the administrative arrangements set up to implement the government's new initiatives. In a penetrating analysis of the machinery of Partnerships, Lady Sharp (former Permanent Secretary at the Ministry of Housing and Local Government) has singled out two particular weaknesses in the approach so far adopted: a failure of central government to achieve an equal degree of commitment from all the departments involved; and a confusion of roles between central and local government, in which the strengths of the divisions of responsibility in the existing system are sacrificed to over-close control from the centre, with no appreciable gain in efficiency to compensate for the loss.[2] The second strand of criticism is more fundamental. Rupert Nabarro and Ian McDonald have recently (1978) analysed four of the initial Inner Area Programmes[3] and reached the conclusion that Partnerships have failed to face up to the key role of central government both as a provider of resources and in setting the policy context. They argue that unless there are substantial modifications in government's approach and the level of commitment that government departments are prepared to make, the prospects of real change are not great. In the case of Liverpool, the sums allocated to the economy in the 1979/80 Urban Programme (£4m) amount to less than the unemployment benefit paid out in the city in a single week. Nabarro and McDonald also criticize what they call 'the continuation of the rather sterile McKinsey/Bains approach to local government management'; they point to the absence of any

---

[1] Speech to Annual Conference of Chartered Surveyors at Harrogate, 26 September 1978.

[2] *Estates Times*, 6 October 1978.

[3] Rupert Nabarro and Ian McDonald: 'The urban programme, will it really help the inner city?', *The Planner* (November 1978), pp. 171–3.

reference to groups in special need, such as immigrants; and they lament the fact that so little money is being devoted to the voluntary sector and more experimental initiatives. They end by calling for 'a firmer framework', and a stronger lead from the Department of the Environment.

Then there are the criticisms of the content of inner-city policy, which has tended to date to consist of a straightforward attempt at reversing those existing policies whose failure has been sufficiently demonstrated. Thus we have all local authorities urged, by Ministerial circular, to adopt a changed attitude towards inner-city industry; and a greatly reduced emphasis in central government's priorities on planned out-migration. One difficulty about this approach has been the extent to which the relationship between new initiatives, introduced to support it, and existing policies appears to have been neglected. An example that stands out immediately is the extent to which the new emphasis on the importance of retaining manufacturing industry in inner-city areas may conflict with the equally important goal of improving the inner-city environment in order to retain the existing population and attract newcomers. Clearly, satisfying the needs of manufacturers for improved communications will involve road construction and improvements of the kind that have already been sufficiently shown to be intensely unpopular. A parallel problem is the extent to which an inner-city policy based on economic regeneration led by the creation of new jobs for the unskilled and semi-skilled could conflict with meeting preferences in the area of housing, which is, as the evidence presented earlier suggests, of particular significance in affecting intentions to stay in the city.

To other critics, the whole concept of an inner-city policy is misconceived. One member of the Greater London Council recently argued that

> a respectable case exists for accepting the dismal truth that manufacturing industry may never reinvest in Dockland and inner-city areas, unless it is propped up permanently by heavy state and local subsidies. So why not turn these windy, desolate areas into public amenity space? In short, grass it over, sell off publicly owned land to the best bidders and let business enterprise take its natural course.[1]

Joe Rogaly of the *Financial Times* has gone further. His argument is quite simply that 'the decay and disintegration of our inner cities has not gone far enough. We should do everything we can to speed up this process; all talk of resuscitation should be replaced by a more down to earth consideration of what people really want'.[2] The alternative proposed by those who advance this line of argument is to

---

[1] Roland Freeman, 'Is inner city renewal a lost cause?', *Investors Review*, 10 November 1978, pp. 19–21.

[2] Joe Rogaly, quoted in David Wilcox and David Richards, *London the Heartless City* (London: Thames Television, 1977) p. 111.

abandon the concept of government intervention altogether and allow the forces of 'natural' regeneration full play. Two strands of argument are distinguishable here. The first takes the line that much of the blame for past failure lies at the door of the planning system, and sees the solution either in the wholesale abandonment of planning controls, or at least in a selective experiment, either in lifting certain of what are seen as the more irksome restrictions (fire and building regulations and the constraints they place on small industry are often cited), or in selecting a particular location (the London Docklands?) as a 'no go' area for the purpose of planning and other restrictions. In the vacuum created in this way the entrepreneur will flourish and small craft industry take root and grow. The second line of argument sees a major source of difficulty in the way in which public sector housing, increasingly the dominant tenure in inner-city neighbourhoods, has frustrated the desire of inner-city residents for control over their own environment. The entire public housing stock (in the extreme form of the argument) should be handed over to the existing residents. Alternatively, as much as possible should be sold off or transferred to a more flexible form of tenure – housing co-operatives, for example.

The exasperation that lies at the root of many of these arguments is understandable, and is well summed up by Alice Coleman. The presumed death of the inner city is not accidental, she suggests: rather, we have murdered it

> by providing 30 years of lavish spending on new housing, new roads and new open spaces. Now we are asked to compensate for this crime by providing *more* lavish spending on *more* new housing, *more* new roads and *more* new open spaces. Is not the invitation to intensify these counter-productive processes merely an invitation to more intensive murder?[1]

However, it is at least arguable that the once-for-all withdrawal of the state (in its various forms) from its involvement in the inner city is likely in the long term to create more problems than it solves. The alternative would be to adopt a far more flexible style of operation, based on the recognition that the problems of the inner city are complex, and the relationship between different aspects of these problems not yet fully understood. Many of the difficulties that we now face are the result of adopting an over-simplified approach in the past. Some key examples of the inflexibility of past practice are: the rigid separation of land uses imposed by planners; rigid boundaries set up between different sectors of the housing market, exemplified in the inability of the system to cope with changing needs; and the compartmentalization of the activities of different institutions working within the same small geographic areas. This is perhaps particularly striking in the case of schools, where Robert Thornbury has recently referred to the teachers' 'ostrich-like

[1] Alice Coleman, op. cit.

unconcern about the need for a total urban strategy';[1] but it is also prevalent in a number of different but equally significant areas. For example, Graham Lomas has argued that one of the main reasons for the current plight of the inner city is that national economic policy has been insufficiently sensitive to the particular needs of the inner-city population.[2] This argument applies with particular force in the case of London, whose growing economic difficulties have been exacerbated rather than helped by the continued operation of the government's regional policy. Another important failure has been the inability, or unwillingness, of government to respond constructively to the attempts of the inhabitants of the inner city to become more closely involved in the decisions that directly affect them.

These past failures may appear to reinforce rather than refute the case for abandoning the attempt at direct intervention. However, the lesson that I, at least, would draw from them is not that co-ordination of activity is impossible – merely that it is difficult and time-consuming to achieve in practice. Using the tools that are available – especially in the planning and housing field, where past experience suggests (if often negatively) that they can have a powerful impact – but in a more systematic way, still seems preferable to abandoning the struggle. However, experience since the war does strongly suggest that if interventions are to be effective in a positive way they should be made selectively. And if such an approach is to succeed, it will need to be squarely based on sustaining and developing the positive attractions that the inner city has for a large proportion of its inhabitants, and for potential newcomers.

To distil (and oversimplify) the evidence presented earlier, the main attraction of the city could be broken down into four elements: accessibility, opportunity, variety and security. However, these qualities will appeal to different people, in different ways and at different stages of their lives. Policies based on them will need to take account of this diversity when striking a balance between alternative priorities.

Accessibility, first of all, implies obtaining the crucial first foot-hold in the city, and relates particularly to provision in the housing field. The crucial step here is to restore access to relatively cheap housing that will serve as the first port of call for newcomers and the children of existing residents striking out on their own. Some such measures are already in operation: key-worker schemes; ready access systems providing local authority housing on a first come first served basis. But while cheap housing (often meaning housing thought to be unlettable by any other means) can be tolerable for a short time, without family pressure, it rapidly ceases to be bearable as a sense of alternative possibilities develops and disposable income increases.

[1] Robert Thornbury, *The Changing Urban School* (London: Methuen, 1978), p. 210.
[2] Graham Lomas, 'Inner London's future: studies and policies', *The London Journal*, vol. 4, no. 1, May 1978, p. 102.

The second and equally important step is therefore to increase the range and variety of housing available to inner-city residents with moderate incomes, and in particular housing for owner-occupation, the preferred tenure of a large majority, as the Southwark study demonstrates.[1] Here a variety of schemes already in the course of being introduced may help: both those that help to bridge the gap between available income and cost of housing (low-start and option mortgage schemes) and those that reduce the cost of the property itself (homesteading). But these schemes need to be reinforced both by increasing the amount of funds available for house purchase (and ensuring that they are available throughout the inner city) and by increasing the amount of new housing for sale. If private developers cannot be persuaded to build in inner areas, local authorities (or even, in certain circumstances, intended purchasers) can be encouraged to build themselves. Finally, movement within the public sector needs to be made easier, by modifying qualifications for entry into the system, increasing opportunities for transfer and by encouraging the introduction of experiments in housing management.

Opportunity relates, in the first instance, to the availability of jobs – always the inner city's strong point in the past, and the predominant factor in drawing newcomers. The loss of staple manufacturing industry has been a severe setback for the inner city: measures are needed that will restore the attractiveness of the inner areas both for those seeking work and for employers. The current emphasis on the revival of craft industry is welcome, both in that it is being conducted on a human scale, and in its concern for the value of the product; but the hundreds of new jobs created in this way do not measure up to the scale of the problems now confronting London, with 150 000 unemployed. Similarly, the job creation schemes, devised as a temporary expedient for rescuing the young unemployed from the dole queue, have their uses in the short-term, but by their nature cannot make any lasting impact on the problem. The longer-term emphasis should be expected to be fourfold: first, persuading a significant proportion of technologically advanced industry to locate on inner-city sites; secondly, stepping up the provision of training facilities available to inner-city residents, and linking them more effectively with current efforts to equip school leavers with the essential skills in numeracy and literacy; thirdly, a more flexible approach to part-time employment which recognizes the growing significance of women in the inner-city workforce and makes more effective provision of supporting services; and, fourthly, improvement of the distribution network and transport facilities generally, whose deficiencies have been cited by manufacturers as one of the major reasons for leaving London. Two other areas of potential

[1] E. Fernando and B. Hedges, *Moving out of Southwark* (London: Social and Community Planning Research, 1976).

significance are experiments with workers' co-operatives, and initiatives designed to 'link' large firms with smaller ones, on the basis of providing advice and assistance in the early stages of operation. This is a form of help that may be particularly relevant in the case of businessmen from ethnic minorities. The experience of the Small Business Administration in the US suggests that this approach could help to provide a much needed source of extra employment for inner-city ethnic minorities, who have proved to be particularly vulnerable to unemployment.

Variety is the third factor, and perhaps the most problematic. Once upon a time, social mix was considered a sovereign virtue, and as such one of the major attractions of the inner-city environment. Now this attraction appears to have evaporated with the credibility of the planners who were its main advocates. Practical experience suggests that to set out to produce a balanced and stable social mixture in any given population is likely to turn into a particularly frustrating pursuit of a particularly evasive will-o'-the-wisp. More-over, more recent evidence suggests that it is in any case only a minority of the existing and potential future population who see social variety in a neighbourhood as a positive attraction – most of them, for what are humanly understandable if not always wholly laudable reasons, prefer to live in close proximity to what they would regard as their own kind of people. Ethnic minorities, on whom integration, often in a crassly one-sided definition of the term, has been enthusiastically urged by the majority, have often tended to find the concept threatening rather than reassuring. If variety in social composition of urban neighbourhoods is to be achieved on terms that all concerned find acceptable, it is likely to be as a consequence of other policies – the creation of a wider range of accessible jobs, the introduction of a more flexible housing policy – rather than as a separate and distinct exercise in its own right. Moreover, it will need to embrace not only a variety of social and ethnic groups but also a mixture of age groups. One of the disturbing features of the contemporary inner city is the tendency (which stood out in sharp relief in the Islington study, as in earlier investigations)[1] of the population to polarize around two extremes, in terms of age: the young single households and childless couples, and the elderly. This points to the importance of retaining the allegiance of young married couples at the stage at which they are beginning their families. Here, the importance of providing a variety of services, public and private, stands out as particularly important – variety in this case implying both access to a range of facilities of good quality and choice within services. Education, health and the social services are all areas where the needs of the inner-city consumer require particular attention. One basic prescription for action is to attempt the reverse of what has happened in the health service in inner London – that is, to use such

[1] Nicholas Deakin and Clare Ungerson, op. cit.

leeway as has been created by population decline not only to improve the quality of the service (rather than as has happened in the health service, to redirect resources elsewhere) but also to provide scope for trying alternative forms of service delivery.

Security is the fourth significant factor. This element directly affects only a minority of inner-city residents, but in a peculiarly important fashion. Leaving aside the attraction of anonymity conferred by the sheer scale of cities, which can be attractive to the young at what David Donnison calls the 'lair' stage, when they first live by themselves in the city,[1] two groups have a particular concern with security: the elderly, and ethnic minorities. Both groups have latterly come to see their security as being under threat in Inner London: indeed, the former, on occasion, have tended to see the latter, as the visible symbols of change, as part of the threat to their own position. Fundamentally, this leads back to issues of housing policy: insensitive allocation systems that leave old people high and dry, out of reach of the kind of informal neighbourly protection still provided by older urban areas. Successes in providing additional inner-city employment, if and when they occur, will also help by cutting down the numbers of unemployed teenagers relying on casual crime to make a living. But, like all fundamental solutions, these ones tend to leave an immediate problem unsolved, and there is little doubt that it is one very strongly felt by the groups affected.

I have stressed the need for a more flexible approach to inner-city policy, based on the information we already have about people's preferences. The suggestions in the concluding part are no more than that: they are not intended to add up to a coherent programme. Still less have I addressed the central issue of resources for such programmes and how they should be allocated as between the various initiatives proposed. But it may be worth stating, as a concluding proposition, that whatever approach is adopted, we ought to be clear on one thing at least: we are never going to 'solve' the inner-city problem, as such. The disparities in the distribution of power and resources that cause inner-city problems have deep roots in our current social system, which are unlikely to be grubbed up in the foreseeable future. On the other hand, I believe that it is possible to make significant progress in addressing the worst of the problems and that we will do so faster if we see the inner city as a place with many positive virtues, providing an environment for living and working that could be unsurpassed in the range of choices and opportunities that it can provide. The city can still be, as it has traditionally been, a place of hope; the essential thing is to ensure that this hope is justified for all its inhabitants, not just a fortunate minority.

[1] D. V. Donnison, *The Government of Housing* (Harmondsworth: Penguin Books, 1967).

4 Family Life in the Inner City: myth and reality

David Quinton

When we consider the problems of the inner city we are part of a long tradition of concern among professionals and administrators with the conditions of life of urban and metropolitan families. This concern has always been prompted by a mixture of compassion for the disadvantaged and fear of social disorder and breakdown. Speaking of conditions in Manchester in 1842 Cook Taylor observed that 'the rich lose sight of the poor or only recognize them when attention is forced to their existence by their appearance as vagrants, mendicants or delinquents.'[1] In 1976 the Caloustie Gulbenkian Foundation, prompted partly by the recent disorder in many American cities, sponsored two conferences on education and the urban crisis,[2] and now we are discussing what we can do about city problems.

There seems to be ample justification for this. The statistics persistently and consistently point out that there are higher concentrations of adverse living conditions in urban areas. There is more crime, vandalism and delinquency; there are more low-status and single-parent families; there is more psychiatric disorder, and so on. Many studies have shown the relationship between these factors and various educational and behavioural problems in children. Thus, low social status, large family size and overcrowded conditions have consistently been shown to relate to delinquency, to poor attainment and to behavioural difficulties.[3] Since the concentration of certain of

[1] R. Glass, 'Urban sociology in Great Britain', in R. E. Pahl, *Readings in Urban Sociology* (Oxford: Pergamon Press, 1968).

[2] F. Field, *Education and the Urban Crisis* (London: Routledge & Kegan Paul, 1977).

[3] R. Davie, N. Butler and H. Goldstein, *From Birth to Seven: a Report on the National Child Development Study* (London: Longman, 1972); M. Rutter and N. Madge, *Cycles of Disadvantage* (London: Heinemann Educational Books, 1976).

these adverse inner-city characteristics (the proportion of poor or
low-status households, for example) is increasing in many areas, it
seems logical to suppose that behavioural and educational problems
will also increase. But the relationship between various disadvantages
and the behaviour and development of children are not as straightforward as they sometimes seem. Families with problems are not
necessarily problem families. Disadvantaged areas do not necessarily
have high rates of delinquency. Schools in similar areas can have
markedly different amounts of difficulty.[1] This does not mean that
the roots of these problems do not lie primarily in social disadvantages, or that we should not remove these, but it does mean that we
need to be careful about our assumptions concerning the connection
between disadvantage and children's difficulties or capabilities. We
may mistakenly blame social disadvantage for school problems when
on occasions the blame should lie with the school. We may expect
lower attainments from children from disadvantaged homes. We may
presume that adverse effects may follow from setting our expectations for these children too high.

There have been many studies of inner-city family life: some
concerned with the problems of multiply-disadvantaged families,[2] or
with abnormal development in deprived areas,[3] and others with
social class differences in patterns of child-rearing.[4] However, in
order to look at the contribution of the city itself to various family
difficulties, comparative studies of urban with other environments
are necessary. There have been a number of important contributions
of this kind both in America[5] and in Europe,[6] but these studies are
limited either in the extent of their information on children or of
information on family life. Our own research comparing one Inner
London borough and the Isle of Wight was designed to examine

[1] M. J. Power, R. T. Benn and J. N. Morris, 'Neighbourhood, school and juveniles
before the courts', British Journal of Criminology, vol. 12 (1972), pp. 111–32; M. L. Rutter,
B. Maughan, P. Mortimore and J. Ouston, Fifteen Thousand Hours: Secondary Schools and
their Effects on Children (London: Open Books, 1979).

[2] W. L. Tonge, D. S. James and S. M. Hillam, 'Families without hope: a controlled
study of 33 problem families', British Journal of Psychiatry, Publication No. 11 (1975); H.
Wilson and G. W. Herbert, Parents and Children in the Inner City (London: Routledge &
Kegan Paul, 1978).

[3] For example, D. J. West, Present Conduct and Future Delinquency (London:
Heinemann Educational Books, 1969); D. J. West and D. P. Farrington, Who Becomes
Delinquent?, Second Report of the Cambridge Study in Delinquent Development
(London: Heinemann Educational Books, 1973).

[4] J. Newson and E. Newson, Infant Care in an Urban Community (London: Allen &
Unwin, 1963); J. Newson and E. Newson, Four Years Old in an Urban Community
(London: Allen & Unwin, 1968).

[5] D. C. Leighton, J. G. Harding, D. B. Macklin, A. M. Macmillan, and A. H.
Leighton, The Character of Danger (New York: Basic Books, 1963).

[6] M. Kastrup, 'Urban–rural differences in 6-year-olds', in P. J. Graham (ed.),
Epidemiological Approaches in Child Psychiatry (London: Academic Press, 1977); N. Lavik,
'Urban–rural differences in rates of disorder', in P. J. Graham (ed.), op. cit.

family, social and environmental factors associated with children's behaviour problems in school and with psychiatric disorder. The two areas were chosen because they were radically different environments: the one, part of a 'decaying' inner city; the other, a settled area of small towns.

It is often pointed out that although such data may reflect the lives of representative samples of families, they deal with just two geographical areas. The London borough investigated is in the middle range of inner London areas in terms of various social problems. It has a number of features which parallel the circumstances of families in the inner areas of other cities but there are also clear differences. London, for example, does not have the problems of adult or youth unemployment to anything like the extent that some provincial cities do. The Isle of Wight similarly has a number of features which distinguish it from other small town areas. The importance of the holiday industry in the island's life and economy is an obvious example. From this it is sometimes argued that the value of such a comparison is limited because the areas are atypical. It is true that these considerations mean that generalizations about city and small town life cannot be made, but it is quite incorrect to imply either that the nature of the area affects the conclusions that can be drawn concerning the interrelationships between social factors and children's problems, or that other areas might be chosen which are somehow more representative. This is the first myth or assumption we need to dispose of. There is no such thing as a typical inner city or a typical inner-city family. The same is true of small town areas. Cities have more of certain problems than other areas and more families are affected by these, but the patterns of association between disadvantages are different in different urban areas and the rates of particular adverse circumstances vary quite substantially between cities.

Nevertheless the accumulation of statistics sometimes leads to a stereotype of a city family which might be summarized as follows. Inner-city families are often large, poor and of low social status. Many of them are headed by single mothers or unemployed fathers. They live in poor quality or overcrowded conditions or on anonymous new housing estates. Stable, supportive working-class communities have been decimated by disruptive housing policies and by the out-migration of the more skilled and more competent. The families that remain are either the disadvantaged and feckless remnant of these communities, in-migrating problem families or minority ethnic groups forced by discrimination into the decaying areas. In these circumstances children are growing up poor and unstimulated with resulting low educational attainments and disruptive behaviour. School problems are exacerbated by the alienation of parents and children from the school system. As the children get older they drift into vandalism and petty crime, they find it hard to get work, have children early and often, and create a cycle of disadvantage.

The comparative study

The inner London–Isle of Wight Study was designed to compare family patterns in different environments and to investigate how these relate to a variety of educational, behavioural and psychiatric problems.[1] A two-stage strategy was followed. First, the total populations of 10-year-old children in each area were screened for possible behavioural problems at school, using questionnaires filled in by teachers. In addition, all children were assessed using group tests of reading and non-verbal intelligence. On the basis of this screening, samples of children were randomly selected to represent both the general population in each area and groups of children with particular educational and behavioural problems. The parents of these children were then interviewed on a wide range of topics concerned with the children's behaviour, family interaction and relationships, social contacts, and so on.

Both official statistics and data from the study confirm that the London borough has more of the adverse characteristics associated with family disadvantage. Thus there are more low-status, one-parent, large and overcrowded families; more children in care; more in-migrants from outside the UK; much less home ownership and many more homeless families. Consistent with expectations arising from this concentration of disadvantage, the London children are twice as likely to have psychiatric problems and to have behavioural difficulties at school. The case therefore seems clear: more social problems, more children with disorders (see Figure 4:1). Paradoxically, however, differences between the areas are not strongly reflected in a range of family patterns which might be expected to connect these two sets of facts.[2] Thus, within the family there are no differences

[1] M. L. Rutter, B. Yule, J. Morton and C. Bagley, 'Children of West Indian immigrants: III. Home circumstances and family patterns', *Journal of Child Psychology and Psychiatry*, vol. 16 (1975), pp. 105–24; M. Rutter, B. Yule, D. Quinton, O. Rowlands, W. Yule and M. Berger, 'Attainment and adjustment in two geographical areas: III. Some factors accounting for area differences', *British Journal of Psychiatry*, vol. 126 (1975), pp. 520–33; M. Berger, W. Yule and M. L. Rutter, 'Attainment and adjustment in two geographic areas: II. The prevalence of specific reading retardation', *British Journal of Psychiatry*, vol. 126 (1975), pp. 510–19; M. L. Rutter and D. L. Quinton, 'Psychiatric disorder: ecological factors and concepts of causation', in H. McGurk (ed.), *Ecological Factors in Human Development* (Amsterdam: North Holland, 1977).

[2] For details of interviewing methods and measurements, see M. Rutter and G. W. Brown, 'The reliability and validity of measures of family life in families containing a psychiatric patient', *Social Psychiatry*, vol. 1 (1966), pp. 38–53; G. W. Brown and M. Rutter, 'The measurement of family activities and relationships: a methodological study', *Human Relations*, vol. 19 (1966), pp. 241–63; D. Quinton, M. Rutter and O. Rowlands 'An evaluation of an interview assessment of marriage', *Psychological Medicine*, vol. 6 (1976), pp. 577–86.

in the frequency of parent–child interaction or communication, no differences in maternal warmth towards the children, no differences in
the amount the parents expect the children to do in helping round
the house, or the amount of control they exert over what they are and
are not allowed to do (see Table 4:1). In much the same way the
similarities in marital relationships and family patterns between the
two areas are much more striking than the differences. Thus, a similar
number of mothers are working; the average amount of warmth
expressed by wives about their husbands is the same; the amount of
wives critical of their husbands is the same; couples share daily conversations to much the same extent; husbands help around the house
to much the same extent; families on the island tend to go out slightly

Figure 4:1   **Psychiatric disorder/deviance in the Isle of Wight (IOW) and
inner London borough (ILB)**

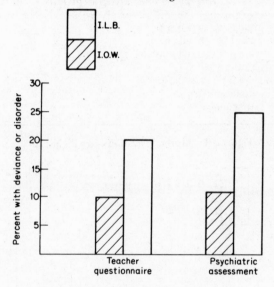

Table 4:1   **Parent–child relationships**

	ILB	IOW
Warmth of mother (mean)	3·7	4·0
Play interactions weekly (mean)		
Mother	6·7	6·9
Father	5·1	5·2
Conversations weekly (mean)		
Mother	3·2	3·7
Father	2·7	3·1
Expectations (mean)	18·1	18·2
Prohibitions (mean)	13·9	13·9

more together but on the whole the level of joint leisure in both areas is quite high. There is a small but significant difference in the quality of marital relationships but the great majority of marriages in both areas are without noticeable problems (see Table 4:2).

In addition, two common assumptions concerning the reasons for problems in the city are not supported by these data. First, although it is true that the London borough is one which has been subject to much redevelopment and to a fall in skilled job opportunities, the idea of a consequent excess of socially isolated or unsupported families is not true. The amount of contact with, or support from, relatives is exactly the same in both areas and the vast majority of

Table 4:2   Marital relationships

	ILB	*IOW*
Mother working in past two years (%)	63	62
Warmth of wife to husband (mean)	3·4	3·3
Wife moderately or markedly critical (%)	20	21
Daily conversations (%)	60	59
Husband helps little in the house (%)	26	29
Frequent joint leisure (%)	42	56
Marriage rating (mean)	2·3	1·9

Figure 4:2   Mother's relationship with her kin

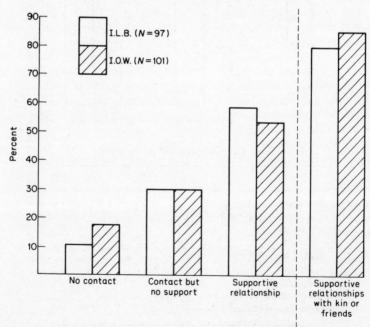

mothers have supportive relationships either with relatives or friends or both (see Figure 4:2). Community change and environmental turnover may have something to do with increased family difficulties in London but the connection is not simply through an increase in social isolation due to the destruction of neighbourhoods. There are many more social isolates in the cities but isolation is not characteristic of families. Multiple-problem families have often been shown to lack support or social contacts or to have poor relationships with kin.[1] However, this seems linked to psychological problems associated with adverse personal histories rather than to lack of potential support as such. Secondly, there is no evidence that selective in- or out-migration is directly responsible for the increased rates of children's problems. It has been suggested that data such as ours can be explained by the fact that 'happy families move out'.[2] This is not the case. In a separate four-year follow-up of families in this area it has been shown that the selective out-migration of families with less disturbed children has not occurred. Nor is the in-migration of problem families an explanation. The rate of disorder in children of in-migrants from other parts of Britain is no higher than that of children born and bred in London of London parents. Moreover, the parents of indigenous children received into care are not significantly more likely to be in-migrants than parents in the general population.[3] Finally, it is known that the semi- or unskilled are not over represented among in-migrants to this area from other parts of Britain.[4]

The question of the effects of in-migration of families from the new commonwealth is important. They certainly suffer more social disadvantages than the indigenous families but there is no evidence that they bring more family disturbance with them. This is discussed below.

In many ways then the patterns of family relationships in this part of London are remarkably similar to family relationships on the Isle of Wight. A number of common assumptions concerning the explanations for the higher rates of children's problems have been shown to be inadequate. Yet the London borough has many of the characteristics of disadvantage common to inner-city areas, and these are known to relate to children's educational and behavioural problems. Moreover, the children in this London area do have more of these problems. We need, therefore, to explain the nature of the connection between area indicators of disadvantage, family life and children's development.

[1] H. R. Schaffer and E. B. Schaffer, *Child Care and the Family* (London: Bell, 1968); H. Wilson and G. W. Herbert, op. cit.; D. Quinton, 'Parents with children in care. I. Childhood experiences and current circumstances', *Journal of Child Psychology and Psychiatry* (forthcoming).

[2] C. Ward, *The Child in the City* (New York: Random House, 1978).

[3] D. Quinton, 'Parents with children in care', op. cit.

[4] E. K. Gilje, *Migration Patterns In and Around London*, Greater London Council Research Memorandum 470 (London: Greater London Council, 1976).

The limitations of official statistics

The first point that needs to be made concerns the limitations of the conclusions that can be drawn from area-based statistics. It is often assumed that because a particular neighbourhood is shown to have high rates of various disadvantages, such as poor housing, individuals of low social status, one-parent families, etc., that there will be a high proportion of low-status single-parent families in poor housing. A number of intervention policies have been based on the identification of deprived areas using such statistics in this way. However, the assumption that such areas contain multiply-deprived families has generally been shown to be wrong. For example, the inner-area study of Lambeth[1] examined the relationship between housing provision and family income. It is commonly assumed that the poorest families are the poorest housed but this proved not to be the case. Overcrowding was related to family size but not to income. Other indicators of basic amenities showed no relationship between income level and housing provision, nor were single parents worse housed than two-parent families. This finding has also been reported in Bethnal Green.[2] The overlap of housing problems with other disadvantage varies from area to area. In this case it is probably particularly affected by the high proportion of local authority housing.

The evidence suggests that even in multiply-disadvantaged areas the proportion of multiply-disadvantaged families is relatively small. Conversely, a number of multiply-disadvantaged families live in areas which are not deprived on the evidence of area statistics. This is recognized by the authors of the Liverpool Inner Area Study who conclude after a careful analysis of census data that

> even in the worst areas the proportions of the resident population in the age, family, social or racial groups most at risk of deprivation are quite small. In virtually no area is the majority of the population actually deprived according to any of the indices of personal, family and social character. The only common form of deprivation shared by the majority of the population is their physical environment and, possibly in some instances, the quality of their housing. In particular the proportions are too small and the areas too large for any conclusions to be drawn about the incidence of multiple deprivation meaning the extent to which a person or family is experiencing a range of different problems. Finally, a large proportion of even the most concentrated indices are to be found not in the worst areas but scattered in other parts of the city.[3]

---

[1] Department of the Environment, *Inner Area Study, Lambeth: Poverty and Multiple Deprivation* (London: Department of the Environment, 1975).

[2] L. Syson and M. Young, 'Poverty in Bethnal Green', in M. Young (ed.), *Poverty Report 1974* (London: Temple Smith, 1974).

[3] Department of the Environment, *Inner Area Study, Liverpool: Social Area Analysis* (London: Department of the Environment, 1977).

Two points arise from this. First, that identifying concentrations of families with problems on the basis of area statistics will generally not be successful. This is clearly shown in relation to Educational Priority Areas by the analysis of the inner London survey by Barnes and Lucas, who demonstrated within designated areas most disadvantaged children were not in EPA schools, but even within such schools most children were not disadvantaged.[1] Secondly, statistical association between area indicators of disadvantage and such problems as delinquency or child disorders can lead to premature causal assumptions. Errors of this sort can arise as Robinson has shown in his discussion of the ecological fallacy when the area indicators of disadvantage do not apply to the circumstances of the individuals who are exhibiting the particular problems.[2]

Nevertheless, it is not the case that numerous studies show direct relationships between all kinds of inner-city problems and children's behaviour and attainments? Yes they do, but these findings need to be put in perspective. Although we now know a good deal about the general correlations between multiple disadvantage and the various problems, we know much less about the processes linking particular disadvantages with the various difficulties of children. Moreover, the kind and extent of overlap of adversities can vary quite considerably between different populations and areas and we know little about the effects of particular combinations of disadvantages. We are certainly not in a position to draw direct causal conclusions from correlations between disadvantages and problems.

Some of these points can be illustrated with our own data. First, in terms of examining general relationships we were able to see whether the adverse factors highlighted in other studies also occurred in our two populations. Secondly, we could examine the effects of the overlap of disadvantages, and thirdly, we could examine whether the differences between the two areas in the rates of children's problems could be explained in terms of these adverse factors, or whether some other city processes seem to be operating.

First, our data do confirm many of the relationships found in other studies. Thus, children's behaviour problems in both areas are related to a number of family adversities such as low social status, overcrowding, large family size, the child having been in care, parental psychiatric disorder and criminality, and marital discord.

The second issue concerns the effects of the overlap between the adverse factors. It has been pointed out that area indices of disadvantage do not tell you the extent to which disadvantages overlap. However, it is apparent that this is of major importance in our

[1] J. H. Barns and H. Lucas, 'Positive discrimination in education: individuals, groups and institutions', in T. Leggatt (ed.), *Sociological Theory and Survey Research* (London: Sage Publications, 1974).

[2] W. S. Robinson, 'Ecological correlations and the behaviour of individuals', *American Sociological Review*, vol. 15 (1950), pp. 351–7.

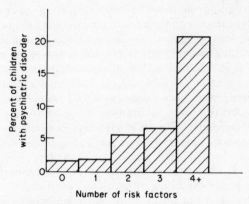

Figure 4:3   Multiplicity of risk factors and child psychiatric disorder

understanding of their effects on family life and child development. It has seldom been possible to look at the effects of isolated stresses. More usually the approach is to take account of the interrelationships between stresses by some statistical procedure. For example, the National Child Development Study has shown that various housing variables have an effect on attainment even when other disadvantages are controlled.[1] However, although this type of analysis shows whether the adversity has an effect over and above other stresses it does not show whether the stress has an effect entirely on its own.

We considered this point using the data from the comparative study. In order to look at this, an index of psycho-social disadvantage was constructed, using the variables mentioned above (see Rutter and Quinton, 1977).[2] We then separated out those families with no adverse factors, those with only one, those with only two, and so on. The results were illuminating. The children with only one risk factor, with only one truly isolated stress, were no more likely to have psychiatric problems than those with no risk factors at all, but when any two stresses occur together the risk goes up no less than fourfold and with even more stresses occurring together, the risk increases further still (see Figure 4:3). The central point here is that an interactive effect occurs – that is, the combination of chronic stresses provides much more than a summation of the effects of separate factors of disadvantage considered singly. This has important implications in terms of social policy since a reduction in the overlap of stress factors could have considerable beneficial effects in the long term.

The third point concerns the extent to which the differences in the rates of children's problems between the two areas can be explained by the excess of family adversity in London (see Figure 4:4). The psycho-social adversity index was again used for this analysis. Over

[1] R. Davie, N. Butler and H. Goldstein, op. cit.
[2] M. L. Rutter and D. L. Quinton, op. cit.

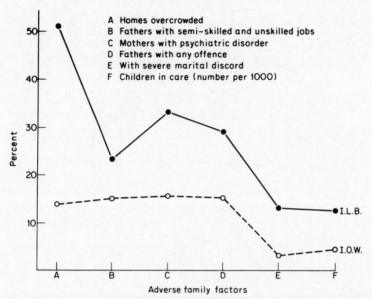

Figure 4:4   Adverse family factors in the Isle of Wight (IOW) and inner
London borough (ILB)

half of the London children were exposed to two or more of these adverse circumstances, compared with less than one-fifth of those on the island. A standardized comparison of the two areas was made: that is, the question was asked if the amount of disadvantage was the same in both areas, would any difference in the rate of children's disorders remain? As Figure 4:5 shows, when such a standardized comparison is made, the difference between the two populations virtually disappears and is no longer statistically significant.

The important conclusion from this stage of the analysis is that behaviour problems in primary-school children in inner London can be largely explained by certain adverse factors operating through the family and, conversely, these factors have similar implications in other reputedly more favourable environments. It is not necessary to invoke any notion of the operation of special direct city processes to explain the differences between the areas.

These analyses raise the question of the mechanisms through which adverse factors have an effect on the family and therefore on the child. Our knowledge here is much less certain. This is both because many stress factors are indicators of an increased risk of family problems but not indicators of family problems themselves and also because stresses do not have a constant impact. As has been shown, the increase in the number of stresses has more than an additive effect. On the other hand, it is known that certain protective factors operate which can ameliorate the effects of adverse

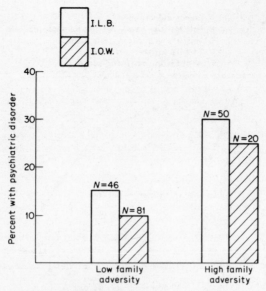

Figure 4:5   Child psychiatric disorder in inner London borough (ILB) and
the Isle of Wight (IOW) standardized for family adversity

circumstances.[1] This means that identifying 'at risk' children or
families or areas on the basis of indicators of disadvantage can lead
to premature conclusions about the probability of particular family
problems. In addition, notions of the importance of a particular
correlation in explaining a particular behaviour or educational
difficulty can lead to premature causal explanations and more
seriously to labelling based on the knowledge of the adverse
indicator.

Social class provides a good illustration of these points. Numerous
studies document the correlation between low social class and all
manner of physical, educational and psychological problems.[2]
However, when other disadvantages are controlled, social class is
only weakly and inconsistently related to children's behavioural
problems.[3] The relationships remain more consistent when

[1] M. L. Rutter, 'Protective factors in children's responses to stress and disadvantage',
in M. W. Kent and J. E. Rolf (eds), Primary Prevention of Psychopathology, vol. 3
Promoting Social Competence and Coping in Children (Hanover N. H.: University
Press of New England, 1979).
[2] For example, Central Advisory Council for Education (England), Children and their
Primary Schools (The Plowden Report), vol. 2 (London: HMSO, 1967); J. W. B.
Douglas, J. M. Ross, W. A. Hammond and D. G. Mulligan, 'Delinquency and Social
Class' (British Journal of Criminology 6, 1966); R. Davie, N. Butler and H. Goldstein,
op. cit.
[3] M. L. Rutter, J. Tizard and K. Whitmore (eds), Education, Health and Behaviour
(London: Longman, 1970).

educational attainments are considered, but these again are much stronger when concurrent stresses such as large family size are present.

The extent to which membership of one class increases the risk of other problems also varies by geographical area. Thus, for example, social class is not related to an increased risk of maternal psychiatric disorder on the Isle of Wight, but it is in London. Similarly, although there are fewer middle-class families in Scotland and although Scottish children have somewhat lower non-verbal intelligence scores, reading attainments in Scotland are known to be superior to those of English children.[1] Whether this is due to educational or family factors is not known, but it illustrates that the connection between indicators of disadvantage and family or children's difficulties is by no means constant.

Research evidence does seem to be accumulating which suggests that many of the educational problems correlated with low social status are related to variations in the quality of a linguistic environment that the child experiences.[2] Nevertheless, this should not lead us to assume that children from the homes of semi- or unskilled parents are generally subject to inadequate stimulation or to other deprivations. Although general social-class differences in parenting styles are apparent, it has to be remembered these are often not characteristic of most working-class homes. This is demonstrated both by our own and by the Newsons' data. Among their families, although a host of statistically significant social-class differences exist, there are no differences for the 4-year-old children in their mothers' responsiveness to demands for attention. The majority of parents in all social classes enforce their views by smacking; there are no differences in maternal warmth towards the children; half of the unskilled fathers rate high on interaction with them. Thus, although social-class differences do exist, these should not blind us either to the variations within classes or to the similarities across classes, or lead us to premature conclusions about the significance of these differences. Many theories exist as to why social-class differences occur and what their effects on children are. It must be realized that our knowledge of the mechanisms linking social class and particular problems is much less certain than our knowledge of the general implications of the overlap between these, social status and other adverse factors.

The implications of more family disadvantage in the inner city have been discussed. Two questions remain. First, why are there more disadvantages in inner-city areas? Secondly, what contributions can schools make to ameliorating their effects?

[1] J. W. B. Douglas, J. M. Ross, W. A. Hammond and D. G. Mulligan, op. cit.; R. Davie, N. Butler and H. Goldstein, op. cit.

[2] M. Rutter and N. Madge, op. cit.

Why is there more family adversity?

As has been shown the adverse effects of inner-city life on children's behaviour can almost entirely be explained in terms of factors operating through the family. No distinct city processes need to be invoked. This, however, is not the case for the adults.

Certain factors such as the greater proportion of semi- or unskilled parents or the differences in housing circumstances are clearly due to various processes in the development of cities. Whether these are inevitable characteristics of city life has not been demonstrated. Similarly, the greater number of large families may be explained through the association between family size and lower socio-economic status, although the reasons for this association remain obscure. However, certain other factors, including ones which may affect family interactions and child development directly, seem to be attributable to adverse city processes, although the ways in which these adverse processes operate remain remarkably elusive.

Maternal psychiatric problems may be taken as an example. Such problems are twice as common in the inner London area as on the Isle of Wight. Now it is generally the case that studies of samples of psychiatric patients have shown a strong association between depression or neurosis and marital and family problems. This is also true in our study. Where marital relationships are poor, the majority of mothers have psychiatric problems both on the island and in inner London. However, a more important fact is that there is a considerable excess of such psychiatric problems in London mothers in the absence of marital difficulties or less satisfactory family relationships. Thus 24 per cent of women in this area in satisfactory marriages nevertheless have psychiatric problems. Some clue concerning the possibility of additional city stresses acting upon adults is given by the association of disorder with social class. On the Isle of Wight there was no association between social class and psychiatric problems in women. Thus increased psychiatric problems are not necessarily a correlate of low social status. Further, there was no area difference in the prevalence of depression in women whose husbands had non-manual occupations. Thus depression is not an inevitable consequence of city life. In London, however, depression was much commoner in working-class women and it was only in this social group that the rate of psychiatric disorder was higher than on the Isle of Wight. The reasons for the increase in disorder in working-class mothers are not yet known but the data suggest that some additional city factors may be operating. What these factors may be is unclear at present. A number of common assumptions about family life in the city have been considered earlier. These fail to explain maternal disorder, just as they fail to explain children's problems. Thus the increase in difficulties for mothers is not related to patterns of selected migration or to lack of community support.

The environment

However, I have yet to discuss the most obvious way in which the city is different from the small town and that is the environment itself. It is necessary to ask whether differences in this explain the differences in individual family problems. The assumption that such environments are somewhat more stressful is commonly made. For example, Milgram has hypothesized that many city behaviour patterns are due to greater information overload in cities[1] and Ward has suggested that a higher level of competence may be needed to handle the city.[2] The fact that inner-city environments are often seen as unpleasant is frequently taken as evidence that they are harmful, but it is important that these two notions should be kept distinct. An unpleasant environment should be changed regardless of whether it has adverse effects or not, but an unpleasant environment does not necessarily cause social problems.

There are a number of problems in investigating the effects of the built environment on the individual and the family. These include the difficulty of taking previous housing and personal history into account as well as considering the ways in which cultural factors affect vulnerability to stresses.[3] Nevertheless, the evidence that the built environment itself is a markedly harmful feature of city life is not clear-cut. For example, psychiatric problems in adults have not generally been shown to relate to environmental circumstances, and do not do so in the present study, nor do they change when environments are improved.[4] Housing styles do not generally appear to affect psychological functioning in the absence of other stresses. It is true that certain environmental features, such as overcrowding, are related to various family problems but this is usually in the context of other overlapping disadvantages. Thus living in flats is not consistently related to adult psychiatric problems[5] but rates are higher for mothers in high-rise blocks.[6] We have yet to produce convincing evidence of direct links between wider environmental variables and the increase in adult psychiatric problems or marital difficulties in urban areas. However, the possibility remains that other features of housing are more important than the nature of the dwellings them-

[1] S. Milgram, 'The experience of living in cities', *Science*, vol. 167 (1970), pp. 1461–8.

[2] C. Ward, op. cit.

[3] D. Quinton, 'Cultural and community influences on child development', in M. Rutter (ed.), *Scientific Foundations of Developmental Psychiatry* (London: Heinemann Medical, 1980).

[4] E. H. Hare and G. K. Shaw, *Mental Health on a New Housing Estate*, Maudsley Monograph No. 12 (Oxford: Oxford University Press, 1965); G. Taylor and G. Chave, *Mental Health and Environment* (London: Longman, 1964).

[5] N. C. Moore, 'Psychiatric illness and living in flats', *British Journal of Psychiatry*, vol. 125 (1974), pp. 500–507.

[6] N. Richman, 'The effects of housing on pre-school children and their mothers', *Developmental Medicine and Child Neurology*, vol. 16 (1974), pp. 53–8.

selves. Thus, Brown and his colleagues[1] have shown that stress, such as threatened eviction or loss, have an effect on maternal psychiatric state. The critical environmental variable may thus be a perceived lack of control over individual circumstances rather than the physical characteristics of the area itself. This feeling may have been exacerbated in recent years by the rapid change in the environment both in the physical sense and in terms of visible population changes, especially with the influx of black families. However, it is extremely unlikely that any straightforward relationship between environment and developmental problems exists. For example, wide variations in rates of deviance are often found in similar physical environments.[2] Nevertheless certain environments such as the Piggeries in Liverpool do seem to have become inimical to habitation. Situations such these have been linked by Newman and others to features of design such as the lack of defensible space or of semi-public areas where safe, informal contacts might be established.[3]

At present the evidence suggests that there are stresses in life in inner London which relate to the increase in maternal psychiatric problems but the nature of these stresses is not well understood. The relationship with social class indicates that city stresses only have an effect in the absence of adequate resources. Material resources are clearly important here but they are not the only ones. For example, Brown's study shows that working-class women in a similar inner-city area are subject to more acute and more chronic stresses than middle-class mothers. However, they are only more likely to succumb to these by developing psychiatric problems if they are further stressed by the presence of pre-school children, or especially if they lack an intimate, confiding relationship with a husband or boyfriend.

From the point of view of the child, however, family values and relationships seem to be the variables which most strongly mediate the effects of the physical environment and the child's view of it. Thus, in the recent study of five capital cities by Lynch, the children in the poorest environment (Mexico City) were the most content with it and those in the best (Melbourne) were the least satisfied. This was related to parental attitudes. Mexican parents had come to the city because they saw advantages in it for their children, particularly from an educational point of view. The Australian parents felt themselves

[1] G. W. Brown, M. N. Bhrolchain and T. Harris, 'Social class and psychiatric disturbance among women in an urban population', *Sociology*, vol. 9 (1975), pp. 225–54.

[2] A. P. Jephcott and M. P. Carter, *The Social Background and Delinquency* (Nottingham: University of Nottingham, 1954); A. Edwards, 'Sex and area variations in delinquency rates in an English city', British Journal of Criminology, vol. 13 (1973), pp. 121–37; M. J. Power, R. T., Benn and J. N. Morris, op. cit.

[3] W. L. Yancey, 'Architecture, interaction and social control', *Environment and Behaviour*, vol. 3 (1971), pp. 3–21: O. Newman, *Defensible Space: People and Design in the Violent City* (London: Architectural Press, 1976).

to be in underprivileged circumstances and they communicated this
negative attitude to their children.[1]

Families with problems and problem families

So far I have discussed some general features of family life in one
inner-city area, the greater amount of disadvantage there and the
consequences of the overlap of adverse factors. The emphasis so far
has been on how this relates to various problems. It is essential, however, to consider the extent to which even multiple disadvantage
places children at risk, since one common confusion which needs to
be disposed of is that between families with problems and problem
families. Take our own data first: the overlap of family problems is
strongly related to child psychiatric disorder, yet over three-quarters
of the children in families with four or more adverse factors had no
psychiatric problems. In Britain as a whole, about one in six children
lives in conditions of extreme social disadvantage, characterized by
poverty, poor housing and family adversity,[2] yet nearly half of these
children are well adjusted and one in seven has some kind of out-
standing ability. In the Newson study mothers in all social classes
valued their children equally and over two-thirds of unskilled fathers
tell their children stories regularly.[3] In general the majority of even
the severely disadvantaged parents manage to bring their children up
in happy and secure homes.

Disadvantage and disturbance in children of West Indian parentage

A particularly good example of the variations in the implications of
social indicators of disadvantage can be given by considering the
West Indian born parents and their children in our study.[4] As has
been shown in many other investigations, these families are much
more likely to be large, to be in shared housing and to have low-
status occupations. These two latter disadvantages are almost
certainly connected with racial discrimination. Nevertheless, this
level of disadvantage means that the families have more of some of
those adverse circumstances which relate to disturbance in indigenous children. However, in other respects the patterns of family
adversity are not the same. Some adverse factors such as maternal

[1] K. Lynch (ed.), *Growing up in Cities* (Paris: UNESCO Press, 1977).

[2] P. Wedge and N. Prosser, *Born to Fail?* (London: Arrow Books, 1973).

[3] J. Newson and E. Newson, *Four Years Old in an Urban Community*, op. cit.

[4] M. L. Rutter, W. Yule, M. Berger, B. Yule, J. Morton and C. Bagley, 'Children of
West Indian immigrants: I. Rates of behavioural deviance and of psychiatric disorder',
Journal of Child Psychology and Psychiatry, vol. 15 (1974), pp. 241–62; M. L. Rutter, A.
Cox, C. Tupling, M. Berger and W. Yule, 'Attainment and adjustment in two geo-
graphical areas: I. The prevalence of psychiatric disorder', *British Journal of Psychiatry*,
vol. 126 (1975), pp. 493–509; W. Yule, M. Berger, M. L. Rutter and B. Yule, 'Children
of West Indian immigrants: II. Intellectual performance and reading attainment',
Journal of Child Psychology and Psychiatry, vol. 16 (1975), pp. 1–18.

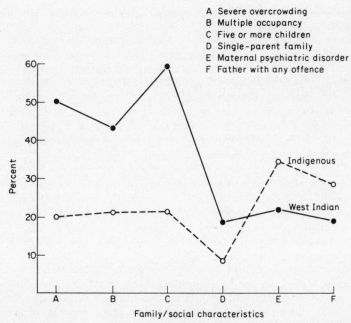

Figure 4:6   Family/social characteristics of West Indian and indigenous families

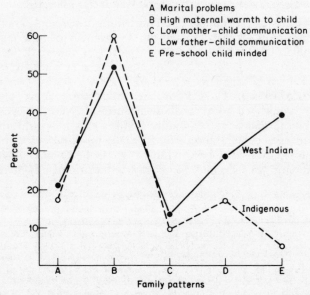

Figure 4:7   Some family patterns among West Indian and indigenous families

psychiatric problems or fathers' offences against the law are somewhat less common in the West Indian families (see Figure 4:6). Similarly in certain aspects of family relationships the two groups are
much the same and in others there are clear differences. The quality
of marital relationships is the same, mothers expressed the same
amount of warmth towards their children and there were no significant differences in the number of single-parent families. However,
patterns are more variable in terms of parent–child interaction.
Fathers, for example, are considerably less likely to have regular
conversations with their children, and many more children have been
looked after by child minders during their pre-school years (see
Figure 4:7).

The different reasons for the presence of certain disadvantages
within this group may explain the fact that the relationship between
disadvantages and children's problems are also different. Although
West Indian families are generally more disadvantaged, many of
those factors which are related to disorders in the indigenous
children are not strongly related to such problems among the West
Indians. For example, overcrowding, family size, maternal psychiatric state and paternal criminality do not increase the risk of
psychiatric disorders. Indeed, despite the increase in many disadvantages, West Indian children are somewhat less likely to show
behavioural problems in the home. The reasons for these differences
are unclear. There may be certain protective factors operating in
West Indian homes, or it may be that the greater degree of parental
expectation and control suppresses possible overt problems.

However, the West Indian children showed more classroom
problems. In addition they were much more likely to have
behavioural difficulties which were entirely confined to school. Once
again, however, these problems were not directly related to disadvantaged circumstances, except that troublesome children were much
more likely not to be living with both natural parents. Thus,
although the West Indian families were more disadvantaged and had
children who were somewhat more troublesome at school, the
disadvantages they suffered were generally not directly related to
children's problems. This may be because the effects of disadvantages
were overlaid by more influential factors. For example, there is some
evidence that West Indian parents, at least at the time of this study,
although rather more concerned about education than their English
counterparts, placed less emphasis on parent–child interaction or on
the importance of play.[1] This difference in emphasis may affect the
general level of cognitive development and relate to the children's
lower reading attainments.[2] It is known that the latter has a strong

[1] M. Pollack, *Today's Three Year Olds in London* (London: Heinemann Medical/SIMP,
1972).
[2] A. N. Little, 'Educational policies for multi-racial areas', Goldsmiths' College
Inaugural Lecture (London: University of London, Goldsmiths' College, 1978).

effect on school behaviour in children from all backgrounds and that
reading problems are probably precursors of behavioural difficulties,
rather than the reverse.[1] Whatever the nature of the mechanisms
leading to the West Indian children's greater behavioural problems
in school, it is apparent that the relationships between disadvantage
and difficulties is not a straightforward one. This is both because the
correlates of disadvantage may vary in different groups and also
because particular ameliorating factors may be operating in some
circumstances but not in others.

The school as a positive factor

The question of ameliorating factors brings me to the last point I
wish to consider and that is what the role of the school might be in
attenuating the effects of social disadvantage. It should be made clear
that I am dealing here with the school's contribution to the general
effects of social problems and not to specific services or provisions for
particularly disruptive or troubled children.

So far I have argued that the excess of children's problems in cities
is largely explained by greater family adversity of various kinds. This
observation is a view not infrequently echoed by teachers when they
complain that their problems walk in through the door. By this is
meant not only that families cause the children's problems but also
that attempts to deal with these at school are frustrated by lack of
interest or support from the home. However, this seems to be too
simple an explanation. First, it is known that schools with very
similar catchment areas have very different rates of problems and
that this is unlikely to be due simply to differences in intake.[2]
Secondly, the research evidence suggests that the majority of parents,
even from disadvantaged circumstances, are not alienated from the
idea of school, although they may be puzzled about its practices.
Thus, 74 per cent of Wilson and Herbert's multiple-problem families
in Birmingham saw the teacher as someone whose authority ought to
be supported. The parents of reading retarded children studied by
Sturge were keen to help their children[3] and among the West Indian
parents in our study 84 per cent had taken their children to a library
in the previous three months. Half had bought the children books
during this time and half had checked the children's homework
regularly. In general their educational aspirations were high. What

[1] A. Varlaam, 'Educational attainment and behaviour at school', *Greater London
Intelligence Quarterly*, no. 29 (1974), pp. 23–37; M. L. Rutter, J. Tizard and K.
Whitmore, op. cit.

[2] M. L. Rutter, B. Maughan, P. Mortimore and J. Ouston, op. cit.; M. J. Power,
R. T. Benn and J. N. Morris, op. cit.

[3] C. Sturge, 'Reading retardation and anti-social behaviour', M. Phil. dissertation,
University of London, 1972. Unpublished.

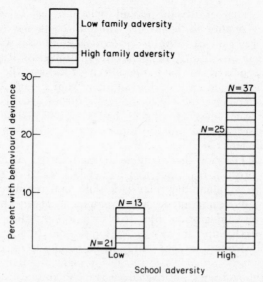

Figure 4:8   Behavioural deviance in London according to family and school
adversity

they may have lacked were techniques. This means that conventional measures of parental interest in school work, such as attendance at open days or PTA meetings, are not adequate. These occasions are often intimidating even for middle-class parents, let alone disadvantaged ones. A study of a thousand disadvantaged families quoted by Midwinter showed that 59 per cent of mothers tried to help with reading and practical work, 74 per cent felt teachers were interested in parental views, but on the other hand 80 per cent felt that they knew very little about the methods being used in the school.[1] Parents in these circumstances may lack expertise or knowledge as to how to help their children, but there is little evidence that they do not care. However, both their lack of expertise and their lack of suitable circumstances for promoting the children's educational development, means that the expectations which schools should have about the possibility of home support must be realistically based.

I would like to conclude with a suggestion that, despite the primacy of home background in determining many aspects of child development, the school nevertheless can act as an ameliorating factor in the face of disadvantage. In our comparative study it was possible to construct an index of school adversity in the same way as we had for family problems, using such indicators as high teacher or pupil turnover, the proportion of children on free school meals, etc.[2]

[1] E. Midwinter, 'Family functioning and educational performance', *Social Work Today*, vol. 10, no. 12 (1978), pp. 12–13.
[2] See M. L. Rutter and D. L. Quinton, op. cit.

When the rates of deviant school behaviour in London were examined in relation to school and family adversity, the results were illuminating. Children from low adversity homes who were in low adversity schools showed no behavioural problems. High school adversity appeared to have the effect of raising the rates of disturbance in children from low adversity homes while low school adversity attenuated the effects of family problems. The ways in which the low adversity schools had this effect could not be determined in this study but the important point here is that schools can have this effect (see Figure 4:8).

I have tried to show that many social disadvantages do not always, indeed do not usually, imply that homes lack warm or supportive relationships – rather they may lack skills and resources to help facilitate cognitive and intellectual development. There is little use in schools complaining about this. It is their job and their claim for special status that they are able to develop skills in children; it is their responsibility to find ways of doing so. This seems to me to provide the clearest way out of disadvantage for many children. The best hope of schools having positive effects is for them to concentrate on promoting those skills which increase the child's mastery of the environment and provide a path out of disadvantaged circumstances. This almost certainly involves developing basic and relevant skills rather than attempting to provide a primarily supportive but not skill-oriented atmosphere. This does not mean schools should not be warm and supportive places, but it does mean that they should not try to be substitute families.

One example in support of this argument can be given. The failure of a child to develop reading skills has well-known adverse consequences. There is another side to this issue however. The development of such skills may have a protective effect. Figure 4:9

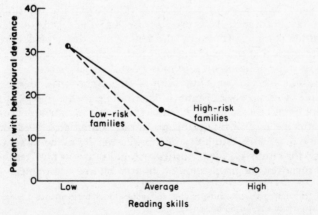

Figure 4:9   Reading skills, family adversity and behavioural deviance

shows the relationship between poor, average and superior reading skills, family adversity and behavioural deviance in school. The upper line shows the findings for children from deprived and disadvantaged homes. The bottom, dotted line shows the results for those in more favoured circumstances. In both cases the rates of disorder are considerably less among children of above average attainment. Of course, this may simply mean that more intelligent children are more resilient to stress, but the study by Rutter and his colleagues shows that behavioural problems in the classroom are strongly influenced by the extent of reward and encouragement for scholastic attainment.[1]

Reading is just one obvious example of the possible positive effects of the development of ability. It is likely that many other skills of both an academic and non-academic sort have similarly powerful effects in ameliorating the effects of disadvantage. This leaves us in a distinctly hopeful situation. Schools can do nothing about low social status or large families or bad marriages on poor housing. It is more than encouraging to know that those abilities they can foster can have a powerful impact in ameliorating the effects of the greater amounts of disadvantage that cities unfortunately contain.

[1] M. L. Rutter, B. Maughan, P. Mortimore and J. Ouston, op. cit.

5 The Limits of Positive Discrimination

Marten Shipman

It is tempting to consider inner-city problems as a mid-twentieth-century phenomenon. But the nature of contemporary inner cities results from the accumulated burden of history upon them. There were inner-city problems as soon as there were cities. Furthermore, the problems are international. In Britain the problems first arose with early urbanization at a time when the technology and administration for coping was undeveloped. But the wider contemporary perspective is also important given the tendency for those in any one city to see their problems as unique. From London the rest of the country may seem to be having it easy. From Glasgow the capital's problems must seem modest.

We have now ten years of British and twenty years of North American experience of active intervention in inner-city education from which to learn.[1] At the start of any review it has to be remembered that these interventions, usually implementing policies of positive discrimination, have employed only marginal resources. The amount likely to be spent on educating the fifth-form leaver is still far less than that spent on the pupil going on to higher education, however well funded the intervention.

Just as the historical weight of previous urbanization affects contemporary urban activity, so prior investment in educational plant, policies and personnel shapes new programmes and ensures that they will receive only resources that can be spared once ongoing commitments have been met. Intervention projects, and arrange-

[1] For the British experience, see J. Gray, 'Positive discrimination in education: a review of the British experience', *Policy and Politics*, vol. 4, no. 2 (1975), pp. 85–110. For the American experience, see H. Averch, *How Effective is Schooling? A Critical Review and Synthesis of Research Findings* (Englewood Cliffs, N.J.: Educational Technology Publications, 1974).

ments for rewarding teachers and others facing adverse social conditions, are best reviewed, therefore, as marginal elements in the total organization of education. With this perspective, the distinguishing characteristic of the successful intervention, curriculum project, nursery-, primary- or secondary-school organization, and of effective resource allocation to schools, can be seen to be the way things are done as well as what is done. It is the planning, implementation and control as much as the curriculum, whether open or closed, structured or unstructured, teacher- or learner-centred, that matters. Indeed, these 'shorthands' often confuse issues in education and over-simplify differences and similarities. In particular, the co-ordination between project and mainstream schooling, marginal resource and ongoing commitment, new and existing investment is often neglected. It will be argued that organization is often poor and can be resisted by teachers as anti-educational. The younger the children concerned, the greater this resistance is likely to be. Yet, while an absence of coherence in education is unfortunate nationally, it is a disaster for the inner-city child.

The common element in much educational policy in the last twenty years has been positive discrimination. This remains a policy unchallenged by any political party. It applies not only to schooling, but to the social services around schools. The RoSLA programmes, Schools Council and other curriculum projects, schemes for differentially allocating central and local government funds, and for building up support services around schools, have, with accompanying secondary-school reorganization, all been influenced by the philosophy that more should go to those who face most difficulty. Yet precise definitions of the objectives of this policy are hard to find. The Plowden Committee asked for schools with low standards to be raised to the national average and then above it.[1] But it was never clear whether this meant standards of provision or standards of attainment. When the Educational Priority Area action research programme was established, four objectives were specified – to raise attainment in the schools selected, to increase parental involvement, to improve teacher morale, and to increase communal responsibility.[2] But only rarely have these objectives been spelt out in detail. In practice the programmes have usually been concentrated on inputs such as improving school buildings or increasing teachers' salaries. The justification for action seemed too obvious to need specification. Children facing multiple social handicaps need the best not the worst of facilities. So do the teachers who struggle with the consequent problems. There is gross inequality between groups of

[1] Central Advisory Council for Education (England), *Children and their Primary Schools*, The Plowden Report (London: HMSO, 1967), p. 57.

[2] A. H. Halsey, *Education Priority*, vol. 1. Problems and Policies (London: HMSO, 1972), p. 1.

children in provision, in attainment and in jobs finally obtained. Without intervention, the rich get richer and the poor get poorer. Education seemed to be an important instrument for ensuring social justice and occupational mobility. Equalize education and a more equal society will result. Today we have to explain why these hopes have not been realized.

The punctured optimism over the role of education in determining life chances is a sad reminder of the cosy sentimentality that lay beneath educational thinking and political action ten years ago. Today we know that we can make little impact on social equality through educational intervention. We are even more pessimistic than this. Reviewers of available evidence have concluded that we do not even know how to raise and sustain test scores through special programmes.[1] As a consequence there is no incentive to detail objectives at output, and resources tend to be injected without any clear specification of the expected consequences. But this absence of specification is a symptom of the absence of the organization that might be the key to successful intervention, particularly in linking new programmes to mainstream activities.

This review of available evidence is limited to the criteria used in the existing evaluations. This usually means scores on objective tests. These give only a restricted assessment of programmes to remedy educational disadvantage. The dimensions of that disadvantage are very difficult to determine, or successful intervention would be easy to organize. But measured attainment is important because it is closely related to other important outcomes, such as length of schooling, entry to higher education and obtaining a good job. It is also given high priority by employers, parents, pupils and teachers. The focus in this chapter may be narrow but it covers the main concern of those personally and professionally involved.

There is no point in agonizing long over the low measured attainment of children in the inner cities. It happened world-wide. Her Majesty's Inspectors who surveyed primary schooling, reported in 1978 that reading scores for 9- and 11-year-olds, and mathematics scores for 11-year-olds, were significantly lower in inner-city schools than in rural or 'other urban' schools.[2] This confirmed existing evidence from tests of reading and mathematics in primary schools.[3] The Institute of Mathematics survey in 1978[4] of fourth- and fifth-year pupils in secondary schools also showed that attainment in city areas

[1] See, for example, H. Averch, op. cit. and J. Gray, op. cit.

[2] Department of Education and Science, *Primary Education in England. A Survey by H.M. Inspectorate of Schools* (London: HMSO, 1978), p. 116.

[3] See, for example, Inner London Education Authority, *Literacy Survey* (London: ILEA, 1971), and Inner London Education Authority Schools Sub-committee, *Monitoring Educational Standards – Comparability Test Scores* (London: ILEA, 1972).

[4] The Institute of Mathematics and its Applications, *A Pilot Test of Basic Numeracy of 4th and 5th year Secondary School Pupils* (Southend: 1978).

was below that in the shire counties. There are also groups that fall consistently below even the poor average level of attainment in the cities. Evidence collected in Redbridge in East London in 1977[1] confirmed earlier Inner London Education Authority evidence that West Indian and other children from minority groups were attaining below the level of indigenous children on verbal reasoning, English and Mathematics. Little,[2] using ILEA evidence, has shown how West Indian children not only attain below the inner-city average on reading tests, but deteriorate relative to their white peers across their schooling. Similarly, children of unskilled and semi-skilled parents fall further behind as they grow older.[3] This relative deterioration probably occurs everywhere. But in the inner cities these children start at a lower level than the national average and the gap increases with age. It is not surprising that educational reforms do not seem to have benefited the children of the poor in access to higher education.

The response to such evidence has tended to be curriculum innovation. But this can adversely affect children through short-sighted planning. Ten years ago I wrote a paper entitled 'Curriculum for inequality',[4] warning that the direction of curriculum innovation was going to harm the very children it was designed to help. This was particularly the case for the inner-city child where innovation was probably most rapid. Innovation for the poor while the curriculum for the rich remained unchanged seemed then to be a more effective way of ensuring inequality than selection at 11 had, as long as the criteria of accepted attainment remained unchanged. Today the situation has been exacerbated by unemployment. Yet in every city, and particularly in London, there are jobs available for the qualified, but they are taken by commuters living outside the central city.

The danger of a diluted education for the inner-city child is aggravated by difficulties in maintaining motivation and discipline in schools. If a subject is difficult to teach, the temptation is to drop it. Marland[5] has pointed out that the word has got around that text-books are too difficult. The Schools Council project on the effective use of reading reports that reading seems to have a low priority in lower secondary-school classes and that teachers are pessimistic

[1] Black Peoples Progressive Association and Redbridge Community Relations Council, *Cause for Concern: West Indian Pupils in Redbridge* (1978). For the Inner London Education Authority evidence, see A. Little, 'Performance of children from ethnic minority backgrounds in primary schools', *Oxford Review of Education*, vol. 1, no. 2 (1975), pp. 127–38.

[2] A. Little, 'Educational policies for multi-racial areas', Inaugural Lecture, Gold-smiths' College, 1978.

[3] K. Fogelman, H. Goldstein, J. Essen and M. Ghodsian, 'Patterns of attainment', *Educational Studies*, vol. 4, no. 2 (1978), pp. 122–30.

[4] M. D. Shipman, 'Curriculum for inequality', in R. Hooper (ed.), *The Curriculum* (Edinburgh: Oliver & Boyd, 1971).

[5] M. Marland, 'Towards a professional synthesis', Address to the UK Reading Association Annual Conference, 1977, reprinted in E. Hunter-Grundin and Hans U. Grundin (eds), *Reading: Implementing the Bullock Report* (London: Ward Lock Educational, 1978).

about the value of reading in learning.[1] Worksheets, often incoherent, were an unfortunate replacement for the book. Her Majesty's Inspectors, reporting on mixed-ability work in comprehensive schools, state that their main impression was that schools 'often underestimated the complexity and difficulty of what they were taking on.'[2] In particular they were worried that schools were usually clear about the social aims of moving to mixed-ability grouping, but were less clear about educational objectives, and that this created a lack of balance in the work of the schools.[3] Mixed-ability grouping in secondary schools can be introduced as a solution to discipline problems rather than as a way of raising attainment. Integrated studies and social studies can be introduced because history and geography are deemed too difficult for most children. The run up to O-level GCE or CSE examinations is delayed so that choices are not made prematurely. Assessment is minimized so that children are not prematurely labelled. But in other schools, often independent, or selective in title or practice, outside the inner cities, and producing commuters for inner-city jobs, the curriculum and school organization remains traditional, subject teaching remains the norm and public examinations determine content down to the first form. The children who need least help are given a few yards start and told to run straight. Their disadvantaged peers start later and run a zig-zag course. No wonder educational investment aimed at greater equality seems to have consolidated inequality. This has nothing to do with comprehensive schooling or mixed-ability teaching or curriculum innovation in themselves. It has everything to do with a tendency to do with other people's children what you are unwilling for anyone to do with yours.

This emphasis on the uneven incidence of innovation in education does not mean that it has been widespread. The evidence on the rate of innovation suggests that it has been modest, even in the primary schools.[4] But the rate of change in inner cities has probably been faster than elsewhere, when, on the analysis above, it should have been slower. This has resulted partly from the urgent need to invest where the need was greatest. Investment in buildings, support services, curriculum materials, lower pupil–teacher ratios and falling rolls provide scope for innovation. Inner-city teachers face greater problems than elsewhere and have to look for solutions. Methods that work in the suburbs, in small towns or rural areas, create

---

[1] *The Times Educational Supplement*, 24 November 1978, p. 8. (The report of the project, *The Effective Use of Reading*, edited by E. Lunzer and K. Gardner, was published in 1979 by Heinemann Educational Books.)

[2] Department of Education and Science, *Mixed Ability Work in Comprehensive Schools* (London: HMSO, 1978).

[3] ibid., pp. 16–21.

[4] See N. Bennett, *Teaching Styles and Pupil Progress* (London: Open Books, 1976), p. 54, showing that under 10 per cent were following Plowden's definition of progressive teaching.

problems when motivation is low and parental support inadequate. The inner cities also attract idealistic teachers willing to face the adverse social conditions and anxious to help deprived children.[1] These teachers are often sustained by strong political views in their efforts in the face of adversity. The desire to lessen competition among and between children who start deprived and have little apparent hope of advancement is a reasonable response where all the cards seemed to be stacked unfairly. In the inner cities there is also a shortage of articulate middle-class parents keeping an eagle eye on the curriculum. It is significant that where there are enclaves of professional people, intervention to limit innovation has occurred.[2]

The impact of programmes for improving inner-city education

Intervention programmes

Every evaluation of a major intervention programme has been followed by confirmations and refutations. These differences of opinion result from the different criteria used. Raising test scores and improving motivation are very different aims. Using test scores is a poor way of assessing a programme aimed at motives or work habits. In the evaluation of Follow Through, the High Scope Foundation's Cognitive Curriculum came out badly on the Metropolitan Achievement Test which measured grammatical correctness, but the Foundation claimed success when their test of communicative power was used.[3] Similarly, short-term and long-term success or failure are not necessarily the same. Head Start year-long programmes only resulted in slight gains on standardized tests and these were not sustained.[4] Yet on criteria such as placement in special education, repeating grades, opinions on education by the pupils and their parents, and on intelligence test scores, there is evidence that early Head Start intervention had beneficial long-term effects.[5] We may have been too pessimistic. It is wise to be cautious. There are a few organizational conclusions that can be reached with some certainty, and some more

[1] See G. Grace, *Teachers, Ideology and Control* (London: Routledge & Kegan Paul, 1978), for an empirical study of teachers in London schools.

[2] See R. Auld, *William Tyndale School Public Enquiry* (London: Inner London Education Authority, 1976).

[3] M. M. Kennedy, 'Findings from the Follow Through Planned Variation Study', *Educational Researcher* (June 1978), pp. 3–11.

[4] See, for example, G. Smith and T. James, 'The effects of preschool education: some American and British evidence', *Oxford Review of Education*, vol. 1, no. 3 (1975), pp. 223–39.

[5] US Department of Health, Education and Welfare, *The Persistence of Preschool Effects* (Washington, DC, 1977).

controversial educational pointers. The organizational conclusions can be stated bluntly:

1. There are no simple solutions to complicated educational problems
2. One-shot, small-investment programmes are unlikely to have lasting effects
3. If programmes are not followed by sustained reinforcement, the final impact may be negative
4. Specific objectives can be attained by specially designed programmes
5. No profound impact is likely from any programme as long as it remains isolated from the mainstream of educational provision, and is not planned as part of it.

This synoptic view involves having to cobble together evidence from very diverse sources. What seems to be lacking is any recognizable sequence of learning across the whole length of schooling. The public examination system provides this for a minority right down into primary schools. But these are the children who have least need of an accumulative sequence. The majority who need it most may experience parts that are carefully organized, but one section rarely leads logically to the next. The most dramatic examples of discontinuity occur when children move up to a new school, but they occur within schools, between subjects, between pre-schooling and the infant class, and between schooling and education outside the school. The most worrying aspect is not that there is discontinuity, but that there is resistance to the organization of the curriculum that would increase continuity. This may be especially disadvantageous to the inner-city child.

The nursery programme provides a convenient example. This has been expanded in a no-growth financial situation because of its promise to provide a base on which education, particularly that of poor children, could flourish. But the systematic planning and provision of such a base has never been accepted professionally. On both sides of the Atlantic there is now pessimism. Smith and James,[1] having reviewed the available evidence, conclude that the idea of the 'magic years' is virtually dead. Barbara Tizard[2] in another review concluded that conventional playgroup or nursery experience had no significant effect on test scores or primary-school attainment, or any other long-term impact on general adjustment or classroom behaviour. But such conclusions are not surprising given the absence of any apparent commitment to using nursery schooling for systematically building a base for later attainment. Furthermore, the absence of impact on primary schooling should be anticipated as

[1] G. Smith and T. James, op. cit.
[2] B. Tizard, *Pre-school Education in Great Britain: A Research Review* (London: Social Science Research Council, 1974).

there seems to be no planned sequence of learning experiences to sustain learning as children move from nursery to infant school.

This pessimism over nursery schooling is a reflection of the disappointing evidence on the effectiveness of intervention programmes designed to raise the attainment of poor children. In retrospect too high hopes were placed on marginal resources and on short-term programmes. Too little attention was paid to the relations between intervention programmes and mainstream schooling. The educational content of programmes also seems to have run into organizational problems. Here the focus should be on programmes designed to provide a base of cognitive skills on which later schooling can be built. The educational pointers derivable from evaluations of such programmes look very like the organizational conclusions on nursery schooling. Crudely, detectable cognitive outcomes require: first, programmes that have been carefully designed to attain them; secondly, sufficient control over the teaching involved to ensure that there is implementation as planned; and thirdly, sustained follow-up.

The success of structured programmes in raising measurable attainment is not surprising. Discovery methods can affect motivation and attitudes towards education and may have less tangible long-term benefits. But if the aim is to teach a definable skill, a systematic approach to this end has most chance of success, and learner-centred methods are very difficult to structure systematically. The early Head Start programmes, especially that of Bereiter and Engelmann,[1] seemed to raise test scores dramatically. But these gains were soon lost.[2] However, the Follow Through planned variations programme has again confirmed that the more structured approaches had most success in raising attainment, and that those modelled on what was erroneously assumed to be discovery-based, English primary-school practice achieved the least success.[3] Furthermore, the latter also produced more negative results. But do these differences derive from the content of the different approaches or from the extent to which they can be thoroughly planned and implemented?

Programmes involving didactic teaching and the use of planned modules of work should be expected to have more success in raising

[1] C. Bereiter and S. Engelmann, *Teaching Disadvantaged Children in the Preschool* (New Jersey: Prentice-Hall, 1966). See also, D. P. Weikart, *Results of Preschool Intervention Programs* (Ypsilanti, Michigan: High Scope Foundation, 1976). For a summary of these early projects, see A. Little and G. Smith, *Strategies of Compensation: Review of Educational Projects for the Disadvantaged in the United States* (Paris: OECD, 1971).

[2] V. G. Cicirelli et al., *The Impact of Head Start on Children's Cognitive and Affective Development* (Washington: Westinghouse, 1969).

[3] Apt Associates, *Education as Experimentation: A Planned Variation Approach*, vol. IV, A to E (Cambridge, Mass.: Apt Associates, 1977). See also, *Harvard Education Review*, vol. 48, no. 2 (May 1978) for a full critique of this evaluation. See also, M. M. Kennedy, op. cit., and G. L. McDaniels, 'The evaluation of Follow Through', *Educational Researcher*, vol. 4, no. 11 (1975), pp. 7–11.

test scores than less structured work. Tests consist of exercises practised on programmed courses. Traditional teaching is also easier to implement than more informal, child-centred methods. The structured programme is tightly focused and task-orientated. Scope for the teacher is limited by the blueprint. Significantly, the structured programmes in Follow Through were implemented; which was not the case with all other models, and these Follow Through programmes did not require the length of training involved in the more open-ended programmes.[1]

American evidence suggests that the use of structured programmes overcomes the inefficiency of much everyday teaching. This tends to be haphazard and ineffective for the children. The common-sense view is that teachers are busy people and that this applies regardless of class size or the teaching style. There is little time for planning. The 'Teacher's Day' studies confirm that much time is devoted to activities that have little to do with instruction or the organization of the work of pupils.[2] The 'How Teachers Plan Their Courses' study concludes that they rarely do this in a systematic way.[3] It is usually hand-to-mouth. The best American elementary-school teachers seem to plan the next step through evaluating the light in the eyes of the children in front of them.[4] Most teachers, particularly in primary schools, would acknowledge the strength of this intuitive, sensitive approach, and resent the introduction of systematic planning of instruction for young children. The opposition to the Bereiter and Engelmann programme, and to the Peabody Language Development Kit[5] when the Education Priority Area action research was being negotiated in Britain, are examples.[6] There is resistance to organizing the nursery programme and infant schooling as an opportunity to prepare children systematically in the cognitive skills that they will need later to keep up in the junior and secondary schools. Given the promise of the methods used for improving attitudes towards schooling and of possible longer-term benefits, this is a defensible position. But it may handicap just those children who need an early boost.

The situation in mainstream schooling as distinct from special projects suggests another reason why the evidence shows discovery-

[1] M. M. Kennedy, op. cit., pp. 7–8. See also J. Stallings and D. Kaskowitz, Follow Through Classroom Observation Evaluation (Menlo Park: Stanford Research Institute, 1974) and W. L. Hodges, in Harvard Education Review, vol. 48, no. 2 (May 1978), pp. 186–92.

[2] S. Hilsom and B. S. Cane, The Teacher's Day (Windsor: NFER Publishing, 1971).

[3] P. Taylor, How Teachers Plan their Courses (Windsor: NFER Publishing, 1970).

[4] P. W. Jackson and E. Belford, 'Educational objective and the joys of teaching', School Review (Autumn 1965), pp. 267–91.

[5] Lloyd Dunn, J. O. Smith and K. Horton, Peabody Language Development Kit (Minnesota: American Guidance Services, 1968). Distributed in UK by Educational Evaluation Enterprises, Bristol, and NFER Publishing, Windsor.

[6] See A. H. Halsey, Educational Priority, op. cit., pp. 86–100. See also J. Barnes (ed.), Educational Priority, vol. 3 (London: HMSO, 1975), p. 71.

based approaches failing to raise measurable attainment, and why local authorities, inspectors, advisors and in-service organizers are organizing model curricula, core curricula, curricular guidelines and learning packages. It is very time-consuming to sequence work for children so that learning is accumulative. Harlen's work on the teaching of science, significantly titled *Match and Mismatch*,[1] gives some idea of the work involved in planning work systematically while allowing for different rates of progress. Class teaching is difficult to organize adequately. Systematically organized individualized learning is a task for a Napoleon. The superiority of structured approaches probably results as much from logistic as educational factors. The real difference in formal and informal teaching styles may lie in the ease with which each can be organized. Both need the structure but this is more difficult to arrange for small-group or individual work.

This is the safest way of looking at Bennett's evidence in England, and of American authors who have reached similar conclusions that formal teaching styles are more productive.[2] The clue lies in the exceptional informal teacher who did obtain excellent results in the Bennett study. She seemed to be able to organize child-centred activities successfully, but was exceptionally skilled and industrious.[3] Such teachers usually move quickly to universities or colleges to promote such methods among students. But such methods may be successful only for the gifted because of the logistic problems. They are more difficult to organize and implement than traditional methods. The talented tend to underestimate their own influence on the methods they favour, and to raise hopes among future teachers that can not always be fulfilled, even if the will to succeed is present. Wragg, using evidence from the Nottingham University Teacher Education Project, comments that it has 'thrown light on several important aspects of class management, which in almost every case turn out to be more vital in informal than in formal classrooms.'[4] Significantly, Wragg has also observed the informal teacher who in Bennett's survey obtained higher learning gains than any other teacher. He reports that she had a very high work-rate, thorough preparation and exceptional clarity in setting up work for her children.[5] But it is not just that a high level of organizing ability is necessary to make informal teaching effective. There is the newness of informal teaching – the absence of the hundreds of years of experience behind traditional methods and the support of parents and teachers. But these traditional methods need not be as mechanical and inflexible as many American packages. Tight

---

[1] W. Harlen, *Match and Mismatch* (Edinburgh: Oliver & Boyd, 1977).

[2] N. Bennett, op. cit. For American examples, see note 3, p. 76.

[3] See E. C. Wragg, 'A suitable case for imitation', *The Times Educational Supplement*, 15 September 1978, p. 18.

[4] ibid.

[5] ibid.

programming and positive reinforcement are anathema to most English teachers. But if the clue to success is in planning and systematic implementation, there is no need for rigidity. As usual the debate has polarized opinion. The priority is to ensure a level of organization that will avoid the time wasting, gossiping and drifting that marks the worst of informal methods. But the organization should not be so rigid that it produces the worst of formally organized classrooms, where children never have to think for themselves or do more than appear to be paying attention.

When the inner-city child is considered, the case for a systematic approach to education becomes even more pressing. In Follow Through, the only programme that worked as well in the cities included (New York and Philadelphia) as elsewhere was the most tightly structured, the Direct Instruction Model, itself based on the work of Bereiter and Englemann.[1] The models of the unstructured type rarely showed any positive effects anywhere, but failed completely in the cities where they tended to have negative effects. Any evidence of this sort needs to be treated with caution. But it is an ominous warning about the danger of not considering that the inner-city child may require a very different education from his peer who does not face the same problems. National surveys may conceal these differences. Inner-city teaching is a tough job. It is likely that the discipline problems among older pupils in inner-city schools make any sustained didactic teaching very difficult. Innovation results from the need to search for alternatives to controlling children in large groups for sustained periods of time. Many teachers also commute alongside others in the inner-city workforce and this further reduces planning time in school. But a deep anxiety should drum in our ears. What if inner-city children are just those who find it most difficult to cope with discovery, child-centred methods that depend on the child being able to find the necessary human and material resources? It is not just a joke that middle-class parents support child-centred schooling because they teach the basic skills at home. West Indian and other minority group parents seem to be taking on the same responsibility by organizing supplementary schools. In school my children can flourish with discovery methods because I make sure that they do discover. But the opportunities for children to benefit from informal classroom organization may differ dramatically between Woking and Wapping.

The evidence on the need for structure, regardless of the extent of formality or informality in teaching style, has played its part in the reaction against innovation at the end of the 1970s. Both in the classrooms and in the training institutions the urge to be in the van of

[1] Apt Associates, op. cit. See also M. M. Kennedy, op. cit., p. 10. For an account of the development of this model, see W. C. Becker, 'Teaching reading and language to the disadvantaged – what have we learned from field research?', *Harvard Education Review*, vol. 47, no. 4 (1977), pp. 518–43.

novelty has been checked. But there is professional resistance to viewing education as a plannable sequence.[1] This resistance is strongest where it matters most, for very young children. Pre-schooling remains an area strong in faith and weak in planning. Yet coherence is crucial from the child's viewpoint and is usually assumed rather than organized. There is often a hollow debate over the pros and cons of structure in the curriculum, as if any method could succeed without being organized. The structure is the guarantee that the content and process has been thought through. Yet even this minimal planning is often distrusted as mechanistic when educating young children. The academic view of child development seems to emphasize natural not planned learning. But the counter-attack on influential figures such as Piaget has been as vigorous as that on progressive teachers who used the interpretations of the translations of Piaget to justify child-centred methods.[2] There is now enough evidence for the practitioner to ignore the academic squabble and act on the principle that there is no substitute for organization regardless of the methods chosen.

Some of the resistance to systematically organizing the schooling of the urban poor arises from attempts to soften the harsh conditions that they face. Teachers in inner-city schools rightly stress that the adverse conditions faced by children require special approaches by teachers. Social and physical skills that can be assumed in more favoured areas have to be taught in the inner city. Under these circumstances teachers feel that children should be insulated within the school from the competitive pressures that are finally going to handicap so many after leaving. But this can become a shirking of responsibility. The older secondary-school child, who suddenly learns that he will leave school unqualified, has been double-crossed. It may not be pleasant to face children with the hard facts of life as these can disturb self-images, but it is necessary if children or parents are to do anything about them. To evade this is certain to widen the gap between rich and poor. The former will get the necessary information and support from the home, and will follow examination syllabuses that will qualify them for jobs. The latter are liable to be penalized by sentimentality. Not everyone can succeed, but the dice should be loaded in favour of, not against, the poor.

The dangers of sentiment weakening a drive to raise attainment can be illustrated by the long history of the failure to improve the relative position of the semi- and unskilled working class since 1944 and the more recent crisis over the education of black children. The response to this low attainment has usually been curriculum innovation. But it has already been argued that this separates disadvantaged groups from their more fortunate peers. Unfortunately, innovation has been backed by a series of psychological and

[1] See note 6, p. 77.
[2] For example, M. Donaldson, *Children's Minds* (London: Fontana, 1978).

sociological concepts which have labelled the problem without explaining it. Teachers have taken action after consideration of theories, only to find that the academics have moved on and are denigrating such action and recommending something new. Intelligence, cultural deprivation, linguistic deficiencies are all put forward as explanations, and end as nightmares as the action penalizes the groups that everyone wants to help. Self-concept theories threaten to follow the same unfortunate cycle. The blame lies with academics being over-enthusiastic, teacher educators lacking scepticism, and teachers innovating selectively to promote greater equality, without looking at what is happening to relative measured attainment.

The innovations to meet the concern over the attainment of black children mirror those for working-class children after the Newsom report of 1963,[1] many of which were organized as Schools Council projects. The Newsom child was given relevance because that was deemed necessary to motivate this type of child. The black child today is given Black studies, steel-band practice and basketball, because that seems relevant to well-meaning teachers and is supposed to boost self-concept. But just as diluted social studies confirmed the low attainment of the Newsom child, so a diluted curriculum will confirm the black child as non-academic. It is right that there should be a concern to promote the worth of all cultures through the curriculum, and that there is still overt and covert prejudice, but black parents and children do not want to be confirmed into the unskilled working class by kindness.

In a critique of self-concept hypotheses, Stone[2] has pointed out that while schools try to compensate black children for negative self-concepts (which probably exist only when viewed apart from the social context of the lives of these children which requires positive self-concept to survive), the West Indian community tries to supplement what they see as the inadequate schooling given to their children. We have the absurd situation where schools cut the time given to basic subjects in order to introduce fringe activities that will interest black children, while their parents organize supplementary schools to cover the basic skills not being learned at school. Teachers blame parents, poor self-concepts and cultural deprivation, while parents blame schools for poor teaching, low standards, racism and prejudice. Stone's research challenges the assumptions behind self-concept theory, but, more importantly, exposes the fear of the black community that their children are being prepared to be second-class citizens.

This concern of parents is widespread. Crudely, they oppose any-

[1] Central Advisory Council for Education (England), *Half our Future*, The Newsom Report (London: HMSO, 1963).
[2] M. Stone, 'Black culture, self-concept and schooling', Ph.D. thesis, University of Surrey, 1978.

thing that lowers targets for their children. They press for an instrumental, basic education that will prepare their children for higher education and for the job market. Parents may have seemed ignorant in denying the immutability of intelligence, in emphasizing the importance of actually teaching the basic subjects, or organizing children's work sequentially, and in demanding order in schools as a basis for learning, but their observations of their own children have usually turned out to be a better basis for action than theories of intelligence or learning. But parents also see the tough world beyond school and mistrust the liberal romanticism that denies their children the skills that are being drilled into the children of just those professionals who seem to be responsible for the innovations to which they object. These parents only want what the more fortunate among us can choose or buy.

Demographic changes will strengthen the power of parents to get the schooling they want. The unpopular school is the first to empty when rolls fall. In many inner-city areas with high net outward migration, about half the school population will be lost within a period of less than fifteen years in the 1970s and 1980s. This gives parents a whip hand over schools. The unpopular can be closed as places become available nearby. Even if there is legislation to enable local education authorities to determine the form entries of secondary schools, and hence to share available children out between schools, there will be limits to the extent to which parents can be denied access to the schools they want for their children, and which they know to have been built for a larger entry than is to be allowed. Schools are already trying to sell themselves, and with parents demanding tighter discipline and a more traditional curriculum with higher standards in the basic subjects as the condition for sending their children, teachers have every incentive to meet these demands to save their schools from possible closure.

Resource allocation on the basis of positive discrimination

Any attempt to allocate spare resources on the basis of positive discrimination has to meet the two inexorable conditions under which public services are financed. First, the available resources are marginal. Existing commitments have to have first call on available money unless large and increasing amounts are given to the service. Teachers appointed for a new programme have to be paid thereafter. Buildings once in use have to be maintained. New services add to those that have to be paid for before the next innovation occurs. The second feature of educational costs follows from the very high proportion that goes to paying teachers. Some 60 per cent of expenditure on education goes on salaries and another 20 per cent on premises. Once other inescapable commitments are included, only some 10 per cent can be varied without affecting salaries or the maintenance of buildings. Out of this 10 per cent are paid the cost of the genuinely educational developments, books and the running expenses of schools. In good times we employ more teachers and build more schools. In bad times we cannot cut the teaching force, and there is professional and public opposition to closing buildings. Hence the crucial 10 per cent is squeezed even further. The marginal expenditure on intervention projects is paralleled by marginal re-allocation within the routine working of the system. The allocation of costs in education, the expectations of those involved in the schools and as parents, and the working of the Employment Protection Act, are all geared to expansion, both demographic and economic. Positive discrimination does not only have to operate with marginal resources, it is squeezed by the pressure to maintain existing commitments in the face of rising costs per pupil as numbers shrink.

The Plowden Report stimulated not only Educational Priority Area action research, but reinforced the arguments that available resources should be used to reward teachers and schools facing the most difficult problems. The start was a building programme in deprived areas and an additional £75 to teachers in schools nominated as in Educational Priority Areas. Most local education authorities have tried to allocate more resources to schools coping with poor children, despite the impossibility of avoiding spending more on those pupils who stay on longest in schools or colleges. At the same time the central government has initiated and financed several schemes for supplementing teachers' pay in schools facing severe social problems and has grant-aided the appointment of teachers to meet special needs. The consequences of basing action on such policies is difficult to assess. But there are four serious concerns. The benefits may not accrue to the deprived children. The policies may soon become redundant and lead to injustice. Insufficient control over the resources once allocated can blunt impact. Sustained positive discrimination can penalize schools which are effective and hence popular.

Programmes to implement positive discrimination tend to be very blunt instruments for affecting educational or social change, not only because the resources used are marginal, but because they are directed at areas or schools indentified as containing children facing severe problems, rather than to the children themselves or their parents. Barnes and Lucas,[1] working on Inner London Education Authority reading scores and on data from the ILEA primary-school index used in the allocation of resources to schools on the basis of deprivation faced, found that disadvantaged children were very widely distributed throughout the inner city. Any policy operated through the designation of areas or schools as in need of priority in the allocation of resources was liable to miss many of the poor. Most

[1] J. H. Barnes and H. Lucas, 'Positive discrimination in education: individuals, groups and institutions', in J. H. Barnes, op. cit.

of the poor do not live in poor areas and most of the people in poor areas are not poor. Extra resources to areas here are taken from, or do not go to, areas there. But within the area or school designated for extra resources there are likely to be a majority who would not qualify for that extra help if the indicators were for individual children or families rather than areas or schools. Barnes and Lucas concluded that policies of positive discrimination through schools would be most likely to benefit middle-class children who were born in this country.

The ILEA no longer allocates additional resources to schools on an all or nothing basis. But extra monies to teachers are still allocated in this way. This means that in schools not designated as facing deprivation there are still many children from deprived homes. The figures given by Barnes and Lucas are remarkable. Three and a half times as many children received free meals outside EPA schools as inside. There were five times as many children of unskilled or semi-skilled parents, three times as many immigrant children, and five times as many from large families, outside as inside those schools designated for receiving extra resources. For every seven children in inner London at risk of being multiply disadvantaged, five were out-side schools receiving extra resources and in which teachers were receiving extra allowances. This evidence was available long before extra payments such as the social priority allowance were made. Local education authorities realized the limitations of area-based and school-based extra payments before central government, but this policy is still popular politically. Yet it was not able to improve the lot of the majority of disadvantaged children even when first imple-mented.

The second worry is that payments once given are rarely redistributed as the conditions faced by the teachers concerned change. It is no tragedy that a payment such as the social priority allowance is kept by teachers who are in schools that have ceased to face exceptional difficulty. It is unfortunate that such a payment was so difficult to apply fairly at the start and was so divisive in action that no way can apparently be found to reallocate it. As the years go by teachers facing extreme difficulties are being paid less than others once in a similar position but now more fortunate. Every new pay-ment of this kind aggravates the injustice between teachers. It is not a minor issue. The problem has been accumulating for ten years, as most payments, once given, remain with teachers as long as they stay in the same school, regardless of the changed situation around it. It involves the original EPA allowance, scaled posts resulting from the scheme to allow extra points to be given to schools facing exceptional difficulty, and other schemes negotiated through the Burnham Committee who determine the structure of teachers' salaries. These are static arrangements in a fluid situation.

The third worry is over the management of resources in education.

Once they are allocated, control evaporates. For example, teachers appointed under Section 11 of the Local Government Act of 1966 may have been earmarked to help with the special needs of immigrants which was the intention of the Act. But from there on these teachers merge into the general staffing of schools, not necessarily even identifiable as meeting any specific need. Indeed, it is doubtful if even the original appointments had any objective rationale, as the Department of Education and Science dropped the collection of immigrant statistics in 1973, and this was the only basis available for allocating the 75 per cent grant for these special needs teachers. Only at the end of 1978 was this lack of control acknowledged in a Home Office Consultative Document. But this was after twelve years without accountability and five years without a factual basis for the appointments. Similarly, intervention programmes may be carefully designed, but once implemented are rapidly modified. The transmutation of curriculum projects by teachers has been well documented.[1] From the outside this merging into the prior curriculum of the school may look like dishonesty. The lack of control over resources once allocated may look like poor accounting. But both are really the result of the exercise of autonomy given to staff within schools. It is a dilemma of a decentralized system of education.

There is another accounting problem resulting from the succession of nationally and locally initiated intervention programmes since the start of the Urban Programme in 1968, to the Inner City Partnerships of 1978. Each of these programmes arrives with a blaze of publicity and then lingers on unnoticed apart from spasmodic evaluations that rarely cost the exercise. Many of these programmes have built up supports for schools in inner-city areas. Project directors, seconded teachers, advisers, researchers, community relations officers, home visitors, curriculum support teams, youth workers, staff in on- and off-site units for disturbed or truanting children and in treatment centres, home–school relations officers, teacher-social workers, and a host of volunteers financed as part of the initiative, all work hard in depressing conditions to advise teachers and to press innovations. But resources are always scarce. A growth industry here means less there. In an expanding economy there are few problems. But in a no-growth situation and with the Employment Protection Act, the squeeze on less favoured areas is intensified. The appointments once made are difficult to terminate. The work being done is valued. But it is difficult even to map where the various agencies are in the inner cities and impossible to account fully for their activities. The Schools Council has recently researched into what happened to all those curriculum projects.[2] Similar

[1] M. D. Shipman, *Inside a Curriculum Project* (London: Methuen, 1974).
[2] Impact and Take-up of Schools Council Projects – Schools Council project (1976–79), based at University of Sussex.

research into the remains of projects initiated under the Urban Programme, the Educational Priority Areas programme, the Community Development Projects, the Inner City Partnerships, and so on, would uncover a mass of uncoordinated, inadequately audited activity.

These accountability problems in and around education are part of a more profound problem. Implementing positive discrimination in rapidly changing urban conditions can ultimately penalize effective schools. Social problems are concentrated in small, scattered areas throughout the whole of the inner city. Here the schools face the greatest problems and rightly receive any resources available once existing basic commitments have been met for all schools in the city. But these run-down areas are the first to be redeveloped, and lose population fastest from voluntary and planned out-migration. Resources are pumped in as the children move out. The pupil–teacher ratios fall rapidly. Some schools have half as many pupils per teacher as others just up the road. But rapidly falling rolls occur in just those schools which are receiving the extra resources on the basis of positive discrimination. Nearby schools which may be only marginally different in the social problems faced, but which were below the cut-off point for extra resources, or lower on the scale for receiving extra resources, and where the population is stable, get more and more relatively disadvantaged. Falling rolls aggravate this situation. The empty places increase parental choice and unpopular schools become vulnerable. Unfortunately there is no evidence that extra resources or smaller classes have any positive effect on attainment.[1] Pumping resources into schools that are losing children also takes resources from nearby, popular schools, which have the reputation, and probably the substance, of higher attainment. They tend to gain the children of the more aware and articulate parents, hence widening the attainment gap further. The resources go to one school, the children to the other. The latter can use any resources given, the former may reach a point where extra resources have little relevance to the problems faced. They may even be used to deflect effort from the very mainstream activities that determine attainment and hence popularity.

Here the limits of positive discrimination are clearly visible. It is just to ensure that schools in run-down areas are given the best of facilities. Their physical condition is in many cases poor. It is fair that teachers in such schools should be rewarded for doing a difficult job. But there is a point beyond which effective and popular schools are starved of resources and in which the morale of teachers is sapped by seeing the less effective receiving the rewards. The internal organization of contracting and possibly demoralized schools further exacerbates the situation. Ambitious staff tend to leave.

[1] For a review of this evidence, see M. D. Shipman, *The Limitations of Social Research* (London: Longman, 1972), pp. 144–6.

Specialists and those capable of leadership become scarce. The proportion of ineffective and unambitious teachers increases. Scaled posts, however generously provided, are likely to be held for long service or looking after the stock cupboard. The school reaches a point where parents desert in increasing numbers, fearing closure. Yet no momentum can be generated internally. The local education authority has to pump in even more resources to try to get things moving through in-service training, curriculum teams, extra supply teachers, advisory support and face-lifts to the building. But these resources have to be taken from other schools, and their impact is often negligible.

This situation exists even where objective indicators are used for allocating the bulk of available resources. These tend to include output factors such as disturbed behaviour of low attainment.[1] But such factors should be under the control of staff. Schools achieving high attainment and good behaviour are penalized. But these effective schools are also popular for this is what parents look for. Positive discrimination, once it has helped overcome the more obvious differences between the resourcing of schools in deprived areas, can start to penalize success. Evaluation is usually focused on innovations. The really important area is the tendency of sustained policies to become redundant in the form in which they were conceived, because the context of their implementation has changed.

The way forward

It would be irresponsible to suggest that dramatic improvement in the performance of inner-city children can come from reforms within education without major changes in conditions around the schools, particularly in employment. Nevertheless, if some schools can be effective in adverse conditions, so can others facing similar problems. In this chapter three major weaknesses have been discussed. The organization of schooling does not ensure sequence within and between the different stages of education. The allocation of resources is starting to reduce incentives to be effective. The net effect of policies to improve the chances of the poor has usually served to penalize them further. Yet the motivation of teachers in inner-city schools remains as a source of optimism. Gray[2] has suggested that these teachers must have found unacceptable the notion that they were contributing to the generation of inequality. Intervention programmes, curriculum innovation and positive discrimination met the desire to deflect resources, however marginal, towards the poor in education. That urge to help the inner-city child remains strong,

[1] M. D. Shipman and H. Cole, 'Educational indices in the allocation of resources', *Secondary Education*, vol. 5, no. 2 (1975), pp. 37–8.

[2] J. Gray, op, cit., p. 104

but the context of education is changing the context in which it is implemented. Demographic and economic pressures leading to contraction and a growing concern to get the mainstream right in the school curriculum are closely connected. Expansion allows for innovation. Contraction forces a reconsideration of the mainstream. Under these conditions, what is the most promising way forward?

The political base

The most extraordinary feature of the current educational debate is that schools are simultaneously expected to work miracles yet are acknowledged to be under-powered when unsupported. The attempt to get rid of corporal punishment is typical. Teachers are asked to give up a sanction yet offered nothing to replace it. Parents demand ordered schools but are often unwilling to control their own children or to back teachers when they try. The equilibrium of inner-city schools is often perilous. Thornbury[1] in his descriptions of the urban school drives this point dramatically home. But this organizational vulnerability is the prime concern of teachers. Grace[2] has shown how 'good' teachers in inner-city schools are typified by their competence in maintaining control and being concerned for the welfare of the children. Their qualities in the teaching situation were considered secondary in most schools. If sanctions, positive or negative, are removed, these teachers are in an intolerable position. So are those who stress the need to raise attainment as a priority in the inner city, when this depends on support from parents, employers and social services that is often not given. Somehow that support has got to be increased.

A way forward would be to strike a bargain between parents and teachers. Parents would offer more support and receive more power to affect decisions about central issues such as the curriculum. Teachers would yield some of their professional autonomy in exchange for support. This would require a major effort of mass communication to spell out the benefits that could accrue. It would require a wholehearted effort by central and local government, and probably the definition of new legal responsibilities for parents and a stronger role for the courts if these duties were not fulfilled. Such a bargain might promote a more consistent and sustained context for the education of inner-city and other children. It would also give the poorer child more of the advantages of his more fortunate peer. Above all it would meet Musgrove's telling summary of the weakness of our schooling that '. . . schools are underpowered in relation to the goals they try to attain.'[3]

[1] R. Thornbury, *The Changing Urban School* (London: Methuen, 1978).
[2] G. Grace, op. cit., pp. 148–69.
[3] F. Musgrove, *Patterns of Power and Authority in English Education* (London: Methuen, 1971), p. 1.

As usual the outcomes of such a political bargain would be unpredictable. Parents have strong and sometimes unwelcome views on education. The political action following attempts to reform secondary education in some West German states is a warning. Even more significant may be North American examples where parents have obtained control. Atlanta has 90 per cent black people. A bargain here exchanged bussing for black control for education. The schools emphasize basic skills, order and hard work. It has been decided to build a new selective school based on admission by academic examination. There would be a risk in really involving parents in education. But they can make it work and a genuine partnership based on shared hopes might produce a service of, rather than for, the public.[1]

The educational base

The tendency for evaluation to be concentrated on new developments rather than ongoing activities has not only meant that more attention is given to marginal activities, but that policies can become redundant or even harmful without being noticed. This applies particularly to positive discrimination where the line between helping those who cope with the most pressing problems in the schools, and harming those who are doing the most effective job for the deprived, is very hard to draw. The line also changes rapidly. This is why there is a continuing need to look for unintended consequences. To examine the impact of any new policies, or enduring policies on attainment, is a safeguard for the poor. To account for the way resources are allocated and used is another. Too often the articulate and the knowing get the best bargain. They probably still will if there is legislation to limit parental choice of school as rolls fall. Education needs hard-headedness not soft-heartedness if it is to be fair.

It is not, however, sufficient to promote greater justice in education. It is also necessary to raise the effectiveness with which resources are used to raise standards all round. This will not be achieved by scattering small sums of money among many ambitious projects. That has been the unhappy history of over a decade of interventions from the Urban Programme to the Inner City Partnerships. High hopes and small sums only go together if there are very limited and clearly specified objectives. If children are to be helped materially, the resources should go to them or their families. If the physical condition of schools need improvement, the money should go to a building and improvement programme. If teachers need compensating, they should be paid more. If attainment is to be raised, targets should be set, and money allocated to teachers who agree to work towards them. In all cases there has to be control over

[1] D. Ravitch, 'The "white flight" controversy', *The Public Interest*, vol. 51 (1978), pp. 135–49.

the way these resources are used, or their specificity, and hence their cutting edge, will be lost.

However, these guidelines for action have to apply to the mainstream as well as to the marginal activities. Over a decade of projects have hardly left a mark because nothing changed in the remaining 99 per cent of schooling. Given the direction of many of these projects this was a blessing. But the effort to improve inner-city education has to go on and this will not happen by tinkering around the edges. The principles of specificity, continuity and accountability are important throughout schooling. There have to be targets. There has to be planning to ensure a sequence of learning for each child. There has to be evaluation of the success of the investment made. Without these too much has to be taken on trust in the face of evidence that inner-city children are losing out in school.

The implication of the need to approach education more systematically is clear. The time has come when we should back winners. The accumulated evidence from evaluations should be used instead of backing every fresh, untried idea. Successful teachers need incentives even if these have to be provided at the expense of compensating the unsuccessful. Resources should be given to schools with a good record in unpromising conditions. Michael Rutter's chapter, 'Secondary-school practice and pupil success', suggests that there are first-class schools in the inner city. They should serve as models. The Schools Council, H.M. Inspectorate, advisors, and especially academia, should forgo their fascination with the frontiers and be more concerned with the effectiveness of mainstream activities and ongoing policies. This should involve identifying good practices so that the best can become the target. Such an emphasis would put the premium where it matters – on raising the relative performance of inner-city and other disadvantaged children in curriculum areas that count in employment and higher education.

There are two advantages in replicating successes, whether derived from curriculum projects, new support services or special payments for special services. The first would be to diminish discontinuity in schooling. Action to implement positive discrimination has been marginal in scope and diffused in impact because resources are already tied to existing commitments, and innovations have been adopted or adapted only if they fit. The evidence on the need for organization in learning and for control over the use of resources has been unwelcome because it went against current educational theory and brought with it pressure to give up some school-based autonomy over the curriculum. It also meant accepting that extra payments should remain earmarked as intended and should be redistributed as needs changed. Teacher autonomy is a bulwark against central control. But the cost has been discontinuity for just those children who need it most, and a lack of incentives for many of the more effective teachers. A new balance is required to preserve teacher autonomy but also to ensure that the central part of the curriculum is organized systematically. This may not be crucial in areas where stable conditions apply, but in the inner cities it is the condition of equity for the children.

The second advantage is that backing winners could raise aspirations for the inner-city child. The danger of the continuing evidence of lower than national average attainment is that targets are lowered. Fortunately there is now a debate over standards, and economic and demographic contraction are forcing us to re-think. But the low aspirations may be deep-seated. The stress on keeping order and maintaining good personal relations that Grace[1] found to be the criteria on which teachers judged their peers in inner-city schools involves a devaluation of academic ability and teaching skill. Teachers who stressed these academic and pedagogic aspects of their work felt that the schools were failing to recognize the ability of inner-city children. The majority of teachers saw pupils as the products of their environments. They used this view to explain the problems of their pupils and as a basis for relations with them. There is an unfortunate determinism in this view. Once again it is encouraged by the way the academic evidence on the relation between schooling and social background is prepared and presented. It results in a downward spiral of expectations.

Giles,[2] looking at the experience of black children in the same areas of London as Grace, reached similar conclusions. He found the teachers sympathetic, concerned to help black children. But these children were seen as future members of the working class. The concern and sympathy still left these children as losers. This fatalism may reflect the surface reality of the inner city. But the most striking feature of cities is their variety, even within small geographical areas. All is not unrelieved gloom, and parents still have high hopes for their children. Yet the opportunities in the commercial, governmental, service and distributive sectors are still taken by commuters. The numbers of inner-city children going on to the wealth of further and higher education institutions still remains low despite their proximity.[3] A winner's, rather than a loser's image would give the inner-city child a brighter future on his own doorstep, and beyond.

What does this mean for educational policies in general, and positive discrimination in particular? We have to take the organization of schooling more seriously, in relation to the allocation of resources and to the way the learning experiences of children are sequenced within and between schools. That organization should be based on three principles. First, it must

---

[1] G. Grace, op. cit., pp. 170–89.

[2] R. Giles, *The West Indian Experience in British Schools* (London: Heinemann Educational Books, 1977).

[3] Department of Education and Science, *Statistics of Education*, vol. 2. School Leavers (London: HMSO, 1975), Table 111, p. ix.

narrow not widen the gap between rich and poor. Secondly, it must give parents more rights and responsibilities to avoid a deterioration of public confidence in education and to bring support to teachers. Thirdly, it must add incentives to be effective to compensation for facing difficulties. Schooling may not be a very powerful force in relation to other social and economic factors. But part of that weakness could be overcome if education was organized systematically for the children, particularly when they are disadvantaged in the inner cities.

PART TWO

Educational Provision

6 Education and Employment: match and mis-match

Pat White

At a time of high youth unemployment it may seem that I am begging the question by the very title, 'Education and Employment'. Both in the short term and the long I would contend I am not. What I am going to do is not only look at employment in today's terms but explore what employment might mean in the future. There are four main aspects I want to discuss:

1. The employment situation today
2. The transitional problems faced by school leavers now
3. Fresh problems which will arise over the next decade or so
4. The implications for schools and colleges as they plan to fit educational provision to the needs of young people.

First, the employment situation. Some figures which relate to inner London as an example of an inner city will set the scene. Although the number of vacancies dealt with by the Careers Service cannot be regarded as a measure of the total vacancies available for young people, a comparison of those figures over the years at least gives some indication of the change in demand for young workers. An examination of figures of vacancies dealt with annually by the Inner London Service shows that demand for young people under 18 remained fairly stable at about 50 000 from the late 1950s to the mid-1960s, declining to 35 000 by 1970 and to around the 20 000 mark in the past three to four years (it dropped as low as 15 000 in 1975). To put this into context, a year-group in the Inner London Education Authority is about 30 000+, of which we reckon about 25 000 actually hit the labour market each year. But it should be remembered that inner London vacancies also traditionally attract young people from outer London and the Home Counties. Thus in the last twenty years we have moved from a situation in which 'notified' demand consistently exceeded the number of young people available, to one in which the recession underlined the fact that no longer could it be taken for granted that the vast majority of school and college leavers would already have jobs to go to at the end of term or after their summer holidays. This has resulted in a dramatic slowing up of the rate of absorption into the labour market of new entrants and at the same time the prolongation of periods of unemployment for those who have worked, but have lost or left their jobs and are hoping to re-enter the labour market.

The drop in absolute terms in the number of vacancies was not the only dramatic event. Particularly over the past decade, the employment structure has been changing at a rapid rate as well. The change bears the marks both of an economic recession and of the various legislative measures affecting employment dating from selective employment tax (SET) through redundancy payments, employment protection and equal opportunities, as well as national and international structural changes. The effects of each are impossible to isolate but their combined effect has been to speed up the changes that were already under way and accelerating.

The backcloth to this is that even by 1961 Greater London was predominantly a service-oriented city with less than a third of the total male workforce employed in the manufacturing sector, and already the number of people working in offices alone exceeding those working on the shop floor. A mark of the additional problems is that redundancies in the manufacturing sector amounted to nearly a quarter of a million between 1966 and 1972 (out of a total workforce in 1966 of just over four million) a rundown which was particularly sharply felt in those areas where such employment in the past had been strongly located, and which had acted as a focal point for the manufacturing industry workforce.

Thus profusion has been replaced by an increasing shortage of skilled craft jobs of all kinds, whether traditional or modern. In every area in London there has been a serious reduction in the number of medium-sized, previously expanding industrial firms which could be relied on each year to recruit and train a sizable group of young people in various occupations. The transplanting of these 'seed-bed' firms (in terms of training opportunities for young people) out of the inner city, however desirable in many ways, is certainly seen by careers officers as one of the major contributory factors leading to the continuing impoverishment of the inner-city labour markets. Only in the very centre of London (the City and West End) is the job profusion of the 1950s still perceptible. Here the commercial and business sector has kept the job market strong. But the growth in the number of jobs available in financial, professional and scientific services, in the public sector and the whole commercial sector, provides no answer to the problem of the educationally less well-qualified proportion of the school-leaving population, those currently hit hardest by unemployment.

Recently it has been proved conclusively that entry requirements demanded by employers tend to rise as the number of employment opportunities decline. Entry levels move up or down a notch in response to supply and demand. This movement has in recent years continued upward from GCE A-level to graduate-level entry; from O-level to A-level entry; from no educational qualifications to 'good' CSEs.

Choice of employment in inner London remained a reality for most school leavers until the mid-1960s. For the next decade the narrowing range in the kinds of work available was masked by the continuing surplus of the total number of jobs available, compared with the number of young people leaving school for employment. Now choice for the academically well qualified remains, but for the unqualified and untrained it is limited to a degree not previously faced in the South East. Nevertheless the predominant pattern, even now, is that relatively few of the total unemployed are out of work because of an over-all lack of job opportunities, but rather that a high proportion are on the margins of employability. For example, in November 1978 there were about 3000 young people registered with Careers Offices in the ILEA as looking for work, while there were over 6000 live vacancies, 5000 of which were in Central London and of precisely the nature mentioned above. Thus the London problem is a compound one, with the evident paradox of serious labour shortages co-existing with unemployment, since industrial dispersal has to some extent been accompanied by skilled and key-workers and their families.

Although I have spent some time outlining the London scene, I make no apologies for doing so. London acts as an extreme example of what is happening in most inner cities or large conurbations in this country. With the exception of the Greater London area, the skilled manual section of the workforce is the most important numerically in conurbations although, as has already been seen, in London there are more managers, professionals and non-manual workers. In general all conurbations have suffered considerable structural changes. In all, the semi-skilled and unskilled numbers have declined, but Greater London has the lowest percentage of manual workers and has experienced the most rapid reduction in numbers.[1]

Thus today's school leavers are facing a rapidly changing scene, in which the number of people without jobs has been steadily rising, a trend quite separable from the cyclical variations in the numbers of unemployed corresponding to periods of recession and recovery. This unemployment has not fallen randomly on the population. It is

[1] Unit for Manpower Studies Project Report, *Employment in Metropolitan Areas* (London: Department of Employment, 1977).

now recognized that it is the younger sections of the labour force which are particularly hard hit. Unemployment for the young is even more selective – the vast majority of the unemployed are unqualified and likely to obtain jobs below craft level if they obtain them at all. There is no easy explanation for the vulnerability of this particular group. Contributory factors inevitably include the fact that tradition-ally employers curtail recruitment as an early means of economy in labour costs; young people enter and re-enter the labour market more frequently than adults, hence the added danger for them in times of recession; and there is a tendency among employers to dispense more readily with the services of those who are regarded as 'supernumerary', and people whose wage costs come under the heading of overheads rather than production. The effects of technological change on the labour force have an accumulative, and sometimes undesirable, effect on job opportunities for the young, particularly where there is de-skilling of an operation. Thus we are beginning to see the immediate situation facing young people, but do we fully understand what processes they themselves are undergoing during the vital stage when this reality breaks through to them?

Occupational psychologists, adopting a developmental approach, maintain that occupational choice is an evolving sequence of vocational decisions. Their line of thinking may be summarized as follows:

1. Vocational development is a developing self-concept as a worker
2. Vocational adjustment is the process of seeking work where the requirements are consistent with one's view of oneself
3. Job satisfaction is therefore related to the degree of this consistency.

There emerge three distinct stages of development in adolescence:

(i) Formation: in the early teens, when development is through iden-tification with key figures and during which choice, dominated by needs and fantasies, gives way to choice from interests and capacities with the increasing social participation and reality testing of the individual
(ii) Translation: when self-concept is translated into occupational terms and tentative choices are modified against this developing self-consciousness
(iii) Implementation: this comes after a trial period of work when effort is made to establish and maintain oneself in a particular career.

That is the theory. What then are the problems faced by the disadvantaged youngster growing up in the modern inner city?

The period of identification often takes place in an unsatisfactory, although not necessarily unconcerned, home background, where often poverty, not only in terms of household income but also in the widest environmental deprivation sense, is one of the main problems. Such youngsters desperately need to be made aware of the choices and decisions which have to be made, and gradually prepared for the transition to adult life, in order to overcome the inherent limitations in outlook. The difficulties of the translation phase for the disadvantaged are largely ones of communication. Restricted linguistic fluency results in an inability to absorb abstract concepts and frequently limits conventional academic progress. Additionally disadvantaged youngsters appears to know a lot about the work available to them from their parents, siblings and friends, because it is traditionally narrow in extent; but this knowledge is in reality scanty, inaccurate and full of family and neighbourhood prejudice.

With these facts in mind adults need to think carefully about the following statements:

> Motivation and personality affect how a person views his abilities and influences how he uses them
> How an individual perceives his own situation is more likely to determine how he acts than how others perceive it.

But

> How others see this contributes to how he sees himself.

What then are the cumulative effects of the employment situation on the aspirations of youngsters, particularly the so-called disadvantaged, or those with a handicap or those from ethnic miniorities?

Indifference by parents, teachers, social workers, employers or 'them' will deaden young people's aspirations. We need to give these youngsters, even in times of normal employment in 1960s' terms, constructive help. They have little natural, ordered sense of the range of employment, nor of the qualities which make a job congenial or a worker successful. How much more important does this become when unemployment could be the reality? The role of vocational guidance in its broadest definition must be to help an individual to develop and accept an integrated picture of himself and his role in the world of work; to test this concept against reality and convert it into reality, with satisfaction to himself within the setting that society provides. At the implementation stage we must ensure that each young person has been helped to understand who he is, rather than simply sprayed with occupational information; that we have helped him broaden his horizons, to see what meaning work has for him and for society; that we have helped him find his level of capability and prepared him to accept responsibility for himself and to make his own decisions. Then and only then will each individual have gained sufficient self-confidence, and the flexibility which grows from such confidence, to face not only the early years in the labour market which can be experienced in or out of work, but also the traumas of the cycle of redundancy, unemployment, retraining and re-entry into the labour force which he is likely to face during his adult life.

It is precisely at this point that we should look at the role of adults vis-à-vis the school leaver. In essence, careers officers, but they should not be alone in this role, see themselves as essential mediators between the educational and economic systems, interpreting schools to employers and endeavouring to influence employers to think more carefully about the way they use the young people they have recruited. This implies we are at the point of conflict between discordant systems, a discordance which can be seen as the result of two major factors. On the one hand, manpower predictions (except in too short a term for educational response to be possible) have a poor record; they should be heeded, but with a proper scepticism. Industry is too vague or ignorant of its own recruitment needs. On the other hand, school systems have failed to respond adequately to the changes in the economic realities of the 'world outside', and there is a need for curriculum reform. I would even suggest that a core curriculum should include at least an appreciation of economic and technological realities as a compulsory element. In other words, on the schools side there must be a quicker and more fundamental response to the changing values of society and not a simple reinforce-ment of traditionally held attitudes.

It would be simplistic to talk only about preparing today's school leavers for today's situation. Anyone who is 19 or under in 1979 will be 40 or under in the year 2000. There is little point in trimming our sails to suit today's wind when I maintain that the storm ahead of us will bring with it winds we have never met before, could find us totally unprepared and present society with a challenge which some of us have never even contemplated.

> Affluence has done nothing to assuage our primal anxieties about shortage. The ecological panic of the past decade has deep psychic roots. And now it turns out that the real problem in the foreseeable future is likely to be lack of work. Metals can be recycled, energy conserved, etc., but work is a much less tangible commodity and although the immediacy of the problem is belied by the bulging briefcases and over-crowded schedules of those whose present job it is to find out how it should be tackled, the anxieties are already mounting.

Thus wrote William Taylor in the *Times Higher Education Supplement*.[1] There is no certainty of growth rates of a kind that would ensure additional employment, and there is continuing concern about our long-term economic performance. For instance, it seems likely that there will be 2·5 million extra workers entering the labour market in the UK between 1976 and 1991. With a growth rate of 2·75 per cent in GDP there would be no expansion in the number of jobs, with resulting unemployment of 3 million by 2000. If the growth rate were 2·5 per cent, the figure would rise to 5 million. A growth rate of 3·5 per cent could result in an additional 3 million jobs. I say could

---

[1] *THES*, September 22, 1978, p. 30.

because, as Mukerjee points out, with conventional wisdom, growth leads to greater investment which in turn can lead to further technology which is job decreasing and not job increasing. It has been said that what we are facing today, is a trilemma – nuclear war, over-popualtion and, if we survive these two, leisure.[1] The problem is can man keep up with his own technology?

Industrial society is increasingly departing from its nineteenth-century base.[2] We need to take stock of its present and think about its future with quite different intellectual concepts from those inherited in the traditional theories of industrialism, as we stand on the threshold of the post-industrial society. Knowing something of likely future needs and aspirations, we should seek to ensure that present decisions do not utterly foreclose the future, that there is sufficient flexibility to allow future generations to alter and perhaps reject the priorities of the present, remembering the future does not arrive with today's problems.

It is not easy to escape from conventional wisdom, and thought patterns can all too easily become obsolete. The past turns imperceptibly into the present and the present into the future. When we reach the time when a minority is able to feed, maintain and supply the majority, it may make no sense to keep in production those who have no desire to be in it or who are unfit for work. People's usefulness to society in economic terms varies with the use to which their labour is put. If full employment, which, like equality of opportunity, has been ambiguous enough to serve honourably as an objective of social policy for more than thirty years, now needs taking down and replacing, what are the implications? Somehow, the concept of work has to be uncoupled from the concept of employment. We must all have work; we may not all be able to have employment. The current contrast between work and leisure is altogether too crude.

David Cockcroft, Trades Unions research head, has said, 'To look at microelectronics in terms of job losses is like viewing the invention of the wheel in terms of an increase in road accidents',[3] and yet are we ready to, and must we, displace employment as the crucial arbiter of distributing wealth? Certainly it would seem that at present our structure of motivations, incentives and rewards is too closely geared to future employment and not enough to present and future work. Yet to all of us the source of income matters, and however adequate that income may be, reward without effort yields little satisfaction and could, within current thinking, demoralize the individual and society. So let us look at the problem of a post-industrial society.

The post-industrial society differs from industrial society principally on the dimensions of economics and social structure. Specifically these are

---

[1] Dennis Gabor, *Inventing the Future* (Harmondsworth: Penguin Books, 1964).

[2] Krishan Kumar, *Prophecy and Progress* (Harmondsworth: Penguin Books, 1978).

[3] David Cockroft, 'How micros could change the role of the unions', *Computer Weekly*, August 31, 1978.

held to be changes in economic activities such that the post-industrial
society is not primarily a goods-producing but a service economy; changes
in occupational structure such that the white-collar workers replace blue-
collar workers as the single largest category in the labour force and, within
the white-collar category, there is an increasing predominance of the
professional, scientific and technical groups; and changes in the form of
technology with the older machine technology supplemented by the rise of
the new intellectual technology, i.e. essentially management and problem-
solving systems making extensive use of the computer. Overarching all
these changes is the centrality of theoretical knowledge as the source of
innovation and policy formation. This theoretical knowledge becomes the
strategic resource and its custodians – the scientists, mathematicians,
economists and the engineers of the new computer technology – become
the key social group replacing industrialists and entrepreneurs of the old
industrial society. Its institutions, the Universities, research organizations,
experimental stations, become the axial structures of the new society
superseding the business firms of the industrial society.[1]

The chief ingredient of 'skill' required will be creativity, originality,
perceptiveness, with manual skill and neat packages of factual
knowledge of less importance. Thus, tool-pushers become unnecessary and change into paper-pushers whose numbers, given
certain social decisions, can grow beyond any limit because they can
always give work to one another. In this sense, a growing
bureaucracy can be seen as the unconscious wisdom of the social
organism unprepared to face growing unemployment.[2]

But what follows from this move to a service economy? The
structural changes involving the continuous growth of the tertiary
sector have occurred both in the USA and the UK from the beginning
of industrialization. The differential rate of expansion of manufacturing and services from the start made it plain the future lay with
services.

From 1750–1850 manufacturing and services expanded at the expense of
agriculture and even then the service sector showed a quicker rate of
expansion than manufacturing both in terms of employment and productivity. The trend continued from 1850–1900 with service employment
increasing faster than manufacturing but with decreasing productivity.
This tendency has continued up to the present day – a majority of the
population is now employed in the service sector and the difficulty of
raising productivity in this sector is an important contributory factor in
inflation.[3]

Thus there will be no novelty in the post-industrial society in the
continued mass emigration from industrial work. There is a
constancy and continuity. What has so far made for dramatic
differences of work is the mass movement from agriculture to service
employment compounded by the fact that this has equally been a

[1] Krishan Kumar, op. cit.
[2] Dennis Gabor, op. cit.
[3] Krishan Kumar, op. cit.

movement from the countryside to the city. But the rise of services has led to a fundamental transformation in the nature of the individual's relation to his work and to his fellows – a reversal from the trend towards alienation and depersonalization in the large corporations of industrial society, allowing greater scope for the development and exercise of personal skills.

The rapid growth of educated and specialized groups (for example, in the UK there has been an extraordinary increase in the number of scientific and technical employees since the beginning of the century; as Toffler pointed out,[1] 90 per cent of all scientists who have ever lived are alive now; and by 1981 the professional and managerial groups will equal one-fifth of the work force, the second largest occupational category only to clerical, sales and service workers) – this rapid growth is transforming the shape of the occupational hierarchy from that of a squat pyramid with a wide base of unskilled and unqualified manpower to that of a tall urn.

It widens out below the top to reflect the need of the techno-structure for admin., co-ordination and planning talent, for scientists, engineers, sales executives, salesmen, those learned in the other arts of persuasion and for those who programme and command the computer. It widens further to reflect the need for white-collar talent; and it curves in sharply towards the base to reflect the more limited demand for those who are qualified only for muscular and repetitive tasks and who are readily replaced by machines.[2]

Thus 'industrial society is the co-ordination of machines and man for the production of goods. Post-industrial society is organized around knowledge for the purpose of social control and the directing of innovation and change.'[3]

Schumacher warned us on this saying 'it might be said that the ideal of an employer is to have production without employees and the ideal of an employee to have income without work'.[4] Can the pursuit of these two ideals, undertaken through science and technology, lead to anything but total alienation and final break-down? The problem is that 'man has refashioned the use of space but has left the use of time unchanged.'[5] Leisure would find man psychologically unprepared. Leisure for all is a complete novelty. And yet, such leisure could be a reality in one generation. It could be here now in the UK were it not for powerful defence mechanisms which delay it. Compulsory work is on the way out, but compulsive work stays until a new generation grows up for whom there is no sharp limit between work and play. Joad once said, 'Work is the only

[1] A. Toffler, *Future Shock* (London: Pan Books, 1971).

[2] H. Wilensky, *The Welfare State and Inequality* (Berkeley: Univeristy of California Press, 1975).

[3] D. Bell, *The Coming of Post-Industrial Society* (New York: Basic Books, 1973).

[4] E. F. Schumacher, 'Survival of the fitter', *Listener*, 1 May 1975, pp. 576–7.

[5] A. Touraine, *The Post-Industrial Society* (New York: Random House, 1971).

occupation yet invented which mankind has been able to endure in anything but the smallest possible doses', and yet we are now faced by modern technology upsetting the 'brains and brawn' market and the long-standing near equilibrium of demand and supply of labour (not that it was ever a fair state of equilibrium).

The increasingly sophisticated uses of micro-electronics could create new industries, more jobs and extra wealth, or could mean 5–6 million in the dole queue at the end of the century. We need a bridge over what could be a one-generation gap at best. We have entered a new phase in the idea of progress and the concrete experience on which it is built. From the late seventeenth century onwards, progress was based on science and technology used to improve the perform-ance of industry leading to the rise of the European middle class. In the nineteenth century the working class rose to self-consciousness and began to demand their own share of the inheritance, although still within the same Western framework of reference. Now the relation of forces has changed again. The extra-European world, denying its own history, has entered the picture to strengthen the traditional conviction of progress and perhaps to modify it in its own direction.

Until recently the majority of people had to work to keep a leisured minority. We are now faced with the possibility of a world in which only a minority need work to keep the majority in 'idle luxury'. The minority could be so small as to be entirely recruited from the most gifted part of the population. The rest will be socially useless by the standards of today, based on the 'Gospel of Work'.[1]

One way out is to arrest technical development. We cannot do this in a competitive world. The world must be co-operative to survive and yet remember the horror with which one read *Brave New World*[2] where a third of the population were on the land, and production methods were arrested to provide seven and a half hours daily work for them, while they were made to believe the methods were the most progressive possible.

What must happen is that man must be brought into equilibrium with his new environment – man can be happy if his security is assured and time is spent between mild work designed as much for occupational therapy as for production, and good recreation. Education for leisure must start early as it equals education for happiness in a complex civilization.

This could lead to the rediscovery of man the individual after the dark age of man the cog. It demands something like the broad educational objectives of the Renaissance – the desire to learn, love of learning, knowing how to learn and where to find information, judgment and compassion. A sense of the one-ness of knowledge, an enquiring mind, an understanding of basic concepts of science, maths and the humanities,

[1] Dennis Gabor, op. cit.
[2] Aldous Huxley, *Brave New World* (Harmondsworth: Penguin Books, 1955).

with a focus on the applications of computing, not its science (except for the few who will meet the shortage of electronic specialists) and above all the development of each individual's uniqueness. Within this the mastering of the access to information is a good deal more important than memorizing it. What we are encouraging is an attitude to learning which is an uncynical attitude of mind which refuses to be bored, a sense of curiosity preserving sensitivity.[1]

The ability of humans to communicate information, ideas and feelings has been the primary factor in man's evolution. Today, when the technology he has created is out-pacing social evolution, it is the skill in greatest need of improvement. It must be remembered that the advance of technology is cumulative, its progression is geometric not arithmetic. It is of paramount importance that we stop producing a population unable to cope with rapid change or in which the change is too slow to be perceptible if measured against the speed of technological change. What we have to adapt to is the concept of leisure. The main difficulty is defining leisure stems from the fact that the concept of leisure has had different meanings for different people. The Ancient Greeks saw it as an opportunity to develop body, mind and soul; the Puritans saw it as a threat of indolence and sin; many workers today see it as release and escape from the routine of work; to the old, it often poses problems of filling time. What is certain is that leisure time is not obligated – it is when behaviour is directed by our own will and preferences, but it can be pure pleasure or work-related activities or voluntary community work.[2]

The effect of the regular organization of work has been to create a common rhythm of life, with leisure occurring in much the same sequence. Enjoying leisure in modern society is almost conditional on having a job. Without work a person's normal rhythm of life and his approach to daily routine is undermined and participation in normal forms of recreation and social relations becomes well-nigh impossible. And yet the hours people work today are long compared with earlier historical epochs. In medieval times people did less work than today, for instance, there were more than 100 public holidays. But the influence of Puritanism pushed up the hours of work, making employment the major determinant of the pattern of life. During this century hours have fallen but they are still in excess of what has been historically normal. Yet the meaningless nature of many industrial occupations has already led some people to centre their lives on leisure. Some people work in order to be able to do desirable things in their leisure time. What we must remember is that adolescence is the period during which interests are aroused and a liking for a particular leisure activity is developed.[3]

Another aspect of concern to us is the considerable extent to which members of modern society rely on the products of organizations catering for a mass market to fill their free time. Thus, it is necessary

[1] Edward Short, *Education in a Changing World* (London: Pitman, 1971).
[2] Kenneth Roberts, *Leisure* (London: Longman, 1970).
[3] ibid.

that society sould be sufficiently affluent to be able to support a group of professional organizers and entertainers whose sole function is to cater for the leisure interests of the remainder. But we could be moving into an era when an individual's self-concept is based upon, and reinforced by, the activities he undertakes during leisure.[1] Should we concern ourselves increasingly with 'preparing the young for their future leisure lives rather than their occupational roles, if education is to continue to be a meaningful experience.'[2] Many young people have no clear goals or values to guide their leisure activities and yet no longer can leisure be treated as an area of life which simply absorbs the tensions created by the other more powerful parts of the social system. Leisure will shortly become such a basic part of people's lives that its use will give rise to problems which entail profound consequences for both the individual and for wider society. Attempts to solve the conflicts and frustrations that are aroused in contemporary society are becoming conditional on a thorough appreciation of the nature of the consequences of the uses to which people put their free time.

We are advising today's young people on two planes – tomorrow and the day after tomorrow. We understand tomorrow and its problems of structural unemployment as it is known today, but the day after tomorrow is more problematic. In other words whether we like it or not today's school leavers face a society which will be different from much that we know unless the present rate of change is arrested. It is their future, not ours, and we must enable them to decide what they want that future to be. We must ensure that they know the options before them, understand the implications and have the ability to influence the choices made.

Clearly, I have been putting forward one extreme of the possible long-term future and, as I mentioned earlier, manpower predictions are so unreliable that they need to be treated with a healthy scepticism. Nevertheless it would be folly to ignore the possibilities. One may wonder what purpose 11 years of schooling has served for the tens of thousands of teenagers who leave school at 16 only to find themselves on the dole. It must cause them to reflect bitterly on the contrast between the opportunities which were promised to them and those which were actually available.

Indeed there is a view that education, like a kind of cerebral cod liver oil, is so good for children that more of it is bound to be better. Equally, there is an almost universal assertion that education is the prime ingredient of economic growth. Could it also be said to be true that very few jobs require eleven years of education and very few of those who compulsorily get only eleven years of education are going to occupy those jobs? Each job requires its own special expertise, but

[1] ibid.
[2] D. Reisman, 'Leisure and work in post-industrial society', in E. Larrabee and R. Meyersohn (eds), *Mass Leisure* (New York: Free Press, 1958).

it is entirely unrealistic to expect school to provide this. The varieties of specialist knowledge are almost infinite and it is both necessary and reasonable that employers should train their own workforce. Maybe the only contribution which schools should be expected to make to the wealth of nations is the teaching of those minimum standards of literacy and numeracy which will qualify children later to benefit from training. It is salutory to remember that 150 years ago, when universal education was still a Utopian fantasy, John Stuart Mill stated the case for it as being 'the increase of wealth and the improvement of morality'. Could it be that the tragedy of today is the concentration on the first to the virtual exclusion of the second. For Mill meant by 'morality' far more than the vaguely censorious Grundyism which we attach to the term today. He meant the intellectual maturity which enabled a person to make reasoned, independent judgements, free from the pressures of herd instincts, and then to accept personal responsibility for the consequences.

Despite the falling proportion of unqualified school leavers since the raising of the school-leaving age, still too many leave school not only lacking the basic skills and knowledge needed for work and adult life in general, but also not attuned to or prepared for work, let alone unemployment. Extended compulsory education has not provided them with the necessary skills for survival, but has just lengthened the period of their dependency. Indeed it has not only not prepared them for the transition from school to work – it may have alienated at least some of them from the work scene altogether.

Currently it is fair to say that most careers education is geared to helping pupils find answers to questions such as: What are my interests and abilities? What are the occupations most compatible with these? What are the future prospects in and of these occupations? How can I prepare for, and later progress in, these occupations? But does this really meet the needs of today's young people? The techniques used can, by implication, be described as cognitive in nature, and therefore we are forced to the conclusion that vocational choice for all must largely be a rational process. In reality it is unlikely that for many it is a process with decisions occurring at only one or two strategic points in time, one of which by force coincides with leaving school. Rather, it is a series of decisions throughout life, influenced strongly by non-cognitive factors. Not 'Can he do it?' but 'Will he?', 'Does he want to?', 'Does it meet his needs?', and even fundamental questions like 'Does he really want to work?', 'Does it fit with his self-image?'. In other words adding attitude to aptitude.

Careers education should be helping young people answer questions such as these:

> What sort of person do I really think I am? (self concept)
> What sort of person would I like to be? (ideal self concept)
> What sort of person do people who matter to me think I am?

And who are these people?
How do I reconcile these self concepts with information from
the cognitive domain? (examination results, etc.)
How important is work to me?
What do I want from life?

Unemployment within the present context is destructive to anyone
and is at its most destructive with young school leavers. The
discouragement of the failure to get a job may permanently alienate
them from the world of work and society. One important aim in
school must therefore be to give youngsters confidence. Confidence
brings with it a lack of fear of failure, which in turn engenders a
wholeheartedness about work and the full use of creative abilities. A
confident person enjoys competition, accepts responsibility. Insecurity inhibits and leads to a fear of failure, of making mistakes,
and the insecure avoid competition and responsibilities and opt out.
The snag is that others tend to accept the opinions we hold of ourselves; thus low esteem anticipates failure, an attitude which is more
likely to produce failure, and we are into the vicious circle of self-ful-
filling prophecies.

It is almost a debate about whether education produces social or
economic man. Let me remind you of some of the remarks made by
James Callaghan in his Ruskin speech 'Children should be equipped
to the best of their ability for a lively, constructive place in society and
also to fit them for a job of work.' Stressing the need for balance he
added, 'There is no virtue in producing socially well-adjusted
members of society who are unemployed because they do not have
the skills. Nor at the other extreme must they be technically efficient
robots.' Yet the responsibility still falls on the shoulders of the
individual pupil, while a mechanistic interpretation of the relationship between education and employment persists. If jobs require an
increasing educational attainment and society provides opportunities
for education, then according to sapient orthodoxy the burden falls
on the individual to achieve the education necessary for employment. Employers contribute to the emphasis on education. Educational achievements are taken as evidence of self-discipline and
potential for promotion. Trainability is presumed to correlate with
educational achievement, as are productivity, personality and adaptability. In industry and commerce, as in nature, those who lack
adaptability for change, like dinosaurs, tend to die and there is an
overriding need for mental flexibility.

But recognizing educational needs applies as we have seen not only
to cognition but also to subtler things like motivation. There is need
to make educational capital of the evident inter-connections between
self, career, work and society in learning. Perhaps it is here that I can
agree with at least some of the evidence produced by Illich.[1] His

[1] I. D. Illich, *Deschooling Society* (Harmondsworth: Penguin Books, 1973).

premise that schools organize the curriculum into prefabricated blocks of learning in order to be more able easily to gauge the results, carries with it the implicit danger that people try to apply the same rule to their personal growth. They put themselves into assigned slots, squeeze themselves into the niche which they think they have been taught to seek, and in the process put their fellows into their places too, until everyone and everything fits. People can be schooled to let unmeasured and unmeasurable experience slip out of their hands.

Children grow up in a world of things, surrounded by people who serve as models for skills and values. Peers challenge to argue, compete, co-operate and understand, and if a child is lucky he is exposed to confrontation and criticism by an experienced elder who really cares. A child needs information and a critical response to it. School is the very vehicle for this experience. Our society believes that social man is born in adolescence and is properly born only if he matures in the school-womb, and with current organization this is largely true. The importance of the task is such that none of us can afford to fail in it.

In a draft report 'Preparation for working life and for transition from education to work', which would become the basis for an education action programme in the European Economic Community, the following paragraph appears:

> Work is a large and important part of life. At the same time, a job is only one centre of an individual's life. Education for living and education as a preparation for work are parallel and complementary arms for educational institutions, but there is evidently a growing concern and necessity to give greater emphasis to certain qualities which are of particular importance in preparing the individual for the world of work. These include, inter alia, a capacity to communicate more effectively in oral, written, numerical and social terms; the ability to exercise initiative and take responsibility, to work in a team on a common task, to handle practical problems involving manual skills and to observe and learn through doing; an understanding of the diversity of the world of work, including the uses and implications of science and technology in society; a comprehension of the human and physical environment in which the individual lives, as well as knowledge of the world beyond the local community; and an understanding of the decision-making processes affecting the young person's working conditions and work environment.

Thus we are talking about preparation for adult life, a preparation which has given each young person the basic standards necessary at least to benefit from further training; the necessary information on which to base decisions – choice cannot be made in ignorance; and the basic understanding of the job market, with an awareness of its structural deficiencies as they apply to him.

7   Primary-school Practice and Pupil Success

Paul Widlake

Introduction

It is not easy to be clear about concepts like 'success', 'practice', 'schooling' or even 'good teacher'. It becomes increasingly obvious to anyone who attempts to investigate these concepts that the autonomy enjoyed by British school teachers permits the co-existence within some schools of a remarkably wide range of curricula and pedagogic principles.[1] If, like Gerald Grace, we attempt to go beyond description and to examine the rationale for these varying practices and beliefs, it becomes increasingly difficult to avoid the possibility that urban schools may (or, as Grace thinks, *should*) become arenas for 'the making visible of conflict of fundamental principles and of a "crisis of validity" in curriculum and pedagogy'.[2]

I am less sanguine about the benefits of making conflict visible. When one party to the conflict takes up an attitude of unyielding opposition and refusal to compromise at any cost, the situations produced may be ugly and unproductive, as the winter of 1979 has made abundantly clear to all the world. Luckily, one does not find ideological warfare in many primary-school staffrooms. The events at William Tyndale School, and the subsequent Auld Report,[3] remain unique. No other primary school has bared it soul to public scrutiny in this way. But is has happened once, and primary education will never be quite the same again.

---

[1] See Gerald Grace, *Teachers, Ideology and Control* (London: Routledge & Kegan Paul, 1978), p. 213.

[2] ibid., p. 212.

[3] Robin Auld, *Report on the Inquiry into William Tyndale School* (London: Inner London Education Authority, 1976).

It is not the differences of opinion between the various interest groups which is alarming but the complete absence of any procedure for helping those most directly concerned in the conflict, and who may legally be called upon to answer for the manner in which they have discharged their responsibilities. My main feelings in reading the Auld Report were of shame and pity. Nobody emerged with much credit. Administrators were seen leaving things to sort themselves out, refusing to accept the responsibility for supporting senior staff in schools, expressing amazement at the outcome of events. The staff, managers and parents, in their various groupings, whatever the intentions, produced disastrous results for themselves and the school they were all claiming to be anxious to save. One and all, they felt they were serving the best interests of the children; they carried on believing this until the school was closed and the children sent elsewhere, and no doubt most of them still believe it today. The fact is that for nearly two years those children were denied anything approximating to a proper education (whether defined after Plato, Marx, or at any station in between).

I have continued to worry about this, because my work with practising teachers, at the Centre for Studies in Educational Handicap, Didsbury School of Education, forces such issues to the surface. Teachers at Didsbury have been provided with opportunities 'to comprehend their own structural location' as Sharp and Green demand; they do not continue 'as unwilling victims of a structure that undermines the moral concerns they profess.'[1]

This process of raising the critical awareness of teachers is one which providers of in-service courses should gladly accept, but it is work which requires a certain level of delicacy if the tutor is not to lose credibility. Looking at the various sources available, one finds by far the largest volume and the most passionate commitment in the work of sociologists, but much of it is very negative. Some seem to spend half of their writings condemning teachers for labelling children, and the other half labelling teachers as conservative traditionalists; liberal pragmatists; evolutionary socialists; child-centred ideologists; radicals of the unattached left; old Marxists and new Marxists. I suppose this helps those who are helped by this sort of thing; but the products, in terms of teachers' writing about their own situations tend to be rather negative, and one is eager to contribute in a positive spirit. I want to effect change in our primary schools; I want to stir teachers, advisers and others directly involved and I believe this can be done within the context of the existing British educational system. I suppose that qualifies me for the label 'liberal pragmatist'.

The immediate concern is how we can manage change in our schools without provoking the degree of conflict which closed

[1] R. Sharp and A. Green, *Education and Social Control: A Study of Progressive Primary Education* (London: Routledge & Kegan Paul, 1975).

William Tyndale; or alternatively, driving the personnel concerned to nervous breakdown. It seems important to explore the possibilities of partnership and co-operation: of fraternity. I shall draw on some personal experiences to support my belief that the British school system could, if the best practice were available to all, make a significant contribution to the lives of children in the inner cities. I shall describe and analyse practice in a school which has a reputation for good teaching and give my ideas on generalizing the methodology and findings to other schools.

Grounds for optimism

I have no belief at all in simple solutions to the problems of the inner city but I believe it is possible, and indeed essential, to maintain optimism: not fatuous optimism, which ignores the facts or tries to make light of them; but optimism based on the observation that in some places and at some times, man has acted corporately and responsibly for the good of his fellows. This is the feeling I have had in reading Mary Tyler's account of her five years in an Indian prison.[1] On many occasions she achieved complete empathy and understanding with the women prisoners, who included people most rejected by Indian society, the Harijans and untouchables.

I should like to say a little more about India, because I was there not long after Mary Tyler's release and visited many of the places mentioned in her book, especially in Calcutta: also because Calcutta has provided a kind of base-line; and if ways and means can be found of making education available and meaningful in just about the worst urban conditions on this planet, the rest of us had better keep trying.

Comparatively few Europeans penetrate the bustees; the tendency is to dismiss the city as unfit for human occupation and to pass rapidly through (for example, John Morris in *Eating the Indian Air*[2]). Those who remain, like Ved Mehta, tend to hysteria: 'I can find no words to describe its filth, its disease and its misery. At first I felt I could accept Calcutta, that it wasn't as bad as I thought it would be. But now I know I cannot accept Calcutta. I fear Calcutta. I reject Calcutta'.[3] But V. S. Naipaul, a calm and dispassionate observer, also refers to the threat posed by the city: 'Compassion and pity did not answer, they were refinements of hope, fear was what I felt.'[4] The educated middle-class deal with the city by ignoring the squalor; they seem able to put distance between themselves and the abandoned children on the streets, the fearfully afflicted beggars, the child

[1] Mary Tyler, *My Years in an Indian Prison* (London: Gollancz, 1977).
[2] John Morris, *Eating the Indian Air* (London: Hamish Hamilton, 1968).
[3] V. Mehta, *Portrait of India* (London: Weidenfeld & Nicolson, 1970).
[4] V. S. Naipaul, *An Area of Darkness* (London: Deutsch, 1964).

prostitutes, the occasional corpses. Physical conditions in Calcutta, even in the 'wealthy areas' around the British Council, are extremely bad: unrepaired roads, inadequate drainage and a tremendous number of homeless people camping on the pavements. In the bustees, where I went after dark with a young teacher, the press of people is unbelievable. There is no sanitation. The houses are shacks made from wattle and daub or any materials which come to hand. Malaria, typhoid, tuberculosis, cholera are common; cockroaches, rats, mice very much part of the scene.

The bustee I visited was regarded as an 'improved' slum – there were pictures of a housing Minister congratulating the residents on their self-help programme. There are at least two other levels of settlement below this: the newly-arrived and the long-established pavement communities. A drive along Chowringhee Road and around Dalhousie Square late in the evening reveals literally thousands of people sleeping unprotected on mats: sometimes whole families, with cooking utensils and fires. Wherever it is humanly possible, they erect some kind of shelter and establish a permanency of occupation from which they can be dispossessed only by the sternest governmental measures.

The observer of this monumental human misery is tempted to take refuge in the belief that anyone living under these conditions becomes so brutalized that normal human emotions are no longer felt. Extreme poverty does produce extreme behaviour, but at both good and bad poles. I saw many examples of community action and I was quite unable to convince myself that most parents were indifferent to the wellbeing of their children though they certainly construe 'wellbeing' in a manner quite removed from Western ways of thinking. The collective indifference to the fate of unattached individuals is what strikes the visitor most forcibly, but there remains a huge population of concerned parents driven to their wits' end by poverty and disease, who are nevertheless willing to make sacrifices for their children's education and welfare. Moreover, there are a few dedicated workers who point the way which others might follow.

One evening 'school' visited was entirely voluntary and charged no fees. The male teacher had been doing this work for seven years, without pay. There was only one room, perhaps 6 × 4 metres constructed of wattle and daub like the surrounding dwellings, and it was situated in the very heart of a Muslim community. To reach it one had to go down pitch black alleys, after leaving a 'main road' congested with traffic and people and tiny shops. Here were forty or so children aged 5 to 8, learning their letters (in English and Bengali, as well as Urdu; many of them also attended in the morning for lessons in Arabic, a religious requirement so that they could read the Koran). They had a Tilley lamp for illumination, and they squatted on the floor with their slates and textbooks. It was very moving; still more, a child sitting on the ground *outside*, painfully completing an exercise by a glimmer of light from a nearby hut: she would not come in because she went to another school in the daytime, but she liked to be near the seat of learning, it appeared.

Again and again, I have found my mind returning to this scene and to the work of others whom I visited – for example, the nuns who ran a class for pavement children. It is enough that they do it. I am grateful because they retain hope and if they can, we in the affluent West are being self-indulgent if we fall into despair about parts of Birmingham, Manchester, Liverpool or Glasgow.

So curiously enough, the technique I would advocate for enabling teachers – and those who write about teaching – to retain the convictions that what goes on in primary schools is worthwhile and not harmful to children, would be to urge them to make more and more contact with the families of the children they teach. Numerous studies have been conducted by the Centre for Studies in Educational Handicap (CSEH) which illustrate the need and the benefits some teachers accrue. For example, one headteacher visited families on a council estate, which for her was new territory, and she concluded:

> I approach this task with trepidation. I wanted to understand these working-class mothers better. I was unsure of my reception. It would have been very easy to regard my pilot study as worthless and change the topic. However, I gained a great deal from it. I overcame my fear of visiting homes, which I had previously done only in cases of illness. I emerged with a feeling of admiration for many of these mothers – they cope with inadequate living accommodation, shortage of cash and material resources, and live in an area where houses are so close together they must of necessity live in everyone else's pocket, and yet they remain remarkably cheerful.[1]

Teachers on both full- and part-time courses now undertake such visits during field-weeks, and similar approaches have been used in initial training.[2] There are elements of culture shock and the consequences are sometimes unexpected, as is inevitable if a teacher enters the course naively unaware of the living conditions of a large proportion of the population of this country. It is easy for teachers to underestimate the interest that the majority of these parents have in their children's welfare and education, because some are very ill-equipped to articulate their love and concern, and reluctant to enter schools even when a warm welcome is assured – which is far from always being the case. Some teachers at Didsbury are currently engaged on a description and analysis of a project in Moss Side, Manchester. This has been established to help bring the schools into closer contact with parents, who – surprisingly – are often well satisfied with what is being done. The benefits to the teachers are obvious. Many parents have become involved in the work of the

[1] Paul Widlake, *Successful Teaching in the Urban School* (London: Ward Lock, 1976), p. 135.
[2] ibid.

school. There is an increase in understanding of one another's problems and a considered attempt by the schools involved to take account of their pupils' particular needs, which sometimes manifests itself in curricula modifications. Of course, the eclectic methods used by most British schools in teaching reading already include a considerable use of the child's own environment, a point which is often overlooked by critics.

These, and many other studies carried out in the Centre for Studies in Educational Handicap have been reported.[1] There is no doubt about the availability of good models, the existence of splendid exemplars, the successes of first-rate teachers. The trouble lies elsewhere, in the attempt to provide an *educational system* in which all children are given opportunities equal to the best available. The differences between the more and the less successful state schools, even when they draw from virtually the same population, have been noted regularly (for example, in the Newsom Report).[2] Progress might be made if we could understand the mechanisms by which 'successful' headteachers define policy and activate their staffs, deal with situations of potential conflict, encourage initiatives from parents, and generally ensure that children in the school are effectively learning.

'Successful' primary schools

To describe any state school as 'successful' is to invite a howl of protest from the far left, who consider the whole system operates to the detriment of the poor and oppressed, and that it cannot be improved, only abolished. It is certainly true that schools as at present constituted in Britain do not, in general, provide a very stimulating learning environment for many pupils; this is more true of secondary schools than primary and the facts have been published many times.[3] One's acknowledgement of this reality is not the same as a blanket dismissal of all schools and schooling. Like all human institutions, our schools are imperfect and fallible and variable, but some are good and caring, and the vast majority could certainly be improved to a reasonable standard if the will and the wit existed.

Success, at one level, is easily observable in primary schools. The children are seen to be happily involved in meaningful activities and their attainments in the basic subjects can be assessed. They are

[1] ibid; Paul Widlake, *Remedial Education: Programmes and Progress* (London: Longman, 1977); Paul Widlake, in Colin Richards (ed.), *Education 5–13* (Driffield: Nafferton Books, 1978).

[2] Central Advisory Council for Education (England), *Half our Future*. The Newsom Report (London: HMSO, 1963).

[3] For example, Department of Education and Science, *A Language for Life*. The Bullock Report (London: HMSO, 1975).

interested, and interesting; literate and numerate, as well as sociable and articulate. It is not too difficult, either, to determine the factors which enable some schools to produce good results and others very poor ones.

A study comparing the initial teaching of reading in four infant schools in a north-western city was carried out by Hylton.[1] Two of these schools were situated in areas of multiple deprivation (A and B) and two in more affluent suburban areas (C and D). It was expected that methods of teaching reading would vary: that teachers in the poorer areas would adopt methods different from and more appropriate to the special educational needs of their pupils – but this was not so. The main difference found was between schools A and B, both of which were in areas of multiple deprivation. School A had very poor reading results, only 24 per cent of the top infant children having a reading age of 7+ prior to going into the junior school. School B, however, showed good reading attainment by the children in the top infants, 71 per cent having a reading age of 7+. There appeared to be three main differences in the way the teaching of reading was approached in these two schools, which could account for such a discrepancy in the reading results. First, school A did not use any systematic method of teaching reading, while school B approached reading in a well organized, systematic way. Secondly, the headteacher of school A had very little to do with the teaching of reading in her school, showing no interest in it and offering no help to her staff on the subject. In contrast with this, the head of school B was very much involved in the reading in her school, helping both staff and children in every way she could. Thirdly, there was the difference in the level of teacher expectation between the two schools. At school A the head felt that the children could not be expected to achieve much in the way of learning to read because of their culture, personalities and home backgrounds: they were not expected to succeed. The head of school B did not see any one section of the school as being less able than another (there was also a high proportion of immigrants at this school) and expected all the children to learn to read by the end of the infant school. The attitude and expectations of the head seemed to be the main determinant of reading standards in the schools. These attitudes appeared to spread throughout the school and were often adopted by other members of staff. The headteacher of school A had negative views towards her children compared with positive views held by the other heads, especially the headteacher of school B whose children were similar to those of school A. The heads of school B, C and D expected most, if not all, of their children to reach a reasonable standard of reading by the end of the infant school. The head of school A expected very few

---

[1] S. Hylton, 'A study of methods of teaching reading in four infant schools', Centre for Studies in Educational Handicap, Didsbury School of Education, Manchester Polytechnic, 1977. Unpublished.

successful readers, especially among the West Indian population of the school. Schools B, C and D had good reading results while school A's results were very poor. The fact that teachers' and headteachers' expectations greatly affect the educational attainment of children was shown in an old and famous study by Rosenthal and Jacobson[1] and would seem to be reflected to some extent by the findings of this study. School A and school B both had children of similar socio-economic status, but the difference in their results was over-whelming. There are other factors to consider, such as the systematic teaching of reading and the relationship between headteacher and staff and so on, but it would also seem that teacher expectation is a most important consideration and not to be underestimated.

A more extensive study conducted by Madeleine Piper,[2] a Cambridge anthropologist working at Didsbury, used an ethnographic approach in a detailed study of a primary school which focused on the central aims and values of the school and how these were communicated to the children: in short, the culture of the school, how this was transmitted and what the implications were for West Indian children being exposed to, and in varying degrees assimilated by, this culture ('culture' here being used in Douglas's sense of the 'public, standardized values of a community').[3] An attempt was made to identify the public values of the school, the central categories around which it oriented itself and how assent to these values was achieved.

Much of the pleasure of such research resides in the amassing of detail and the dense picture of school and classroom life which emerges. This school is revealed as an institution where order prevails and the activities of the head, and to a slightly lesser extent the deputy head, set a strong example to pupils and other staff. The school is outgoing and welcomes, even encourages, visitors. During the study, friends of teachers came in to help, student teachers came in on visits and practices, 'ethnic' dance teachers came in to teach the children, policemen on public-relations duty came in and helped with routine activities, an ITV camera crew came in to film the big band, the staff and children were interviewed on local radio. In many ways the school is a show-piece – an 'active multiracial school'. The children also go on numerous visits outside the school: the Athenaeum, the Science Museum, limestone caves in Derbyshire, an outdoor pursuits centre, and Salford Art Gallery, to name a few. The children are used to meeting outsiders and to being on display, This

[1] R. Rosenthal and L. Jacobson, *Pygmalion in the Classroom: Teacher Expectation and Pupil Performance* (New York: Holt, Rinehart & Winston, 1971).

[2] M. Piper, 'West Indian children in primary schools', Centre for Studies in Educational Handicap, Didsbury School of Education, Manchester Polytechnic, 1979. Unpublished.

[3] M. Douglas, *Implicit Meanings: essays in anthropology* (London: Routledge & Kegan Paul, 1975).

made the presence of an observer and helper rather unexceptional and the school's readiness to use any available help facilitated assuming the role of participant observer. One of the children mentioned in interview that one of the aspects of the school he particularly liked was the exciting things which happen: filming, being interviewed, going on trips.

The headmaster has a very outgoing approach, promoting the name of the school whenever possible. He was generous in inviting us into his school after only short discussion of his few reservations. As already mentioned, he allows frequent visitors to the school in a variety of capacities. His claims for the school are in terms of its atmosphere rather than in terms of 'success': he claims that there is no gloom in the school and that expectations of all pupils are high. He encourages activities which enrich the children's lives and provide them with interests outside the narrowly defined academic. It is felt that music channels energies and discovers talents, and provides high self-esteem and confidence which affect the child's other work. While music is his own main interest, the head in choosing his staff has selected four people who have an extracurricular interest they could introduce to the children. As a result there is one teacher who takes an Olympic gymnastics class, one who takes the chess team to matches, one who has a pottery class, and one who takes an English folk-dance class. All these activities take place after school hours and are enthusiastically attended. The children, therefore, have a range of contents in which they can discover talents and succeed; and energies can be focused on co-operative school activities. The children are encouraged to do constructive things and to do them for pleasure and self-development.

The headmaster also encourages parents to come to the school, and this is physically declared by a welcome notice. They are always greeted warmly, and come in the normal course of events to watch the shows, which provide at least three opportunities a year, in addition to the two parents' evenings. When a child is severely disciplined, a note is sent home asking the parents to come in. If this is inconvenient some special arrangement is made to see them.

The headmaster, then, seeks to raise the self-esteem of the children through practical means, by providing a range of directions in which they can accomplish. He places great emphasis on effort and deals lightly and often humorously with mistakes: the children are encouraged to do and to try. It is difficult to speak of the head as an isolate as many of his decisions – and virtually all the enactments of these decisions – are made with the full, active co-operation of his deputy. They have been in the school for the same length of time and have really created the school as it is now together. Most of their ideals for the school are similar. The deputy has told us of a crisis period the school experienced at the time when the present head-master took over six years ago. There was very poor discipline in the school, with children refusing to co-operate in lessons and very poor literacy. For the deputy the deciding crisis came when she was unable to finish the week due to a constant headache caused by the noise. Over the weekend, she thought of setting up a major central activity to direct the children's energies; she also thought that the best way to make a start on improving literacy would be to make the children practise daily. Further, over this same weekend, she read some Open University units discussing behaviour modification, and decided she would set up incentive schemes in her own class encouraging all behaviour regarded as positive. The headmaster enthusiastically took up the suggestions which came from this 'crisis weekend' and some of the most notable aspects of the school as it is now were initiated.

This, then, is how educational 'policy' is initiated at primary-school level. It begins with a long, cool look at the available skills and attainments of both staff and children and it is transmitted to other members of staff by example, enthusiasm, persistence and (where a member of staff is weak or recalcitrant) flexibility and tolerance. The results, in this school, are impressive. Reading ages (as measured by standardized tests) are high, and children with both high and low intelligence quotients achieve scores well above their chronological ages. Children of different races are encouraged to learn together, and emotionally disturbed children are provided with a firm structure which enables most of them to contribute to the life of the school. The vast majority leave in better shape, affectively and cognitively, than they were in when they first started at the school. This is a definition of 'success' which the 'reasonable man' beloved of lawyers would be glad to accept.

Certain features of the organization of the school, teaching methods employed, and the way attitudes implicit in these are expressed, accounted, at least in part, for the success of the school. The main features isolated were:

1   *High expectations*
    (a) In activities, notably in orchestra, and concerts.
    (b) In work – indicated in the display of large amounts of children's work.
    (c) In behaviour – children are not expected to misbehave. Disappointment and surprise are expressed when they do so.

2   *Consistency – in expectations through the school and through time*
    (a) In incentive and sanctions – good work/behaviour is praised and rewarded with full inclusion in the school's activities; poor work/behaviour is answered with exclusion from some activities, and with displeasure.
    (b) In what is valued and what is devalued; staff co-operate in conveying a more or less uniform set of values.

(c) In the teaching of each particular teacher. Values are consistently conveyed, and work on the wall reflects, in more pragmatic terms, what the children have studied. An example would be that only cursive script is used on the board, which reinforces the learning of this skill. The children are expected to transfer the learning from one situation to another: what is expected is made quite explicit; the world in which they live and work directly reflects the world they are set as their goal, in both academic and behavioural terms.

3 *Continuity*
   (a) Behaviour modification is long-term. Children know they are being observed all the time by all the teachers. They know that present behaviour will affect future treatment.
   (b) There is continuity between home and school. Parents attend school functions, come in when a child has seriously misbehaved, and are referred to by the teacher. The children also have homework twice a week which is signed by the parents. The teacher also refers to brothers and sisters she has taught.

4 *Directness and openness towards errors and failings*
   It has been explicitly pointed out by one teacher that most of the West Indian children she teaches are evangelical Christians and place great emphasis on honesty and frankness. This may predispose the children to respond favourably where they are treated with directness.

5 *Relatively formal teaching*
   (a) Clarity of expectations.
   (b) Emphasis on procedure, setting out.
   (c) Much support.
   (d) Clear constraints on behaviour.

6 *Humorous and caring environment*
   (a) The children are relaxed by the constant humour of the head and deputy and are put in a position to feel equal, to banter good humouredly.
   (b) Care is shown in knowing of family troubles and showing concern over them, in caring for the children when troubled and sick, in spending time on extracurricular activities and taking the children on outings and courses.

7 *Resourcefulness*
   (a) In using tendencies and tastes to involve the children, for example, saying the 'Our Father' daily with disruptive children who take religion seriously.

(b) In offering a variety of fields in which children with different tendencies can participate and excel, for example, the big band and gymnastics.

8   *A heavy emphasis on literacy*
Throughout the school, and monitored using the child's own record card.

Ways forward

It has been shown that many primary schools are effective in providing learning opportunities for the bulk of their pupils. It has been fairly easy to establish certain procedures of good management into which it would seem possible to inculcate less gifted and determined headteachers. Why then, are there so many poor schools and so many children abandoned to illiteracy and innumeracy, their bleak prospects rendered yet more hopeless through their years at school? More specifically, what can be done to effect transfer of the best practice to more schools?

I think the beginnings of all such changes have to be established through increased openness and painful self-appraisals. When one looks at other schools renowned for excellence of a particular kind – for example, the Royal Ballet School – what strikes one is the complete willingness of the tutors and pupils to expose themselves to the most rigorous criticism. The pupils here seem singularly adult, and the adults retain respect because they live within the same awe-inspiring discipline. The contrast between such attitudes and those pervading much of British society is very painful. What a contrast between the athlete at the barre – reiterating movement after movement in a frenzy of disgust although each one would represent a peak of achievement to the average person – and the tetchy self-righteousness of many of the characters depicted in the Auld Report. It is not enough merely to become aware of ideological differences; we should consider explicitly *the nature of conflicts in schools* and how to develop mechanisms for their resolution.

An attempt has been made to describe and analyse techniques used by some primary schools designated by the local authority as 'successful'. Because we have been fairly explicit in our descriptions, one can be sure many readers will feel that their idea of a successful school is rather different. In fact, in a multi-cultural society, it is inevitable that this should occur, and it can be healthy for us to differ if the right framework can be provided. When there is substantive agreement within the community, an ecological approach such as that which prevails in Denmark and Norway, can be very productive. For example, features on which Norwegian parents and primary teachers seem widely agreed include:

Children should not commence schooling until the age of 7.

There are inherent dangers to children's development in an emphasis on early reading – children have more important things to be doing in these early years than learning to decipher the strangulated language of specially written primers.

Schools should be small, completely unstreamed and make provision for handicapped pupils; team teaching is the norm within the main stream.

It is unlikely that a representative group of English parents, managers and primary-school teachers would reach anything like this degree of unanimity. This is certainly not the fault of the head and deputy, who are the personnel ultimately held responsible if some kind of unified theory is not achieved. The free expression of a diversity of opinions is a cherished ideal of the open society. But the strong movement towards 'accountability' is indicative of a feeling among the British people that the schools, like other institutions, should be able to offer a reasoned statement of the manner in which its responsibilities are discharged. There is nothing sinister in this, but in fact it was easier to obtain such details about Ballygunge Circular Road Evening School in Calcutta than about some schools in our own country. These 'fee-paying' institutions in India (paid in addition to the cost of buying textbooks and materials for children's education from the tiny wage earned from jobs like pulling rickshaws) produce quite a good brochure for parents.

This is not too difficult a task for many teachers on our courses at Didsbury. They often choose to write something along these lines for one of their assignments. But it becomes a mighty challenge for some headteachers faced with deep divisions of opinion among their staff. Whose view should prevail when there is a major ideological conflict? So it is suggested that local education authorities should set up machinery for advising heads (who carry the can, after all) and for offering support in a practical manner before a crisis develops. Madeleine Piper's report is intended to be used in staff discussions and it may be that these would be best conducted by someone who can be perceived by the teachers as neutral in the authority structure.

Next, comes the delineation of objectives. Primary schools ought to welcome the work of the Assessment of Performance Unit. There is no threat of monitoring or intervention by the Department of Education and Science, but the requirement to devise tests which will assess standards nationally has forced the subject committees into published statements which are of the utmost value. The Language Committee, for example, has delineated tasks appropriate to an 11-year-old child in reading, writing and spoken language. If used properly, the document provides a starting-point for staff discussion and might lead to the writing of a policy statement. Really, primary schools should start doing this and in-service courses can provide the necessary support. We are doing something like this at Didsbury in conjunction with the Stockport LEA.

When conflict occurs, there would seem to be good scope for consultancy about its origins, causes and resolution, conducted in a supportive rather than an inquisitorial manner. One is concerned with improving the standards of primary schools, and not at all with interfering in other people's jobs or lives. But the trouble lies with those schools which do not or, more accurately, cannot respond to gentle persuasion. This is where the teaching profession's demand for autonomy is at its weakest. The achievements of the best schools cannot necessarily be set against the failure of the worst, or the mediocrity of the many. Some Scandinavian schools achieve brilliance but within a system which ensures that the *average* standard is extremely high; and it is certain that more guidance is required in our schools. Perhaps the teachers' unions could do more to encourage the weaker members. If a positive response is not made, there is a grave danger that parents will begin to look to the courts, and that all the horrors of a legalistic approach will be let loose. A further suggestion is that all schools should try to produce a written statement of their aims, philosophy and methods, which can be presented to managers and parents and defended without embarrassment by members of staff.

Finally, there should be closer links with the community. Our Manchester school study provides a vivid account of how to do it. Another very fully documented account of how to spend an Urban Aid grant has been written by the late Ted Whitehouse.[1] Very full accounts exist of techniques for linking school to family, school to teacher training, school to economy and school to school.[2] The role of the home–school liaison teacher has been explored, documented, re-examined: a dissertation exists at Didsbury which is a kind of manual on how to carry out this work.[3] Broome[4] has indicated dozens of ways in which it is possible to encourage parents to join in the educational process. The idea is to take education into the home and to bring parents into school; there is no doubt at all that it can be done, is being done, that the results are beneficial and that it should be done in all schools.

---

[1] In Paul Widlake, *Successful Teaching in the Urban School*, op. cit.

[2] A. H. Halsey, *Educational Priority* (London: HMSO, 1972).

[3] P. Brown, unpublished dissertation, Centre for Studies in Educational Handicap, Didsbury Faculty, Manchester Polytechnic.

[4] In Paul Widlake, *Remedial Education: Programmes and Progress*, op cit. p. 46.

8 Secondary-school Practice and Pupil Success

Michael Rutter[1]

All too often inner-city schools have received a bad press, with the regular painting of a picture of homogeneous, failing institutions full of aggressive, illiterate pupils, making life miserable for demoralized teachers. In fact the evidence shows this picture to be false. Inner-city schools vary enormously. Some are doing a good job in spite of the most difficult circumstances; and schooling can constitute a positive experience for deprived children. In this chaper I will outline some of the research findings which indicate those aspects of schooling which seem most likely to facilitate pupil success.

During the last two decades schools, and especially inner-city schools, have been under vigorous attack from all sides. Critics have described them as institutions which foster inequality and racism; which are repressive, non-creative and alienating; and where the teaching is dull, boring and meaningless.[2] Even the titles of books on schooling stand out as messages of condemnation – *The Urban School: A Factory for Failure*,[3] *School is Dead*,[4] *Compulsory Miseducation*,[5] *The*

[1] The work reported here was undertaken in collaboration with Barbara Maughan, Dr Peter Mortimore, Dr Janet Ouston and Alan Smith. The author is also grateful for the help of other colleagues and in particular for the generous help received throughout the study from the headteachers and staff of the schools involved. He is grateful to the Inner London Education Authority and the Department of Education and Science for financial support of the research.

[2] See A. Lightfoot, *Urban Education in Social Perspective* (Chicago: Rand McNally, 1978), for a survey of these views.

[3] R. C. Rist, *The Urban School: A Factory for Failure* (Cambridge, Mass.: MIT Press, 1973).

[4] E. Reimer, *School is Dead: An Essay on Alternatives in Education* (Harmondsworth: Penguin Books, 1971).

[5] P. Goodman, *Compulsory Miseducation* (New York: Horizon Press, 1964).

Underachieving School,[1] *Death at an Early Age*,[2] *Crisis in the Classroom*,[3] and *Pedagogy of the Oppressed*.[4] In Britain, Thornbury[5] has recently provided a lively and thoughtful critique of the various myths and messages pressed on teachers in urban schools by cult figures of the Left and Right, and in the United States, Lightfoot has sought to place urban education in a social perspective. Both authors point to the growing violence and unrest in city schools and note the apparently declining levels of achievement by pupils – the main topics of concern to most writers on urban education.

However, both Lightfoot and Thornbury are basically optimistic in seeing solutions to these problems. They argue for changes in social policy, for a reduction in the inequalities between rich and poor educational authorities, for better integration in the community, and for better social and racial balance in the intakes. Thus, Thornbury maintains that 'the individual teacher could say loud and clear in the staffrooms that putting the social composition of school intakes last in the educational priorities of the school was burying professional heads in the sand.' Lightfoot also stresses the importance of reducing class sizes, of eliminating standardized testing and of abolishing tenure for teachers. They differ in their views of compensatory education; Lightfoot wants more spending in this area, whereas Thornbury wants a reduced emphasis on this approach. Both are very sympathetic to the many difficulties faced by teachers in inner-city schools but both feel that it is important for school staff to have a greater involvement in the social issues faced by the community within which they work. Thornbury puts it like this:

> Teachers had had a hard time – indeed the strenuous conditions of their work had often blinded them to wider issues. Many teachers who had subscribed to the EPA myth, believing that massive extra educational resources would put things right, had worked themselves into illness or early retirement ... They were willing to break their backs planting roses in the window boxes of the poor – but they weren't prepared to demand schools with adjacent playfields or houses with gardens.

Ann Jones,[6] on the other hand, has provided a rather different analysis. She fully recognizes the importance of social and family influences on pupil behaviour and on school functioning, but nevertheless, she argues that the vogue for basing much of the school curriculum on the 'here and now' social situations in which the pupils live, often serves only to encapsulate those pupils in a circle of deprivation. Instead, she emphasizes the importance of an over-all school ethos which is positive, challenging and geared towards

[1] J. Holt, *The Underachieving School* (Belmont: Pitman, 1969).

[2] J. Kozol, *Death at an Early Age* (Harmondsworth: Penguin Books, 1971).

[3] C. E. Silberman, *Crisis in the Classroom* (New York: Random House, 1971).

[4] R. Freire, *Pedagogy of the Oppressed* (Harmondsworth: Penguin Books, 1972).

[5] R. Thornbury, *The Changing Urban School* (London: Methuen, 1978).

[6] A. Jones, 'The school's view of persistent non-attendance', in L. Hersov and I. Berg (eds), *Truancy: Problems of School Attendance and Refusal* (Chichester: Wiley, 1979).

learning, and outlines the various measures within the school which may serve to promote such a climate.

The problem, then, seems to be how to decide which solutions have most to offer. But first there is a prior question: 'Do schools matter at all?' If they do not, might we not do better placing our resources elsewhere, letting schools survive as best they may. That seems an odd question to ask when education is compulsory and when such a high proportion of our national resources is poured into schooling. However, it has to be asked if only because there has developed a widespread acceptance among academics that schools make little difference. This view stems in large part from the American report by James Coleman[1] on equality of educational opportunity and on Christopher Jencks'[2] reassessment of the data. Jencks concluded that 'equalizing the quality of high schools would reduce cognitive inequality by one per cent or less' and that 'additional school expenditures are unlikely to increase achievement, and redistributing resources will not reduce test score inequality'. At much the same time, Jensen[3] concluded that 'compensatory education has been tried and it apparently has failed'. Bowles[4] maintained that 'educational inequalities are rooted in the basic institutions of our economy' and Bernstein[5] urged that 'education cannot compensate for society'. Accordingly before considering the positive steps schools might take in order to foster pupil success, it is necessary briefly to review the contradictory claims and findings about the influence of schooling on children's development.

Do schools matter?

It is appropriate to begin with the large-scale cross-sectional surveys which have been most influential in creating the impression that education made little difference. In essence these showed that school variables such as average expenditure per pupil, number of books in the school library and teacher–pupil ratio, accounted for very little of the variation between pupils on standardized attainment tests. The

[1] J. S. Coleman et al., Equality of Educational Opportunity (Washington: US Government Printing Office, 1966).

[2] C. Jencks, M. Smith, H. Acland, M. J. Bane, D. Cohen, H. Gintis, B. Heyns and S. Michelson, Inequality: A Reassessment of the Effect of Family and Schooling in America (New York: Basic Books, 1972).

[3] A. R. Jensen, 'How much can we boost IQ and scholastic achievement?', Harvard Educational Review, vol. 39 (1969), pp. 1–123.

[4] S. Bowles, 'Unequal education and the reproduction of the social division of labor', Review of Radical Political Economics, 3 (1971). Reprinted in J. Karabel and A. H. Halsey (eds), Power and Ideology in Education (New York: Oxford University Press, 1977).

[5] B. Bernstein, 'Education cannot compensate for society', New Society, vol. 387 (1970), pp. 344–7.

studies were carefully conducted and the data rigorously analysed, both in the original reports and subsequently again by independent investigators.[1] It may be accepted that the findings are well based. Nevertheless, it would be quite wrong to suppose that the results mean that schooling makes no difference. Serious caveats are necessary as a result of three rather different issues. First, it should be noted that the measures of attainment in the original American studies mainly relied on verbal ability – measures which bear very little relationship to anything most schools would aim to teach. More recent studies[2] have shown that there are considerably greater school effects when the measures concern *taught* subjects such as mathematics or science.

Secondly, the surveys have examined a very narrow range of school variables – most of which have focused on one or other aspect of resources. As Jencks pointed out, the measures failed to take into account anything about the internal life of school; its attitudes, values and mores; or its qualities as a social organization. As we shall see, later studies have indicated that these were grave omissions. It is just these social, rather than financial, variables which *do* account for much of the variation between schools.

Thirdly, Jencks' analyses were primarily concerned with the issue of how far an improvement in the quality of schooling would make children more alike – that is reduce inequalities in attainment. The clear answer was that it would make very little difference – the differences in attainment within any one school are far greater than the differences between schools. Raising the quality of education will not, and could not, have the effect of making all pupils the same. But, as other studies to be considered in a moment show, it may have a decisive impact in raising over-all standards of attainment. Surely that is the more realistic and appropriate goal. The task of schools is to help all pupils develop in the most advantageous way possible. It is *not* to achieve some kind of homogenization. '

These three caveats necessarily lead to major reservations about the Coleman–Jencks conclusions. Such reservations are greatly strengthened by the rather different findings from a number of more recent studies. These have shown quite large differences between schools, not only in academic attainment but also in attendance rates, behavioural difficulties and delinquency. Thus, Michael Power and

[1] See, for example, F. Mosteller and D. P. Moynihan (eds), *On Equality of Educational Opportunity* (New York: Random House, 1972).

[2] See T. H. Postlethwaite, 'The surveys of the international association for the evaluation of educational achievement (IEA): implications of the IEA surveys of achievement', in A. C. Purvis and D. V. Levine (eds), *Educational Policy and International Assessment* (Berkeley: McCutchen, 1975); G. F. Madaus, T. Kellaghan and E. A. Rakow, 'School and class differences in performance on the leaving certificate examination', *Irish Journal of Education*, vol. 10 (1976), pp. 41–50: D. Davis, 'Where comprehensives score', *The Times Educational Supplement*, 25 March 1977; M. A. Brimer, G. F. Madaus, B. Chapman, T. Kellaghan and R. Wood, *Sources of Difference in School Achievement* (Windsor: NFER Publishing, 1978).

his colleagues[1] found large and stable differences in delinquency rates between inner London secondary schools; and Dennis Gath and his research team[2] found the same in outer London. David Reynolds[3] found major variations between South Wales schools in rates of academic attainment, attendance, delinquency, and also unemployment four months after school leaving. Heal[4] found that primary schools differed significantly in their level of pupil misbehaviour; we found the same and also showed substantial school variations in levels of reading attainment.[5] A variety of statistical checks and corrections showed that the school differences could not be accounted for in terms of differences in the schools' catchment areas. Nevertheless, because their data were cross-sectional, none of these studies was able to show that the schools had led to *changes* in their pupils' behaviour and scholastic attainments. The inference of a school effect was necessarily circumstantial and uncertain.

The essential next step was a longitudinal study in which the children could be systematically assessed both before entering secondary school and again during and after secondary schooling. An investigation undertaken with my colleagues Barbara Maughan, Peter Mortimore and Janet Ouston[6] provides just such data. In brief, some 1500 children in one inner-London borough were assessed through group tests and teacher questionnaires in primary school at age 10 years; were reassessed on the same measures at age 14 years, in their third year of secondary school; and were then reassessed once more at the time of school leaving, with regard to their success in national examinations. Measures of behaviour, of delinquency rates and school attendance were also obtained. Further data on employment are now being gathered by Grace Gray one year after leaving school. Finally, a detailed study was made of the twelve secondary schools which took the bulk of the children.[7]

[1] M. J. Power, M. R. Alderson, C. M. Phillipson, E. Schoenberg and J. M. Morris, 'Delinquent Schools?', *New Society*, vol. 10 (1967), pp. 542–3.

[2] D. Gath, B. Cooper, F. Gattoni and D. Rockett, *Child Guidance and Delinquency in a London Borough*, Maudsley Monographs No. 24 (London: Oxford University Press, 1977).

[3] D. Reynolds, D. Jones and S. St Leger, 'Schools do make a difference', *New Society*, vol. 37 (1976), p. 321; D. Reynolds and S. Murgatroyd, 'The sociology of schooling and the absent pupil: the school as a factor in the generation of truancy', in H. C. M. Carroll (ed.), *Absenteeism in South Wales: Studies of Pupils, their Homes and their Secondary Schools* (Swansea: Faculty of Education, University College of Swansea, 1977).

[4] K. H. Heal, 'Misbehaviour among school children: the role of the school in strategies for prevention', *Policy and Politics*, vol. 6 (1978), pp. 321–32.

[5] M. Rutter, B. Yule, D. Quinton, O. Rowlands, W. Yule and M. Berger, 'Attainment and adjustment in two geographical areas: III. Some factors accounting for area differences', *British Journal of Psychiatry*, vol. 126 (1975), pp. 520–33.

[6] M. Rutter, B. Maughan, P. Mortimore, J. Ouston and A. Smith, *Fifteen Thousand Hours: Secondary Schools and their Effects on Children* (London: Open Books, 1979).

[7] Most of the children attended one or other of twenty non-selective secondary schools. Information on the children's attainment at 14 years was obtained for pupils in all twenty schools, but limitation of resources meant that it was possible to make the more detailed study of functioning and practice in just twelve schools.

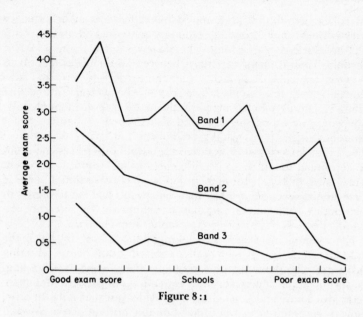

Figure 8:1

The findings are striking in showing large and important differences between secondary schools in each measure of pupil success or outcome, even after all possible due allowance had been made for variations between the schools in the proportions of behaviourally difficult, socially disadvantaged or low-attaining pupils they admitted. The differences between schools also could not be accounted for in terms of variations in the schools' catchment areas. The size and meaning of these differences is best conveyed by considering two examples.

Figure 8:1 shows differences between schools in national examination results. The vertical shows the average weighted exam score per child – the score being based on one point for an O-level GCE equivalent and half a point for a grade 2 or 3 CSE. The horizontal gives the findings for each of the twelve study schools in turn (all schools being non-selective). The data are given separately according to the children's verbal reasoning ability as measured at age 10 years – the top 25 per cent in band 1, the middle 50 per cent in band 2, and the bottom 25 per cent in band 3. The figure shows two main findings. First, examination success is strongly correlated with the assessment of intellectual abilities prior to entering secondary school. Thus, the average number of passes for band 1 children was over 3, for band 2 it was 1·5 and for band 3 it was less than 0·5. This finding is, of course, in keeping with all earlier research and emphasizes the importance of individual differences between children. Secondly, the same data show marked variations between schools such that, at the

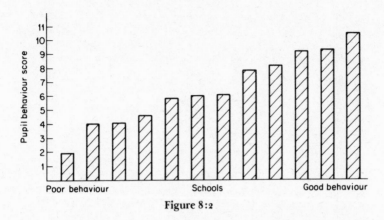

Figure 8:2

extremes, the average score for band 3 children in the most successful school was as good as that for band 1 children in the least successful school! In other words, even after taking into account individual differences between pupils, some inner-city schools were strikingly more successful than others. It is also evident that the pattern of results for each school was broadly similar in all three bands. In general, in schools where the less able children had better than average examination results the more able children also had superior exam success.

Similar differences between schools were found with respect to our measure of pupil behaviour. A twenty-five item scale was created by combining self-report data from the pupils and observational measures for several different age-groups of children. Direct observations of first- and third-year lessons, for example, were used to assess late arrival at lessons, the extent of off-task behaviour, chatting and calling out in class and instances of overtly disruptive behaviour. Damage to school property and the extent of graffiti were systematically noted by observations about the school. Self-reports tapped aspects of behaviour not easily observed, such as truanting, absconding and skipping lessons. The mean rank scores of the twelve schools are shown in Figure 8:2. Scores ranged from under 2 to nearly 11 indicating very great variations between schools in pupil behaviour. Interestingly, there was no significant association between the secondary schools with the worst pupil behaviour and those with the 'worst' intakes of difficult pupils at the age of 10 years. It appeared that the large variations between schools was a response to some aspect of secondary-school experiences rather than simply a continuation of patterns of behaviour previously established in primary schools.

In summary, after more detailed statistical analyses than there has been time to outline here, it was found that the marked school

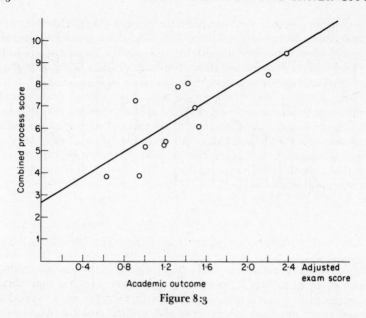

Figure 8:3

variations in each different type of outcome could not be accounted for in terms of any of the available measures of individual intake characteristics. As such measures included not only pupil behaviour and attainments at primary school, but also social background, it seems likely that the school variations in outcome were linked with characteristics of the schools themselves. Of course, the finding that the outcome differences between schools were not due to differences on any of the intake measures, only means that they were due to 'something else'. In order to show that something else concerns features of schooling there must be at least one further step. It is necessary to determine how far school variations in outcome are consistently associated with measured differences in school structure, organization or functioning.

The over-all findings on this point are summarized in Figure 3 which shows the correlation between what we have termed the 'combined school process score' and examination success. The process score is simply a convenient way of pooling all the various school features found to be important in relation to outcome. Figure 8:3 shows that there was a very substantial correlation (0·76) between the over-all school process score and academic attainment. Significant correlations of a comparable level were found with the other measures of outcome – pupil behaviour, attendance and delinquency. Later in this chapter I will consider which variables went into the process measure – and hence which features of school life were most likely to influence children's development. But for the present the point to be made is that the differences between secondary schools in outcome *were* systematically associated with characteristics of the schools themselves. Firm conclusions about causation can only come from controlled experimental studies – by altering school practices and determining if this results in changes in the children's progress. Such investigations have yet to be undertaken but meanwhile there is the strong implication that school processes *do* influence pupil outcomes. In short, it appears that in a part of inner London, known to be socially disadvantaged in numerous ways, some schools were better able than others to foster good behaviour and attainments. Before turning to a consideration of *which* school features make good outcomes more likely, I want to dispose of two prevailing myths.

The myth of the overriding importance of the pre-school years

The first concerns the supposedly overriding importance of family influences during the pre-school years. This view is largely based on the observations that so many difficulties and problems have their roots in early childhood and that interventions in later childhood have so often been rather unsuccessful. Both observations are correct but the inference that the first five years are critical for all aspects of development is false,[1] as a review of the empirical evidence clearly indicates.[2] Children's intellectual and behavioural development is sensitive to environmental change during *all* stages of childhood and adolescence. The school years are certainly early enough to have an important impact on development.

A related aspect of this same myth is that family influences are so powerful that there is no room for schooling to make much difference. This view is wrong on two separate counts. First, as we have seen, there is strong empirical evidence pointing to the high likelihood that schools *do* have an important influence. Second, family variables do *not* explain the whole, or anything like the whole, of children's behaviour and attainments. All studies of deprived or disadvantaged children have noted very wide variations in response. Even with the most terrible homes and the most stressful circumstances some individuals come through unscathed and seem to have a stable healthy personality development. Elsewhere I have

[1] However, although there is good evidence that experiences in middle childhood can and do have an important impact on development, there are a few features such as the development of social attachments which appear particularly sensitive to events in the first two to three years.

[2] See A. Clarke and A. Clarke (eds), *Early Experience: Myth and Evidence* (London: Open Books, 1976); M. Rutter, 'Maternal deprivation 1972–1978: new findings, new concepts, new approaches', *Child Development*, vol. 50 (1979), pp. 283–305.

considered the few research findings on this topic[1] – with the conclusion that *positive* experiences or *protective* factors can go some way towards making up for, or enabling children to cope with, stress and deprivation. Schooling provides one such opportunity by which disadvantage may be to some extent mitigated – or, of course, strongly reinforced.

The myth that all inner-city schools are similar and terrible

The second myth concerns the view that all inner-city schools are both similar and terrible. The evidence clearly negates this pessimistic and condemnatory picture of inner-city schooling. Of course, there are real problems which must be recognized and faced. Academic attainments – as shown both by reading skills[2] and by national examination results[3] – are often poor. In many schools absenteeism is very common, especially in the fifth year. Delinquency rates are high; in some schools nearly half the boys have received an official conviction or caution. These are indeed matters of concern. But it is important not to exaggerate the difficulties. In the first place, the statistics themselves can be misleading. The high delinquency rate tends to convey a picture of rampant violence, but this is wrong. Only a small proportion of delinquency involves any kind of physical aggression and about half of all delinquents only receive one conviction. Not a cause for complacency but not a picture of mayhem either. Thus, in our own study we observed over five hundred lessons in secondary schools serving a socially disadvantaged inner-city area, but during the course of twelve weeks' observation there was only one incident so serious as to stop the course of a lesson completely. It is true that some teachers, especially probationary teachers, experienced considerable difficulties with some of their classes, but the overall impression was far from the 'blackboard jungle' image of city schools.

The second point is that not all city schools are alike. We have already seen the major variations between schools in rates of examination success and of good classroom behaviour. The same applies to attendance.[4] It is true that in some schools daily attendance falls from nearly 90 per cent in the first year to 65 per cent in the fifth

[1] M. Rutter, 'Protective factors in children's responses to stress and disadvantage', in M. W. Kent and J. E. Rolf (eds), *Primary Prevention of Psychopathology*, vol. 3. Promoting Social Competence and Coping in Children (Hanover, N. H.: University Press of New England, 1978).

[2] M. Berger, W. Yule and M. Rutter, 'Attainment and adjustment in two geographical areas: II. The prevalence of specific reading retardation', *British Journal of Psychiatry*, vol. 126 (1975), pp. 510–19.

[3] M. Rutter *et al.*, *Fifteen Thousand Hours*, op. cit.

[4] See M. Rutter *et al.*, *Fifteen Thousand Hours*, op. cit.

year. But also there are schools where fifth-form attendance is still maintained at a rate above 85 per cent. In some schools graffiti are widespread and broken windows and furniture common. But in others old buildings have been transformed by attractive decorations, pictures and plants; and by immediate repairs of damage and rapid removal of graffiti. In some schools morale is low but in others there is an atmosphere of vigour, enjoyment and success. It is crucial to appreciate that, despite the many difficulties they face, there are many good things going on in inner-city schools.

So much for the myths. I shall now consider the reality and the various remedies and solutions which have been proposed by different writers in order to improve inner-city schooling (other than those involving teaching methods or curriculum which I shall not consider here). In doing this I shall first dispose of those which seem to be misconceived.

School features with a limited effect on pupil outcome

Resources

First, there is the matter of resources. It is often supposed[1] that the lack of resources in inner-city areas constitutes the main problem and that increasing resources would provide an effective solution. The research evidence indicates that both suppositions are wrong – at least in Britain. National statistics[2] show that inner-city areas are not necessarily particularly badly off in terms of the financial resources allocated to education. Supplementary funding of various kinds has meant that in some cases they are actually rather better off than rural areas and the suburbs. Thus, the estimated per capita expenditure for 1977/8 in secondary schools in inner London was the highest in the country. Of course, the figures cannot be taken at face value because high spending may reflect higher local costs or the need to repair buildings left dilapidated from earlier years. However, this is unlikely to be the whole explanation as the Inner London Education Authority also spends more per child each year on books, educational equipment and materials. Lack of finance may well have been an important factor in the past but it is not the main issue today. Moreover, variations in financing (either in this country or in the USA) do *not* account for differences in pupil behaviour or attainments.[3] This appears to be so both within and between local authorities. I do not propose to enter the debate on whether we spend enough on

[1] A. Lightfoot, op. cit.

[2] See J. Pratt, 'Calculating your LEA's generosity', *Where*, No. 136 (1978), pp. 73–5.

[3] See M. Rutter and N. Madge, *Cycles of Disadvantage* (London: Heinemann Educational Books, 1976); M. Rutter *et al.*, *Fifteen Thousand Hours*, op. cit.

education – my point is simply that variations between schools in resources do not explain differences in outcome, and it seems unlikely that, in itself, an increase in resources would do much to foster success. More of the same is not an effective answer.

Size of school and size of class

Another popular solution lies in an elimination of the very large comprehensive schools and in a reduction of average class sizes.[1] Both remedies are likely to be ineffective. The evidence from several studies[2] indicates no consistent association between school size and pupil success, however measured. Of course, it is likely that the size of a school does have an impact on its character and style, but the most successful schools include both the large and the small. The same applies to the space available. In our own study the degree of over-crowding (either in terms of the buildings or the over-all site area) was largely unrelated to outcome.

Interestingly, many investigations have shown that average class size or the over-all pupil–teacher ratio is also unrelated to pupil success.[3] At first sight this appears surprising – surely it ought to be easier to teach well in a smaller class? There are a variety of reasons why caution is needed in taking this finding at its face value – popular schools are likely to have larger classes just because they are over-subscribed and schools with a high proportion of disadvantaged children may be given extra teachers just because of the low levels of attainment. In addition, there is some suggestion that low ability pupils have a particular need for small classes.[4] Nevertheless, in spite of all these caveats it is clear that it is possible to run a very well functioning school with fairly large classes. It may be that there are educational advantages in having *very* small classes which allow a different approach to teaching, but with the general run of pupils there seems to be little to gain from cutting class sizes by just a few pupils – from, say 30 to 25. If extra funds are available for schools, there are probably better ways of spending them.

Organizational structure

There is much debate in schools on the most advantageous system of academic and pastoral organization, but the available evidence suggests that no one system has overriding advantages. Much passion, for example, is aroused over the pros and cons of mixed-

[1] See A. Lightfoot, op. cit.

[2] See M. Rutter *et al.*, *Fifteen Thousand Hours*, op. cit.

[3] See M. Rutter and N. Madge, op. cit.; M. Rutter *et al.*, *Fifteen Thousand Hours*, op. cit.

[4] A. A. Summers and B. L. Wolfe, 'Do schools make a difference?', *American Economic Review*, 1977.

ability teaching versus streaming. In general, the evidence suggests that the average academic performance of children in streamed and unstreamed schools is broadly comparable.[1] On the other hand, within streamed schools there is some scholastic advantage in being in the top stream, even after initial differences in achievement and social background have been taken into account.[2] It seems that pupil subcultures and teacher attitudes tend to become polarized along the lines of streaming arrangements so that lower-stream children may become labelled as failures and perceive themselves as such.[3] As a consequence, mixed-ability teaching may have some advantages for less able children without any appreciable lowering of standards for the more able.[4] The data on behavioural consequences are somewhat contradictory but mixed-ability schools may have a reduced tendency to develop delinquent subcultures. However, not all studies have found differences in either behavioural or academic outcome according to streaming or mixed-ability teaching,[5] so the effects are rather inconsistent.

There may be greater difficulties in teaching some subjects (such as mathematics) to mixed-ability classes, particularly higher up the school. To the extent that this is so, some streaming or banding according to pupil skills in particular subjects may well be desirable and advantageous over all. On the other hand, the evidence from studies of teacher expectations,[6] as well as from observations in schools,[7] certainly indicates that children are likely to suffer if they are dealt with in ways which create a sense of failure. This is particularly likely to arise with bottom-stream children, and if streaming is used it is important to ensure that the bottom-stream pupils get ample opportunities for encouragement, reward, responsibility and participation in the life of the school.

There has been less systematic study of contrasting patterns of pastoral care. However, in our own study[8] we found no differences in

[1] A. H. Passow, M. Goldberg and A. J. Tannenbaum (eds), *Education of the Disadvantaged: A Book of Readings* (New York: Holt, Rinehart & Winston, 1967); J. C. B. Lunn, *Streaming in the Primary School* (Windsor: NFER Publishing, 1970); C. Jencks *et al.*, op. cit.

[2] H. Acland, 'Social determinants of educational achievement: an evaluation and criticism of research', Ph.D. thesis, University of Oxford, 1973; J. C. B. Lunn, op. cit.

[3] D. N. Hargreaves, *Social Relations in a Secondary School* (London: Routledge & Kegan Paul, 1976).

[4] C. Lacey, *Hightown Grammar: The School as a Social System* (Manchester: Manchester University Press, 1970); C. Lacey, 'Destreaming in a "pressured" academic environment', in J. Eggleston (ed), *Contemporary Research in the Sociology of Education* (London: Methuen, 1974); K. Postlethwaite and C. Denton, *Streams for the Future? The Long-term Effects of Early Streaming and Non-streaming — the final report of the Banbury Enquiry* (Banbury: Pubansco Publications, 1978).

[5] M. Rutter *et al.*, *Fifteen Thousand Hours*, op. cit.

[6] See D. Pilling and M. Kellmer Pringle, *Controversial Issues in Child Development* (London: Paul Elek, 1978).

[7] See D. N. Hargreaves, op. cit.

[8] M. Rutter *et al.*, *Fifteen Thousand Hours*, op. cit.

outcome between schools organized on a year-based system and those utilizing a house-based system. It was important that some form of pastoral care be readily available, but the administrative organization for providing it seems less crucial. Indeed, it appeared that the informal sources may be particularly important. Pupil outcomes tended to be better in schools where the ordinary teachers were available to see children about problems at any time (not just at fixed periods), and where the pupils reported that, if they needed to, they would talk to a member of staff about a personal problem.

Social mix

The next misconceived, or rather partially misconceived, solution concerns social mix. There is a widespread assumption that a high proportion of socially disadvantaged pupils in any one school impedes children's scholastic progress. The suggestion is certainly plausible; schools constitute social organizations and because of this they are likely to be influenced by the composition of the social groups in them. Moreover, the American data provide some support for this notion.[1] But the evidence from Britain is that social mix makes a difference only at the extremes.[2] Our own data[3] give some pointers to possible explanations for the contradictory findings. We examined the influence of various different aspects of mix or balance in terms of parental occupation, the children's intellectual performance and behaviour prior to entering secondary school, and their ethnic background. Three main findings stand out. First, none of these measures of balance of intake was associated with school differences in pupil behaviour. Secondly, none of the balance variables was associated with our overall measure of school process or functioning. It appears that in so far as social mix (or any other form of mix) has an impact, it does so through the peer group rather than through any direct effect on teacher behaviour. Thirdly, although the balance of intake did not correlate with pupil behaviour, it *was* associated with our other outcome measures. But the most influential balance variable concerned intellectual ability groupings and not the child's social or ethnic background.

Sometimes it is thought that these amount to the same thing; after all it is well known that, *on average*, groups of working-class children and black children have mean IQs below middle-class groups. Of course that is so, but it is important to recognize that the findings

[1] J. S. Coleman *et al.*, op. cit.

[2] C. Mabey, *Social and Ethnic Mix in Schools and the Relationship and Attainment of Children aged 8 and 11*, Research Paper No. 9 (London: Centre for Environmental Studies, 1974); J. H. Barnes and H. Lucas, 'Positive discrimination in education: individuals, groups and institutions', in T. Leggatt (ed.), *Sociological Theory and Survey Research* (London: Sage Publications, 1974).

[3] M. Rutter *et al.*, *Fifteen Thousand Hours*, op. cit.

refer to group differences, the associations are of only moderate size, and there are many exceptions. Plenty of socially disadvantaged black pupils have above average attainments. Socio-cultural background and intellectual ability are far from synonymous.

However, it does appear important that schools have a reasonable balance of intellectually able and less able children, even if it matters less how these are distributed in social or ethnic terms. The mechanisms remain ill understood but it is probable that the explanation lies in the achievements open to pupils. At present, examination success is the most public indication of success. But the exams are so arranged that some 40 per cent of the population are expected to fail. If a school has mainly less able children, then of course the proportion will be higher still. When a preponderance of pupils in school are likely to fail, it must be expected that many children will not identify with school goals and aims. In this way peer group contra-cultures may develop within schools.[1] The suggestion is necessarily tentative in the absence of empirical data on the processes involved. Nevertheless, in so far as it is at all valid, the implications extend beyond questions of social or academic mix to the much more central issue of the nature of school goals and the availability of rewards and success for *all* pupils. Do examinations need to be set in a way which ensures failure for nearly half the population? And do competitive examinations[2] have to be the only sign of school success? The maintenance of academic standards is important (see below) but the use of examinations with a high failure rate in order to do this carries with it substantial disadvantages.

Punishment

The last ineffective solution I will consider is punishment. There are those who see the main need in inner-city schools as one of firmer discipline – and by this is usually meant more consistent and more severe punishment. There has been surprisingly little systematic research into the effects of different patterns of discipline in schools but what evidence there is clearly indicates that more punishment is unlikely to help. Thus, Reynolds[3] found that a low use of corporal punishment was most likely to be associated with good attendance; Heal[4] showed that misbehaviour was worst in schools with formal punishment systems; and Clegg and Megson[5] noted that delinquency

[1] See D. N. Hargreaves, op. cit.

[2] Strictly speaking the national examinations are not competitive in the sense that candidates compete for a finite number of passes. Nevertheless, failure rates are generally seen as a guide to examination standards. In this respect they are different from, for example, tests to check whether pupils have reached a defined level of competence in reading or arithmetic.

[3] D. Reynolds and S. Murgatroyd, op. cit.

[4] K. H. Heal, op. cit.

[5] A. Clegg and B. Megson, *Children in Distress* (Harmondsworth: Penguin Books, 1968).

rates tended to be highest in schools with a great deal of corporal punishment. In our own study[1] we found no significant associations between the number of detentions or the amount of corporal punishment and any of our measures of pupil success. The over-all amount of punishment seems of only minor importance, but certain forms of discipline may actually aggravate the situation. We found that frequent disciplinary interventions in the classroom were associated with worse pupil behaviour. It seemed that constant checking and reprimanding by the teacher perpetuated behavioural disturbance by the innumerable interruptions to the flow of the lesson. Unofficial physical sanctions (such as slaps or cuffing) were also associated with worse behaviour – perhaps because they set a model of violence or perhaps because they bred pupil resentment about personally humiliating treatment. Whatever the explanations, and the findings are in keeping with family studies[2] showing that physical punishment increases the likelihood of social aggression, it is evident that more punishment would not help and might hinder improvements in inner-city schools.

Does that mean, then, that good standards of discipline are unimportant? To the contrary, the same studies show the value of good discipline. It is just that *frequent* punishment is not the most effective way of establishing discipline, although, of course, *some* punishment is an essential part of discipline. Thus, Reynolds[3] found that good attendance was associated with good rule enforcement and with the involvement of pupils in discipline through the use of a perfect system. We, too, found that group-based discipline standards were helpful.[4] Kounin[5] showed that teachers needed to be aware of what goes on in all parts of the classroom; and Brophy and Evertson[6] found that the most successful teachers tended to spot disruptive behaviour early and to deal with it appropriately and firmly with the minimum of interference with the lesson. These are the skills of good classroom management, so well outlined by Michael Marland in his book, *The Craft of the Classroom.*[7] Good discipline is essential in any well run school. This must involve some sanctions and punishment but it is seriously misleading to see more punishment as a way to improving standards.

[1] M. Rutter *et al.*, *Fifteen Thousand Hours*, op. cit.

[2] G. R. Patterson, 'Accelerating stimuli for two classes of coercive behaviors', *Journal of Abnormal Child Psychology*, vol. 5 (1977), pp. 335–50.

[3] D. Reynolds and S. Murgatroyd, op. cit.

[4] M. Rutter *et al.*, *Fifteen Thousand Hours*, op. cit.

[5] J. S. Kounin, *Discipline and Group Management in Classrooms* (New York: Holt, Rinehart & Winston, 1970).

[6] J. E. Brophy and C. M. Evertson, *Learning from Teaching* (Boston: Allyn & Bacon, 1976).

[7] M. Marland, *The Craft of the Classroom: A Survival Guide* (London: Heinemann Educational Books, 1975).

So much for the school features with only a limited effect on pupil outcome. Which are the school characteristics that *do* matter? Seven main variables may be singled out.

School features fostering pupil success

Rewards and praise

The first of these features concerns the ample use of rewards, praise and appreciation – all of which tend to be associated with better pupil outcomes. We found that those schools where the staff took more opportunities to praise pupils' work during lessons, or where there was frequent public praise for good work or behaviour by commending individual children in assemblies or other meetings, tended to have better behaved children.[1] The display of children's work on walls was another means of showing appreciation of the value of their accomplishments and hence an indirect form of reward or encouragement. Schools which used much display of pupils' work tended to have a somewhat better level of examination success. It is probable that praise and encouragement are important for two rather different reasons. First, they are necessary as a means of feedback to pupils on what is and is not acceptable behaviour and achievement.[2] Experimental studies of teacher–child interaction in the classrooms show that teacher approval and attention when the children are behaving appropriately encourages its continuation.[3] Secondly, they are likely to be influential in setting the emotional tone of the school and hence in influencing pupil morale. Many studies have shown that people with a positive view of their own worth tend to be more successful and achieving; and furthermore that people's self-esteem is much influenced by the manner in which they are treated by others.[4] It appears that pupils behave better and achieve more when teachers treat them in ways which emphasize their success and good potential rather than in ways which focus on their failings and shortcomings.

Pupil conditions

Secondly, quite apart from rewards for specific pieces of work or behaviour, our results show that a pleasant and comfortable environ-

---

[1] M. Rutter *et al.*, *Fifteen Thousand Hours*, op. cit.

[2] See J. E. Brophy and C. M. Evertson, op. cit.

[3] See W. C. Becker, 'Applications of behavior principles in typical classrooms', in C. E. Thoresen (ed.), *Behavior Modification in Education*, The 72nd Year Book of the National Society for the Study of Education (Chicago: University of Chicago Press, 1973), pp. 77–106.

[4] See R. Helmreich, 'Stress, self-esteem and attitudes', in B. T. King and E. McGinnies (eds), *Attitudes, Conflict and Social Change* (London: Academic Press, 1972).

ment is associated with better pupil outcomes.[1] As discussed earlier, this is not a question of spacious new buildings or small classes. Rather, the significant variables included items such as good school decorations and good care of the school buildings; good working conditions as reflected in children's freedom to use the buildings during breaks and the lunch period, access to a telephone and the availability of hot drinks; the provision of school outings; and the teacher's ready availability for pupils for advice, help or consultation about personal matters. These variables have not received much attention in previous studies but investigations of other institutions have suggested that people work and behave better when they are well looked after and feel that those in charge understand and respond to their personal needs.[2] Pupils are more likely to accept school norms if school is perceived as a pleasant and rewarding place in which to work.

Responsibilities and participation

Thirdly, ample opportunities for children to take responsibility and to participate in the running of their school lives appear conducive to good attainments, attendance and behaviour. Reynolds and Murgatroyd[3] showed this in connection with the use of a perfect system; Ainsworth and Batten,[4] with pupil opportunities for formal status; and we found it with respect to proportions of children who had been form captain, homework monitor or some equivalent position; with high proportions of pupils taking a special part in school assemblies, house or year meetings; and with the expectation that pupils look after their own books, folders and writing materials.[5] Of course, much is likely to depend on how responsibilities are given and on how far the opportunities are taken to link these with particular goals. However, there is some indication that holding positions of responsibility at school may help students' commitment to education.

Academic emphasis

Fourthly, there is evidence that children tend to make better progress both behaviourally and academically in schools which place an

[1] M. Rutter et al., Fifteen Thousand Hours, op. cit.

[2] See R. L. Kahn and D. Katz, 'Leadership practices in relation to productivity and morale', in D. Cartwright and A. Zander (eds), Group Dynamics: Research and Theory, vol. 2 (New York: Harper & Row, 1960); C. J. Holahan and S. Saegert, 'Behavioural and attitudinal effects of large-scale variation in the physical environment of psychiatric wards', Journal of Abnormal Psychology, vol. 82 (1973), pp. 454–62; I. A. C. Sinclair, Hostels for Probationers (London: HMSO, 1971).

[3] D. Reynolds and S. Murgatroyd, op. cit.

[4] M. E. Ainsworth and E. J. Batten, The Effects of Environmental Factors on Secondary Educational Attainment in Manchester: A Plowden Follow-up. Schools Council Research Studies (London: Macmillan Education, 1974).

[5] M. Rutter et al., Fifteen Thousand Hours, op. cit.

appropriate emphasis on academic matters. Several studies have shown modest but positive associations between the time spent actively involved in particular subject work and attainment in those subjects.[1] Other investigations[2] have shown that academically successful schools tend to have an emphasis on examinations and homework. In our study of secondary schools in inner London we too found that children had better academic success in schools where homework was regularly set and marked, where the teachers expressed expectations that a high proportion of children would do well in national examinations, where a high proportion of the children used the school library and where there was group planning of the curriculum. Of course, it might be thought that these items simply reflected an intake of intellectually able children but this was by no means the whole explanation. Some schools with particularly favoured intakes had rather low academic expectations. It is probably difficult for teachers to know how their pupils compare with children at other similar schools. Whatever the explanation, it appears that children make better progress when clear goals are set and where they are taught in an atmosphere of confidence that they can and will succeed in the tasks they are set. Teacher expectations influence pupils' academic progress[3] and, of course, in turn the children's good work will tend to reinforce and support the teachers' high expectations of them.

Models provided by teachers

The fifth school feature related to pupil outcome concerns the models of behaviour provided by teachers. There is an extensive research literature[4] which shows that children have a strong tendency to copy the behaviour of people in positions of authority whom they like and respect. Not only do they copy their specific actions but more importantly they come to adopt what they perceive to be their values and attitudes. The importance of staff models of behaviour in schools was noted by Clegg and Megson[5] when they observed that attention to staff punctuality was an important element in raising school standards. We also found that pupil outcomes were worse in schools where teachers frequently started lessons late and ended them early. If teachers disregard time-keeping, they can scarcely expect

---

[1] See S. N. Bennett, 'Recent research on teaching: a dream, a belief and a model', *British Journal of Educational Psychology*, vol. 48 (1978), pp. 127–47.

[2] For example, E. L. McDill and L. C. Rigsby, *Structure and Process in Secondary Schools* (Baltimore: Johns Hopkins University Press, 1973); M. E. Ainsworth and E. J. Batten, op. cit.

[3] D. Pilling and M. Kellmer Pringle, op. cit.

[4] A. Bandura, 'Social-learning theory of identificatory processes', in D. A. Goslin (ed.), *Handbook of Socialization Theory and Research* (Chicago: Rand McNally, 1969), pp. 325–46.

[5] A. Clegg and B. Megson, op cit.

good time-keeping and attendance from the pupils. Another example of a negative model was the teachers' tendency to react to provocation and disruptiveness by slapping the pupils. *Positive* models were provided by good care of the buildings and by the willingness of teachers to see pupils about problems at any time.

Group management in the classroom

The sixth set of variables concerns management in the classroom. The individual school class constitutes a social group and, as with any other social group, skills are involved in its management. We found that children's classroom behaviour was much better when the teacher had prepared the lesson in advance, so that little time was wasted at the beginning in setting up apparatus or handing out books and papers, and when, if the lesson was planned as class-oriented, the teacher mainly directed attention to the class as a whole. Our research[1] has suggested that one of the hallmarks of successful class management is keeping pupils actively engaged in productive activities rather than waiting for something to happen. Smooth transitions from one activity to the next are important and when dealing with the class group as a whole, it appears crucial to keep all the children involved and interested. Discipline needs to be unobtrusive with quiet reprimands rather than shouting,[2] with a focus on good behaviour rather than disruptive acts,[3] but with swift action to deal with disruption when this is necessary.[4]

Staff organization

The seventh set of variables is concerned with staff organization and the checking of teachers' work. We found[5] that pupil outcomes tended to be better when both the curriculum and approaches to discipline were agreed and supported by the staff acting together. It was not just that the group planning of courses facilitated continuities in teaching (although it did) but also that it provided opportunities for teachers to encourage and support one another. Much the same applied to discipline – outcomes were better in

---

[1] See P. V. Gump, 'Operating environments in schools of open or traditional design', *School Review*, vol. 82 (1974), pp. 575–94; S. N. Bennett, op. cit.; J. S. Kounin, op. cit.; J. E. Brophy and C. M. Evertson, op. cit.

[2] K. D. O'Leary, K. F. Kaufman, R. E. Kass and R. S. Drabman, 'The effects of loud and soft reprimands on the behavior of disruptive students', *Exceptional Children*, vol. 37 (1970), pp. 145–55.

[3] W. C. Becker, C. H. Madsen, C. R. Arnold and D. R. Thomas, 'The contingent use of teacher attention and praise in reducing classroom behaviour problems', *Journal of Special Education*, vol. 1 (1967), pp. 287–307.

[4] J. E. Brophy and C. M. Evertson, op. cit.

[5] M. Rutter *et al.*, *Fifteen Thousand Hours*, op. cit.

schools where discipline was based on general expectations set by the
school (or house or department), rather than left to individual
teachers to work out for themselves. The particular rules which are
set and the specific disciplinary techniques which are used are
probably much less important than the establishment of some
principles and guidelines which are both clearly recognizable and
accepted by the school as a whole. The importance of some kind of
school-wide set of values and norms of behaviour was also reflected
in our findings that in the more successful schools teachers reported
that their senior colleagues were aware of matters such as staff
punctuality and that they checked that policies were being maintained. It appeared that an efficient system within which teachers
worked harmoniously towards agreed goals was conducive to both
good morale and effective teaching. This was also implicit in our
findings on the pattern of decision-making associated with good outcomes. Pupil success was associated with schools in which there was
the combination of leadership with decision-making at a senior level,
and a decision-making process in which all teachers felt that their
views were represented and seriously considered.

Conclusions

In reviewing the school variables associated with pupil success it has
been striking that the main source of variation between schools does
not lie in factors such as buildings, resources, class size or
organizational structure. Instead the essential differences seem to lie
in the school's functioning as a social organization, and as a setting
for teaching and learning. The important factors in schools can be
conceptualized in terms of features which establish the nature of
school values and norms, those which determine their consistency
throughout the school, and those which influence the extent to which
the school aims and objectives are accepted by the general body of
pupils.[1] Studies in settings other than schools have shown that the
effect of social norms are more powerful when they are clearly
established as applying to a whole social group and when the group
itself is cohesive and supportive of its members.[2] The same seems to
apply to schools.

Schools serving a socially disadvantaged inner-city area face many
problems. Moreover, schools are necessarily shaped and constrained
by a variety of societal forces outside their immediate control. Nevertheless, research findings show very striking differences between
inner-city schools in the extent to which they succeed in fostering

[1] See M. Rutter et al., Fifteen Thousand Hours, op. cit.
[2] See V. H. Vroom, 'Industrial social psychology', in G. Lindsey and E. Aronson
(eds), The Handbook of Social Psychology, 2nd edn, vol. 5. Applied Social Psychology
(London: Addison-Wesley, 1969).

good pupil outcomes. To a considerable extent these differences are associated with factors within the schools' control. Schools have a degree of choice in how they are organized and teachers have a similar choice in their decisions on how to respond to the children they teach. The evidence suggests that these decisions on how to respond are likely to affect the chances of the children improving in their behaviour and attainments. We are far from knowing all that needs to be known about what makes for successful schools but there are sufficient leads and pointers to make a beginning. I am not arguing that schools are the most important influence on children's progress – they are not – nor am I suggesting that education can compensate for the inequities of society – it cannot. Nevertheless, the findings do show that schools constitute one major area of influence, and one susceptible to change. Schools can do much to foster pupil success and even (perhaps especially) in a disadvantaged area, schools can be a force for the good.

9 Working Together: problems and possibilities

Maurice Kogan[1]

The inner city has taken on connotations of squalor, dirt and despair. That it has done so is one of the saddest trends of modern social and cultural history. For successive generations throughout recorded time, the city has been a magnet of opportunity and development. It promised to provide a secure base against the unpredictable forces of nature, against hostile strangers, monarchical tyranny, ignorance and ineptitude. It allowed commerce and culture, peaceful government and education to grow in a haven of relative peace and tolerance. It was not only Hardy's Jude the Obscure who looked towards the city as a centre of hope, but also many a young and highly motivated southern state black looking for an end to discrimination and for opportunity in the American north.

To make sense of how different groups might work together within the inner city we need to think about what has caused the present decline. Certainly market forces have driven out residents and their jobs. The hopes of a better life, health and opportunity incorporated in new towns or green-belt enlarged villages have seduced even the most convivial of occupations, like publishing, away from their old urban haunts. But, more relevant to my theme, large tracts of the city have been sterilized by well-meaning planning. Planning is not driven on by any motive of profit, but by a conviction that there are shared values that can be incorporated in fast motorways, high blocks of flats and shopping centres. These are the politicians', planners' and developers' communal ethic writ large. It is they, as much as the office-block millionaires, who have debased acres of

[1] The author wishes to acknowledge the considerable help he has had in preparing this chapter from some of his colleagues – Len Davis, Mary Henkel, Daphne Johnson and Tim Packwood of the Department of Government and Educational Studies Unit, Brunel University.

streets that should have been rehabilitated. Hence I find myself cautious about too strong a faith in planning, rationality, co-ordination and all the other intellectual gadgets of social engineering.

Inner cities certainly have problems. Efforts must go into the revival of these areas. This means that we stop seeing them as cesspits of social problems and instead recognize them as major assets in brick and stone, and as social networks that can be identified and revitalized.

We live in a bad time for social action. The reaction from the cruder and more optimistic collective ethos has produced a healthy concern with what is acceptable, democratic and what will be most relevant to the people most affected. But that should be different from a low-level determinism which invests no faith at all in systematic social intervention. The danger is that we will be so frightened of doing the wrong thing through the best possible intentions that we will, to paraphrase the preacher, tread the middle path between right and wrong. The social services must play a very delicate game. They must do a lot, but with a light hand so that the primary groups in the inner cities are able to build from the bottom up and not within the holes left by others. The service planners must enable others to do their work. They must enable groups of individuals to enhance their own life patterns within supportive frameworks.

It is for this reason that we have to worry about the stronger attempts at corporate planning. It is not a good thing for local authorities to lack properly integrated policies. They need efficient mechanisms for working out their budgets, their manpower and other priorities. But budgets and finance are really only a different way of stating other and more fundamental things, such as the amount of effort that will go into one service as against another, and the values placed on different priorities. Corporate planning too easily takes on a life of its own. It is worth nothing unless it is concerned with establishing a framework for development between the primary workers in the field. Increasingly, we know that there is no single view of how the inner city should be developed. It ought to be capable of being all things to all men. The corporate planners who go for one-minded or single-value concepts of the good life are squeezing out the real world of conflict, pluralism and decent dissent in favour of a false consensus and synopsis.

The cities and pluralism

Cities have often been thought of as places where there will be happy consensus on values. The underlying conceptions of much of town planning have been, in the past at least, that the normal state of society is an integrative and co-optive system based on generally agreed values. Utopian town plans in post-industrial Britain reflect a concern for order and meaning attached to life.[1]

One need not follow the critics of town planning the whole way as when some attribute to it a feudal and organic view of society in which each member had his allocated, understood and accepted place. But one can certainly see that any attempt to incorporate human relationships into prescribed spatial relationships would inevitably produce a static concept of the city which would be unable to cope with the processes of growth and change in society. Planning paternalism has led, it is claimed, to the spread of the garden suburb, low density housing developments and urban sprawl, and to an urban bias in British town planning. But when we say planners we must be cautious. The politicians, at least as much as the professionals, were behind the rejection of the eighteenth- and nineteenth-century model of the city.

The critics of town planning make, then, several points relevant to our main theme. Town planning assumes a strong convergence of values. Indirectly, therefore, it turns its back on the potential pluralism of the densely populated urban centre in which access to many more people, many more social groups, and many more forms of recreation and employment are potentially available. But it is the pluralistic and non-covergent form of society upon which we increasingly have to build our plans for social relationships. In the city there will be, as there has always been, several life styles jostling with each other. The planners and those responsible for other forms of social control will, therefore, have to look for minimum consensus and not assume that there is one mind about recreation and culture. In effect, they had better recognize and accept pluralism rather than attempt to build unitary societies.

The schools

The schools in the inner cities increasingly have had to recognize that they do not have strong, let alone complete, control over their pupils. They have to mediate a minimum consensus on behaviour and on social control and are blamed if that minimum gets too low. They have to tolerate a range of life styles and a range of values.

The concepts of deviance become, thus, more eclectic – to each norm of behaviour there is its own deviant counterpart – but increasingly the schools accept that deviance will probably have to be met by different forms of acceptance and containment rather than prescription or opposition. In our own research at Brunel[2] we are

[1] J. M. Simmie, *Citizens in Conflict: Sociology of Town Planning* (London: Hutchinson Educational, 1974).

[2] Brunel University Education Studies Unit project on disaffected pupils.

beginning to note how the school works alongside a whole range of opting out. Thus, one of my colleagues is tracking down the extent to which school is, in effect, a part-time occupation. Pupils may leave the school at lunch time and have an entirely separate cultural and social group with whom they relate. Other groups do not thus desert the school but instead maintain their own territory within the school where their own idiom, musical preferences, and sets of relationships are built up. They have no official space for their subcultural activities but operate in the interstices of school routine. They do not conflict with the school but simply work alongside it. It is rather like the role that is predictable for our student unions in universities and polytechnics – not so much a conflicting agent within the university as a counter institution running parallel with it.

Other and more structural divergencies are expressed in specialization within the schools. The divide between the academic and the pastoral is the most important expression of multiple objectives which carry with them multiple values.[1] Within the non-academic area there are the specializations of the pastoral, the disciplinary and the counselling functions, which entail different assumptions about the school's relationships with pupils, different degrees of prescription and support, and different degrees of empathy or resistance to pupil autonomy and control.

This is a contrast that must be emphasized. Schools contain so much divergence, yet are strong looking institutions. They are large buildings dominating a neighbourhood. A secondary school brings together, for quite a few hours a day, for all of the working days of the week, a large number of adults and adolescents. The external imagery is that of a strong unit. The head is a public figure, appearing at meetings with parents or outside agencies as a personality and with a distinctive role. He is named on the school note paper and on the board outside the school. There are not many other public institutions now which can require inmates to wear a uniform. The outward signs of unity and convergence may be fading – school songs, ritualistic attempts to enforce school unity of one sort or another. But a school is a school and membership of it is an important part of the build-up of the personality of a pupil or of a teacher, and of the status that adheres to them throughout the rest of their working lives.

Yet the observer quickly sees how the school contains not only congruencies but also divergencies.

Thus, teachers are specialists in the development and teaching of the curriculum. No other of the welfare state groups claim any preeminence in this role. But even that is an artefact, and not necessarily created in heaven. For example, school social workers in some US

---

[1] D. Johnson, *et al.*, *Secondary Schools and the Welfare Network* (London: Allen & Unwin, 1980), Chapter 3.

schools[1] regard it as their role to provide a critique of the curriculum in terms of the affective development of the pupils and the relationship of the school to the community. In Britain, too, health education specialists from the area health authority, members of the Juvenile Bureau, and others from outside the school, might be providing an input to the curriculum. None the less, the teachers specialize in it. Teacher also care for pupils, largely though not wholly through the pastoral system. They have specialized resources for these purposes within the school building – house rooms and so on – and the power given by the compulsory attendance of pupils, with control over them through predetermined hours.

Now even within the specialized teaching role – of devising, developing and administering the curriculum – there is a whole range of values. Skill-training for use in employment, skills to be used in developing better social relationships and skills related to cognitive development emerge within different modes of teaching, and these divisions do not always simply follow the subject areas. The areas of craft and technology, for example, can contain quite strong divisions on the question as to what the skills are being taught for. Within the non-curriculum areas, the pastoral teacher may or may not be responsible for discipline but, if he is, there are different techniques and different underlying value positions as between administering discipline, acting as the pastor who protects and advises, and counselling pupils on future employment and choice of subjects, or on their personal problems. All of these complexities make coherence and identity in the school important, if difficult to achieve.

The web of services

Now it would be easy to show how the school represents certain values which are different from those of the other welfare services. But all areas of the welfare state share the same range of values. Some degree of assent would be given by teachers, social workers, education welfare officers, psychologists, psychiatrists, and members of the Juvenile Bureau, at least while they remain with it, to such banner slogans as respect for the individual, freedom of life style, equality of civic status, advancement of good interpersonal relationships, collective wellbeing, and defending social arrangements for the sake of everybody.

[1] Examples of literature exploring the closer involvement of social workers in schools include: Lela B. Costin, 'An analysis of the tasks in school social work', *Social Service Review*, vol. 43 (September 1969), pp. 273–85; B. H. Gottlieb and L. J. Gottlieb, 'An expanded role for the school social worker', *Social Work* (October 1971), pp. 12–21; and M. Radin, 'A personal perspective on school social work', *Social Case Work* (December 1975), pp. 605–613.

Teachers and social workers are particularly close together. They both specialize in human development. They both attempt to build from a knowledge of how human beings act and grow and inter-relate. They both try to be non-judgemental. They both try to address themselves to the individual. They both have to mediate the full range of social values, from autonomy to control. The similarities could be extended to the other groups as well. In housing manage-ment, for example, attitudes have changed from a somewhat aseptic belief in tenants' duties and the defence of the rate-payers' assets, to attempts to involve tenants in the management of housing estates, and to provide counselling services on housing matters to non-tenants. These services, too, have changed, as legislation such as that on homelessness promotes an emphasis towards individualism and social justice.

Yet we know, and in my view should not deplore, conflicts of values that exist not only between professional groups but within them as well.

Is it too functionalist, too devoted to the status quo, to say that we ought to be glad that the professions present such a wide range of views? Thus, it is now commonplace in the sociology of health[1] that the range of assumptions goes all the way from the bio-scientific view of the patient as a system to which can be attributed norms of good performance, to social concepts of health that start with the human being's ability to cope with his social, family and work environment, and build on his ability to be an equal participant and agent of his own health care. The one attitude seems to emphasize the clinical aloneness of the patient. In that case, highly specialist skills are devoted to him and to him alone, and incidentally bolster up the power of the doctor through his unique authority to prescribe treat-ment. The other attitude looks to a far more communitarian view of the way in which human beings operate, and takes health well beyond medicine.

I feel we ought to be quite glad that medicine has given us facilities for renal dialysis, for radical surgery when we need it, but that it is at the same time giving us the encouragement and the prods and the knowledge to resist socially and culturally induced illnesses. The problem becomes one of ensuring that both sets of medicine get the finance and public support that they need and that we do not all get bewitched by the high technology to the extent that the less clearly and powerfully formulated precepts of social health are overlooked.

I have already referred to the range of functions of the school and can simply say again that education helps individuals to get what they

---

[1] Margaret Stacey, 'Concepts of health and illness: a working paper on the concepts and their relevance for research', in *Health and Health Policy* (London: Social Science Research Council, 1977), Appendix III.

want, and helps them as well to give society what it needs them to have. Moreover, good education enables people to be critical about themselves and about society and to want to cause change, at the same time as it inculcates an appreciation of what already exists.

Within social work, too, the dichotomies are classic and strong. Clients are accepted at their own valuation. At the same time, a strong theme in social work is the enhancement of self-esteem in the face of institutions and their transactions which tend to reinforce a low self-image. The social worker is chary of imposing values but at the same time is expected to make clients responsive to the norms which are derived from social expectations of control.

These value conflicts are not to be deplored. Inasmuch as the full range of values is available to those who work with the services, they respond to the make-up of the individuals they serve. Individuals have to walk a tightrope between control and freedom, between personal autonomy and the claims of society. The caring professions must, therefore, also reflect the value ranges of their clients.

Now there are several other divergencies that can be pinpointed. You will notice that, so far, I have dealt with the subsidiary matter of how *within* professions there are divergencies. The contrasts *among* professions are, of course, more dramatic. Thus doctors tend to be trained to leadership in hospitals where many professions work together. Social workers tend to think in terms of co-ordination and accommodation of alternative perspectives. The police are trained to investigate innocence as against guilt and these are always, be it noted, events in the past rather than hopes and predictions for the future. Social workers try not to particularize but to assess all round strengths and their clients' limitations with a view to building up confidence for the future. The social worker in field services goes out to meet an individual, often within the family, or in his own setting. The school represents social authority written in bricks and mortar. Its specialized buildings incorporate assumptions about functions, and ways of working. They speak about the style of instruction. Modern school architecture has been a struggle to subordinate physical structures to educational purposes. But educational purposes will change again, and the brand new functions of the 1950s and 1960s will still remain in immovable buildings in thirty years' time.

The history, the working sites, the relative status, the technologies involved, the value congregations, all make for specialization. But that need not be a bad thing. Integrated planning not only takes time and effort. It can also make it more difficult for good style to develop. The issue is not whether professionals should be able to do their own thing. The question is whether they can do their own thing with due observance of other specialists' own things, and in accordance with what clients need.

Working together

I think the observer can see that the different groups have reduced their 'uptightness' at working together. But not enough. Sometimes the most disastrous things happen from lack of co-ordination. And how interesting it is that lawyers and judges who never need to co-operate with anybody else are always called in to point out the virtues of working together.[1]

There are different ways in which working together can occur. One person or one institution may incorporate more than one role; the teacher as pastor and as academic is an obvious example. People can work in interdisciplinary teams as is the case with some child guidance clinics. Or roles can be used reciprocally. So, for example, a teacher may act as a pastor and as a disciplinary agent. But the same pastoral teacher might protect a pupil from a somewhat daunting academic structure. He might also protect the pupil from challenge from outside the school when, for example, the Juvenile Bureau is forming a view of the action to take. The teacher takes up a particular stance – supporter or controller – in response, not only to what he reckons the pupil needs, but also to the challenges that may come from other agencies. We all act in this way. We are all, in the best sense of the words, two-faced in working through our multiple-role relationships.

Those reciprocities can, obviously, lead to conflicts rather than co-operation. But the tendency is always for groups to advocate their specialist competence and power – that being the index of status – at the same time as they necessarily broaden their actual functions so as to make sure of connections outside their own specialist domain. The education welfare service is one of the oldest statutory social services.[2] While its historic function has been to ensure that all children have access to school, if necessary compulsorily, EWOs go far further, in some local authorities at least, in counselling parents about educational resources for their children. They take appropriate action on non-attendance that can be far more than the mechanical application of the school attendance law. There is not room here to go into the vexed and longstanding question of whether and how the EWOs might become school social workers in the full sense of the word and, if so, whether they should remain within the education rather than the social work department. It is certainly the case that both the actualities and the potential of the educational welfare service have been both underestimated and under-researched.[3] The responsibilities of EWOs in relationship to school placement and

---

[1] Department of Health and Social Security, *The Report of the Enquiry into the Care and Supervision provided to Maria Colwell* (London: HMSO, 1974).

[2] D. Johnson *et al.*, op cit., Chapter 5.

[3] K. Macmillan, *Education Welfare: Strategy and Structure* (London: Longman, 1977).

handicapped children have been particularly underrated. They have been shown to have responsibility, in nursery education, with handicapped children and in school placement, of an allocation and support kind as well as in providing clothing and free meals and their traditional regulatory duties.

The relationship between the educational psychologist and the teacher, and the school psychological services generally, are again extremely various. Sometimes a team can consist of educational psychologists, social workers and remedial teachers, in which case much of the work can be undertaken by the team. Where, however, only educational psychologists are employed, the greater number of referrals have to be made to some other remedial team. If the process goes well, the educational psychologist can work with teachers and provide them with an over-all goal for the child which takes account of emotional needs and long-term learning abilities. Learning programmes may be suggested or teachers' attitudes might be modified on the advice of the psychologist. By contrast, the child guidance clinic contains inter-disciplinary teams, which may well come together from different departments of the local authority and the health authorities. The clinic team most often advise that social workers continue to work with the parents. Psychotherapy can be adopted but is severely limited by the resources available. Special education might be recommended. Hospitals might be brought into play.

The health services for young people are part of the health authority provision and include the school health service, the health visiting team and health education. This range of provision demonstrates the complexity of any one area of work with which co-operation should be expected. Screening for health defects is one function. Health-care programmes are another. Health education brings the health services directly into contact with the educational role of teachers.

The Juvenile Bureau is a fascinating example of how each role faces both ways.[1] It represents the full majesty of the law and the normal criteria of police action. But it also protects pupils from what might otherwise be the mechanical application of police norms. It adopts a role which is both reciprocal with the schools, but also quite distinct from them in several of its working modes and assumptions. For one thing, it deals with a small minority of pupils. Less than half the juveniles referred to a Bureau are prosecuted. But the treatment given to those who are not, if they are considered to be guilty of a minor offence, provides some nice anthropological comparisons with the way in which the school behaves. A summons to a police station to have a caution administered by a senior police officer is not, after all, too far distant from the summons to the traditional

[1] D. Johnson *et al.*, op. cit., Chapter 5.

healmaster's study. The same processes of social labelling go on. The file is kept until the child becomes 18 and is then destroyed if no further offence is logged. No doubt those of us who were caned in our youth are now forgiven as well by our schools. But there are fascinating differences, too, in the way that these different organizations behave. For example, the investigating officer will not make a judgement on whether to act. This decision is deliberately removed to another more senior officer so that an objective view can be taken. Now objectivity is the name of everybody's game. But professional work in the other areas considered here usually predicates judgement by the person who knows the case best rather than by someone else within the hierarchy. Here, in fact, there is an interesting conflict of norms.

Resources

I have indicated that there is both hope for working together, because the differences need not be fundamental when values are stated in general terms and because, specialist though roles become, there is sufficient overlap to make reciprocity possible and meaningful. But I have also indicated that there are enough differences in role stances for co-operation to have to be worked for.

It would be feeble to leave this point without referring to the difficulty of resources. I have mentioned elsewhere[1] how transactions have to be worked out in extremely difficult circumstances. One difficult case can knock the bottom out of a whole morning's work in school. One school where we worked, and it was a school without particular difficulties, had perhaps a third of the senior staff's time spent on pastoral problems of 5 per cent of its pupils. Similar figures were worked out for child-care officers in a study made some time ago. Social workers are no better off. A team of perhaps eight social workers might have to relate to a total of fifty educational institutions as well as the services covering all the rest of their clients. The number of problem children in each of those schools, if all is going well, can be as many as a hundred or as few as forty. Not all need social workers. But the need becomes obvious for selective and intensive action that will demonstrate that change and development are possible. And it is to that theme, of differential action within the inner city, that I now wish to turn.

Some solutions

Many solutions are not relevant to the inner city alone. On the issue of working together, first of all, there are already important sign-

[1] Co-operation or conflict?', paper given to the Annual Social Services Conference, Bristol, 1978.

posts of how this might happen. The multi-purpose teams represented by the child guidance clinic have already been referred to. The extremely effective arrangements brought in to deal with non-accidental injury to children are another. There are, however, a far wider range of models now being developed as part of the set of techniques known under the umbrella name of 'intermediate treatment'.

Intermediate treatment can be defined as attempts to reach young people in need of help that fall short of stronger modes of control, although it may be specified as the result of a supervision order. There are now 12 000 youngsters in IT programmes. 1500 of these are as the result of a court appearance.[1] Many of the techniques are simply those already in use by teachers and social workers but brought into new settings. Carefully planned recreational and self-development facilities ranging from mountaineering to youth clubs are one set. Group discussions, in which there is an implicit therapeutic process at work, are another. I do not need to elaborate on the whole range which are well covered in a series of DHSS documents, as well as in some academic writing.[2]

The most important point about intermediate treatment from our stance is that it shows teachers and social workers coming out of their institutional corners and working together. And it is interesting how combined work might form a new specialization with at least some of the status, resources and potential power of old specializations. It is rather like the development of hybrid academic subjects such as biochemistry. The concept of intermediate treatment, and the important principle of hybridity, need to be used in many more contexts than they are now.

Those pupils who become most alienated from the school are often those who finish up needing counsel about employment, and the generation of a good social and family life later on. It is within the lower further education and upper-school setting that combined educational, employment and personal counselling services are most needed. We know how pupils who have been alienated from a school come back to it when they find life outside even less appealing. We know how social work is sometimes rejected by clients unless it comes to help them on a particular issue about which they themselves feel most keenly.

Indeed some of the most important things that will happen in the inner city will start not from the schools or the social services departments or the clinics, but from new small factories where people can learn to enjoy work. They might then learn to reject Clive Jenkins' invitation to forget the work ethic, and learn to enjoy what a good pay-packet means in terms of self-esteem and enjoyment of

---

[1] *Social Work Today*, 5 December 1978, p. 3.

[2] Department of Health and Social Security, Local Authority Circular, LAC(77)1, contains a useful bibliography on intermediate treatment.

goods and services. Social workers have not been too clever at getting into the juvenile employment scene. The schools have tended to lift up their skirts and run when skill-training for specific employment is mentioned. The harder nosed training-for-employment lobby has won out on government funds for job opportunity schemes – an area for which further education and the modern, multi-purpose sixth form are well equipped.

There are not enough social workers and skilled teachers to work with those who can identify new employment possibilities, and work for the right institutional forms in which these possibilities can be taken into account. And so we have to look for what I have called the multiplier effect. Social workers can counsel teachers, when they have not enough resources to do the social work themselves, on the issues of home background, behaviour and family life which the teachers should take into account. Teachers, too, can bring what they know about pupils in the classroom into the work of agencies outside. Psychiatric social workers operate in the schools through child guidance clinics, but they are only a minority when they do so. But if all this happened, what effect would it have, valuable though it might be, on the areas of distress? The answer is nothing very much unless the professionals of the welfare state begin to work decisively, and together, on some of the environmental and structural issues of the inner city which will then put their own work into a stronger and better rooted context.

It is for that reason that we should be exasperated at the way in which the Joint Partnership Schemes seem to be working in London. One school[1] put up a splendid scheme for converting itself into a genuine community school. In so doing, they rightly quoted Henry Morris, the former chief education officer for Cambridgeshire and founder of the Cambridgeshire village colleges.

> As the community centres of the neighbourhood ... the village college ... would provide for the whole man and abolish the duality of education and ordinary life. It would not only be the training ground for the art of living, but the place in which life is lived, the environment of a genuine corporate life. The dismal dispute of vocational and non-vocational education would not arise in it.[2]

And so the school wanted to develop an arts centre with catering facilities close to the school. The building would provide a social gathering place, a place for musical and dramatic entertainments, and a place to eat and drink. It would provide a workshop to learn theatrical, musical and possibly film skills, and a training centre for City and Guilds catering industries foundation courses. It would thus equip young people for many jobs in central London based on the entertainment and tourist industries. And it would serve the whole

---

[1] Suggestions from the Governors of Islington Green School for use of Inner City Partnership Funds (13 July 1978).

[2] Memorandum 1924, Cambridgeshire Local Education Authority.

community in all sorts of ways – vocational, counselling and training for work. That imaginative scheme was not thought appropriate for the Joint Partnership Scheme.

What we need are some demonstration projects in the inner city. We do not want to distribute pound notes from helicopters. We need to have schemes that start with an analysis of what makes a block of streets dismal. The dismalness can be enumerated in many ways. Unemployment would be one of them. Bad physical environment would be another. And then public resources should be brought in to establish centres which provide training for work but which should be linked firmly to the school and FE system of the areas. The other social services should make their diagnosis of need and state their plans for counselling and family support in co-operation with the institutions, both economic and welfare, that are likely to be most grounded within the neighbourhood. The identification of those problems should not be out of the professionals' heads alone but should be the product of analysis with the people affected.

We cannot do without systems and institutions. Many of those have sought to deinstitutionalize schooling, or to avoid the bureaucracy created by our electoral system, have finished up with changes indeed, but no way of sustaining them over time. I am unashamedly a believer in the power of British welfare state institutions to do good. But we have learned much about the need to adopt the right style and to respect the values of those for whom the good is supposed to be done. It is for this reason that systems must be supportive and not prescriptive. The ablest people in the local authorities know that they cannot do everything, armed though they are with legal powers and duties, and empowered to manage massive resources of manpower and physical plant. The good politician, the one with the gift of prophecy and a good administrator, will identify those who can do the real work and do it creatively and well. It is not simply that localized and individual effort seem the democratic way of doing things. Quite often they are not particularly democratic. Small community groups do not necessarily heed the common good as it might be reconstructed over a larger geographical area. So there has to be a balance between those who allocate for social justice and those who implement it on the ground.

That is why we need to turn again and again to the demonstration of good practice. Demonstration projects could show the way to spending money well. We ought to start getting tired about the generalized rhetoric of improvement. That rhetoric always goes into an incantation about the need for a better building, more staff, more money. But until we can find something with roots in the problems that really affect people in the inner city, until the pattern of employment becomes satisfying because it earns money but is also based on skills that can be developed, the green fingers will not make the plants grow. And when people have learned to earn and take pride in the fact that they are doing so, and when they see that education and the rest of the welfare state services are part of the rights which they inherit as contributors to the society, then the dirt of uncared-for neighbourhoods, the good training grounds for urban guerrillas, the good seed-beds of crude and lumpen sociology which so eagerly creates the lumpen proletariat, will begin to go. In all of this, we need to continue to respect the multiplicity of values in the inner city. But the minimum consensus underlying all this is that all need work, all need to enjoy their work, all need education and encouragement in finding that work and learning how to do it, and that all are then entitled to spend their money and find enjoyment within the cities which still remain in Britain potentially beautiful, capable of inducing joy rather than despair.

PART THREE

The Ingredients of a Programme

10 A Programme for a Community of Schools

Michael Marland

Characteristics of a programme

From analysis we need to move to a programme of development. Such a programme does not have to be radical just for the sake of the appearance of progress, nor is it likely to have features that have hitherto been seen as belonging together in one philosophical or attitudinal package. For instance, Reynolds'[1] studies of absenteeism show a correlation between good attendance at school and the enforcement of uniforms, a prefect system, and a *low* level of corporal punishment. The last factor is not one that the crude polarizer of education would normally link with the first two. Indeed, one reason for the difficulties in British inner-city education has been a tendency to judge components of a scheme being proposed according to the supposed 'political' labelling of the component as 'progressive' or 'traditional', two hopelessly loaded and unhelpful labels. What is likely is that a successful programme would be a synthesis, and involve action at a variety of levels: central government, local school system, community of schools (a concept to which I shall return), individual school, teacher team, and individual teacher. It is unlikely that changes at any one of those levels will be sufficient.

There is a core question in all of educational administration, and it is one which is of special importance in the inner city – that is, how to resolve the tension between coherence and freedom. Freedom offers scope for the individual teacher to flourish, to use his imagination, to use her enthusiasm, and to develop what is suitable for the moment.

---

[1] D. Reynolds and S. Murgatroyd, 'The sociology of schooling and the absent pupil', in H. C. M. Carroll, (ed.), *Absenteeism in South Wales: Studies of Pupils, their Homes and their Secondary Schools* (Swansea: Swansea Faculty of Education, 1977).

Coherence offers interrelatedness, continuity, accountability and relationship to needs. It would be dangerous to think that the longer we debate the more we will end up on one side or the other. What we have to produce somehow is an amalgam of, not a compromise between, those two things. If inner-city education is to be related to needs, it must find a way of maintaining both qualities. A system that leaves too much to the individual teacher sacrifices continuity of learning, development and reinforcement. A system that takes too much away from the teacher or teacher team removes both personal involvement from the teacher, and reduces the likelihood of satisfactorily matching lesson to pupil. I fear that many of the American school districts suffer from this second failure, with very little planning power at teacher-team level. I fear that many British school authorities suffer from the former, with very little continuity or curriculum leadership across the years.

Such a programme will be impossible if we work with the crude counters of the educational polarities that have been commonplace so far. These polarities have thrived in the tense conditions of inner-city education. The distinction between 'pastoral' and 'academic' has been exaggerated. Each is merely a point of view that lies within every teacher, but requires focusing from time to time. Pastoral care is meaningless without a strong commitment to a curriculum, and 'academic' is nothing without the guidance and support that lie at the heart of pastoral concerns. At its worst, this split has been seen as 'caring' and 'demanding' – the first task of those with pastoral roles, the second the task of 'the subject teacher'. In fact the two are only different ways of putting the same thing: a teacher has to care for a pupil or his demands will be fruitless; equally, it is a poor kind of caring that makes no demands on the growing child.

One of the weaknesses of American schooling is its separation of discipline from guidance, and both from teaching. A typical junior or senior high school in America will have 'discipline' handled by a deputy principal; 'guidance' handled by a 'guidance department', whose task is to guide barely known pupils into courses over which the department has no influence; 'homeroom teachers', whose tasks are limited to information processing;[1] and 'teaching' – which is sharply different from guidance or discipline which are both thought of as 'administration' and handled by those who do not teach! A parent or a school community cannot sensibly divide discipline from guidance, nor either from teaching, and a positive programme will have to keep the expertise which is possible with the American

---

[1] A few schools are attempting to build up the role of the homeroom teacher, and by this to weld the functions together somewhat. For example, Evanston High School, in the suburbs of Chicago, has an elaborate new 'homeroom programme' devised by a committee of teachers, parents and pupils. This considerably broadens the responsibility of the homeroom teacher, and in effect provides her or him with a curriculum and set of pupil materials very like that attempted in British schools.

division, but produce the cohesion possible with the British amalgamation.

Perhaps the worst of all the polarities is that which is rarely articulated but lurks in the hidden theories of those who work in many British schools; it is the supposed contrast between 'humanity' and 'efficiency'. There is too often a romantic notion present at the back of our minds that the teacher who loses his folder a week before the end of term, or writes to a child's dead mother, gets a girl's first name wrong on a report, or arrives late at meetings, is probably a more feeling and humane teacher than the rest of us. In fact, of course, this is another false polarity. There can be no true humanity without efficiency. Offering help is of little use without carrying out the offer; sympathizing is an insufficient professional reaction to distress; and action is required – often action that requires hours of follow-up in marshalling the practical help required by the pupil. Conversely, there cannot be true efficiency without humanity – for not to take into account the human needs of the pupil, the family, and the community is to ignore part of the data, and thus to be inefficient.

The diagram of school achievement devised by Michael Rutter (page 130) illustrates the possibility of what I should offer as the central philosophy of such a programme. The diagram goes against what many people take for granted: that a school working hard with one section of its pupils is unlikely to be able to succeed also with another, contrasting one. In fact, Michael Rutter and his colleagues have shown that the schools that did best by their most able also did best by their least able. Thus it is possible to work right across the ability range equally successfully. The philosophy which that finding relates to is that which has been most clearly defined by Pat Daunt:

> I believe that there is one essential principle of comprehensive education which can be clearly identified; that without it there is ultimately no clear way of understanding what comprehensive education is or is not, no final court of appeal before which we can test whether comprehensive education is succeeding in its own terms or not; that it is the fount of all comprehensive objectives, and therefore of all comprehensive policies . . . The guiding defining principle of comprehensive education is that the education of all children is held to be intrinsically of equal value.[1]

Now, our early comprehensive schools in this country, and I suspect the American urban school, did not work by that principle. At their best it could be said that they worked by the principle that every pupil would be given the opportunity to get into the highly valued sector. In Daunt's philosophy we are likely to find an underlying principle for our programme, one that will lead to our institutions being

[1] Pat Daunt, *Comprehensive Values* (London: Heinemann Educational Books, 1975), pp. 15–16.

'familial' in that they may vary what they offer from time to time, but
they value, and thus resource, equally.

Finally, in searching for the characteristics of an inner-city
programme I turn to E. M. Forster's famous aphorism for us all:
'only connect'. That was his epigraph for a novel in which he
explored his vision of life. It was one in which good living would
come from connecting 'the passion and the prose'. Educators require
both, but too often have only one or the other: our programme needs
to connect them.

Organization of schooling

Finance

Obviously education is expensive. Michael Rutter has shown that
variations in resources are less potent in their effects on pupil success
than school organization. However, his arguments could not be
extended to cover the huge variations that there can be between
areas. In Britain the use of the rate support grant is a way by which
central government can equalize resources in broad terms, or even
establish deliberate policies to favour areas with special needs. This
has allowed poor inner-city areas to be as well off in educational
provision, or even better, than the lusher suburbs. Without some
such financial machinery those parts of inner cities with a declining
financial base could not support a proper education system, and
would thus spiral still further downwards. This can be seen
dramatically in some American cities. For instance, Cleveland, Ohio,
on the banks of Lake Erie, has affluent suburbs on three sides,
including such famous school districts as Rocky River and Shaker
Heights. These suburbs were built by and for the better-off Cleveland
worker and, indeed, the rapid transit system for Shaker Heights to
the centre of down-town Cleveland can be seen as demonstrating
Shaker Heights' complete dependence on the entrepreneurial life of
Cleveland's banking, financial, retail distribution and entertainment
heart. Yet Shaker Heights has one of the highest per capita
educational spending figures in the entire United States, while
Cleveland is on the verge of bankruptcy and is reducing school years
to save teachers' salaries!

Clearly this is an unreasonable version of the pre-urban American
belief in local school districts financed by locally raised school taxes,
and run by the local people. The people of the suburbs of Cleveland
are there and flourishing only because of the existence of urban
Cleveland; most of them travel in daily, for work and for major
entertainment. It cannot be right that when they return home in the
evening they vote high taxes for 'their' schools, while the city down
the line has very poor schools. Other American cities are working
towards metropolitan-wide taxing schemes and fair distribution over

the schools. Certainly inner-city education requires government wider than that of the inner city itself to establish a sound financial provision. Apart from requiring a method of equalization to ensure that the global sum for an inner-city area is sufficient, there is a difficult technical question of how to ensure that it gets to those who need it. Tessa Blackstone, Marten Shipman and Maurice Kogan have addressed themselves to this question. How would I see it being answered in an inner-city programme?

There are two philosophies, local and central, and the choice between them involves working out in detail what I described as the tension between freedom and coherence. The philosophy that has been developed very sensibly in the Inner London Education Authority is the philosophy of allocating according to the objectively measured need of the school, but largely allowing the school to make its own decisions about how to spend the money. There are certain cases that can be made for certain extra activities; there are certain ear-marked grants; and there are certain controls; it is not a complete freedom – however, it is a very great deal of freedom at school level, probably more than in any other part of the world. The opposite extreme is what you find as a result of specific Federal or State funding in the USA. All the extra money has come in for specific programmes. Thus the heart of the school, its main activity, and its main body of pupils, is untouched by the extra funding because the programme comes in for this or that: this teacher is funded to teach grades three through five, pupils whose verbal reasoning is below 65, and to use only the programme that was devised elsewhere. While the money gets to 'the right pupil', a great deal is stopped off on the way by the most elaborate controls over how the money is spent. Even more serious is the fact that the money does not help the school do what I think the school needs to do, which is not add on a whole lot of extra little bits, but to look at its central activity and refurbish that. You would not improve the over-all performance of a run-down college or a run-down hospital by adding on little bits. You would look at its *central* function. Very often an American elementary school funded in this way by specific Federal funds reminds me of these teenage customized cars, where the car has not been changed, but lots of bits have been bolted on without altering the structure in the middle. We have to find a way of getting the money up to the right pupils without taking away what I have been asking for – a strong measure of local teacher-group planning in relation to the environment, the pupils and the institution.

Control

The question of who controls the planning of teaching is a constitutional question, and it is the central question of educational administration, which I think has been badly tackled in discussions over the last ten years. In general one could say that in this country there is nothing in any government discussions or in the Taylor Report[1] that alters the basic fact that the node of power is in the schools, which thus have great autonomy. Indeed you could argue that the Taylor Report's plea for the strengthening of governing bodies would be totally unnecessary if that were not so. Why trouble to have a strong governing body if, in fact, all the dictates come from afar anyway? This autonomy is barely affected by the loving persuasion of HM Inspectorate. Interestingly, even the Schools Council can be seen as actually facilitating this autonomy: its task is not to dictate but to help teachers decide for themselves.[2] In the USA, the node of control is in the school 'district', which varies from a single school to a huge area, but in a large conurbation is usually the whole inner-city area. There is also extensive State legislation, which is very precise indeed in certain cases, and there is also considerable Federal intervention, even though there is alleged not to be. Federal control is exercised by the fact that funding is given only for specific programmes, for specific kinds of teachers, to specific students. That is a kind of control which is arguably the most important and powerful and quite unlike anything in Britain.

I consider that we have not properly worked out an appropriate dispensation of power and decision-making. If that decision-making is taken too far away from the classroom, it lacks reality; it lacks responsiveness from the teachers; it lacks vigour. However, if it is left too near to the classroom, it becomes bitty. The fragmented nature of educational planning in Britain is appalling. Despite our commitment to responsibility in team leadership enshrined in the salary differentials and arguments of the Houghton Report,[3] and despite the fact that curriculum planning is put firmly in the hands of those with such responsibility posts, all the evidence is that most courses are underplanned, until the examination course virtually plans the teaching. In one junior school, for instance, the deputy head confidently declared that the school did not know what was being taught in the fourth year because the new fourth-year teacher had been in the school for only a term and a bit! In a secondary

[1] Department of Education and Science, *A New Partnership for our Schools* (London: HMSO, 1977).

[2] This 'central' role of helping teachers and schools to plan and decide for themselves was more clearly defined in the paper 'Schools Council Principles and Programmes' produced by the Council in July, 1979. For instance the first of 'the five main programmes' is described as: 'Purpose and planning in the schools. This programme is intended to develop the effectiveness of a new school's staff as a professional team. It will be concerned with such questions as how schools: (1) decide their curriculum aims; (2) plan the curriculum ...' (p. 5). I am not sure that the profession in England and Wales fully realize the implications of this important clarification.

[3] Department of Education and Science, *Pay of Non-University Teachers* (London: HMSO, 1975).

school, to take a contrasting example, there were four heads of the English Department in ten years with, by ill luck, a term's inter-regnum before each. The result was that every change was virtually a fresh start. The Bullock Report[1] established that many teams of secondary teachers of English were living from hand to mouth, with no over-all aims and objectives, and no 'instrument of policy'.

We need a distribution of planning power that is more equally dispersed. In the US the node is too heavy at district level; in Britain it is too heavy at teacher team[2] level. We need power with individual teachers, teacher team, school, and a level which I shall call 'the community of schools', smaller than an urban US district and than a British local education authority, but near to the small school districts of the American suburbs. It is a tragedy of the history of American education that the pattern of 'local' freedom so dearly and tenaciously cherished should have left the ideal unit for planning only in the suburbs, while the inner cities struggled with massive systems. Many a suburban district has one senior high, two junior high and six elementaries. Having one over-all management, such districts can be seen as true 'communities of schools'.

The American mini-school movement, as for instance seen in New York, is a reaction above all to the remoteness of a huge city district. Mini-schools are a part of the organizational structure of the conventional high school, though they have a separate life of their own. The Independent Alternative High Schools, on the other hand, are entirely separate and report directly to the Division of High Schools of the Board of Education. Many of the features fought for by this movement and proclaimed as among the special virtues of the independent or mini-school are the commonplace of the British system. Indeed by British standards the schools are not especially free: 'The alternative school administrator is responsible for the selection of the staff... All selections are made from city-wide teacher lists'![3] Most of the features said to be listed as special are things such as: establishing the range of resources in a school, flexibility of teaching to allow teachers to work in a variety of subjects, flexible hours, close involvement in pupils. It is surprising to have to state as an *alternative* that 'the school administrator [that is, the principal] is often intimately involved in such student problems as attendance, health, discipline, guidance and admissions. Some administrators also devote considerable energy to community relations.'[4] Only a system characterized by remoteness and immense sub-professional separation would prevent these things being the norm.

---

[1] Department of Education and Science, *A Language for Life* (London: HMSO, 1975).
[2] In most British primary schools, this will be the whole staff.
[3] 'New York urban coalition', *Mini-School News*, vol. 5, no. 1 (April 1976), p. 2.
[4] ibid.

I suggest that the large British and American inner-city school districts or authorities should be retained as over-all planning and resourcing bodies, but that they are too large to take much curricula-planning power out of the school. We need to insert an intermediate level for detailed planning. I have mentioned the US suburban district as one model; the nearest model in this country is the 'federal' school of Lord Williams at Thame in Oxfordshire, or possibly North Westminster School in London, though those start only at eleven plus.

The planning unit

Financially I have argued for large-area control to give poor inner-city areas a fair share, or more; but I have also argued for delegation of as much as possible of the spending decisions down the line. In terms of curriculum control and planning mechanism I have argued for something like the small US school district within the large inner-city authorities. In speaking about finance and control, I was emphasizing the constitutional aspect. I want now to emphasize the curriculum-planning aspect, once again in an attempt to find the right mixture of coherence – that is, interrelated planning; and freedom – that is, spontaneous relationship to the immediate or the local.

Probably local planning is always important, but it seems even more so in the inner city. This suggests more than merely the decentralization practised in some of the largest American districts, such as Portland, Oregon or Chicago. That procedure substitutes an average size administrative unit for a huge one, but it still keeps the node of curriculum-planning power well away from the closely related schools. Conversely, the kind of curriculum guidelines now published by British authorities such as the ILEA are, as a result of their distance, far too generalized and vague to make any impact on the autonomy of the school.

It is difficult to exaggerate the extent of the curriculum fragmentation that this autonomy produces, for it is then replicated internally, with lack of continuity from year to year. In some inner-London areas there are breaks of institution after infant school (at 6+), after primary (at 11+), and after secondary with a move to further education colleges (at 16+). At each of these breaks there can be serious discontinuities of learning, resulting not primarily from a move of site, but from discontinuous, discordant syllabuses! Even between infant and junior schools on the same site, but under different heads, there can be total changes in regime, teaching approaches and syllabus in such fundamental intellectual skills as reading and numeracy! An apparently small example epitomizes the larger one: an infant school organizes its library stock into various classifications, using colour codes as keys. The junior school that takes the pupils from the infant school, organizes its stock into a different group of categories, not in anyway concordant with the first, but with the same colours used for different purposes. The secondary school to which the same pupils then go starts them on Dewey classifications! Compare this with a small American school system in which centrally classified stocks are fed into the libraries 'K through 12'[1] with the same classification throughout. Reading skills, library research skills, study skills, computation, concepts in humanities – all these require 'through planning'. A good American school district will have such curriculum continuities specified for each aspect of the curriculum.

If there is to be 'through planning', however, it must have local relevance. Inner-city areas are very different indeed in their characteristics, and while guidelines may appropriately be established city-wide, curriculum must be established locally. For instance, 12-year-olds at Woodberry Down School study the eighteenth-century town house, a topic which acts as a vehicle for many concepts and skills we have built into the curriculum, and which can be seen in all stages from restoration to decay around us. Furthermore it is an introduction to urban town planning – a key subject for the urban pupil. Such a topic would not function in this way in other areas.

It is really impressive to sit in with a superintendent of a small American district and see the coherent co-ordination possible, with one person as over-all leader, but ample scope for individuality and varied personality down the line. Further, such a district can relate to its community in a way which an individual school never can. As Chris Webb, Director of the Notting Dale Urban Studies Centre, has said:

> The notion of school consortia or clusters seems to offer a real strategy for both internal improvements and a more coherent relationship with the hinterland within which the schools are situated. The former offers a whole range of intelligent resource, time, and space sharing, as well as allowing a more local unitary approach to language, numeracy, and the creation of learning materials. Equally, the local character would allow for a serious and prolonged look at the curriculum in all its sociological meanings. This is where the latter possibility for creating a working relationship with the locality would become clear.[2]

Thus, both for the continuity of learning of the pupil and the relationship between the learning institutions and the locality, I argue strongly for a 'community of schools', whether to be known as a sub-district (to adopt US terminology), a consortia or a federation.

[1] This is the standard American phrase, meaning throughout the years of compulsory schooling. 'K' is kindergarten (at the age of 5) and '12', grade 12, the last year of high school (at the age of 17).

[2] Chris Webb, private communication.

Age divisions

Within any schooling system there virtually has to be one or more age breaks. Where these are to come and the arrangements made to maximize the benefits of a break but minimize the disadvantages is one of the most taxing questions of educational administration. It is true that the significance of the breaks has been given undue stress in this country simply because of the almost total lack of curriculum continuity – so that a change of site is a change of learning pattern and curriculum. However, even if there is to be the planning unity for which I have argued in the last section, the age-range of pupils within each institution needs very great thought.

The crucial break, in my view, is the last one before the end of schooling. In Britain we have found ourselves for historical reasons with a cut-off point at 16+. The heavy age-layering of British education, together with the 16+ examinations, which have become an inevitable key target for all students (and terminal target for most), makes the step after the summer examinations of the fifth year of secondary schooling a major one, as into a new educational phase. Indeed, we often use that step to increase the psychological contrast between the fifth form and the sixth. In this pattern it is extremely difficult to run one group of students against the grain. Years ago selective grammar schools did it for their least able by having a 'fifth remove', a group of pupils of sixth-form age doing fifth-form work. It has become very rare indeed.

This is the crucial moment on which to focus, for it is likely that the bulk of pupils in the inner city will be behind their peers elsewhere in the country in their earlier years. There are two obvious ways of hoping to right this: the first is to make schooling more effective, and Michael Rutter's paper gives real hope that this is possible. The second, however, is to complement the first by lengthening school-ing. It seems reasonable that those who start with handicaps might need longer to cover the ground! That simple need, however, is extremely difficult as the British have a system that stops new teaching at the Easter of the fifth year, gives revision up to late May, then spends a month testing, and provides a complete break until the pupil signs on and gets going again (with new teachers and new subjects often) in mid-September, or later if she or he has moved to an FE college. No wonder 17+ exam results are uniformly poor in school and college.[1] The American grade retention system does offer one way of making longer schooling possible – the pupil is 'kept back a year'. However, this has three disadvantages: it is psychologically threatening; it usually involves repeating courses rather than elongating them; it is anyway used infrequently.[2] Paradoxically, the

[1] Denis Vincent and Judy Dean, *One-Year Courses in Colleges and Sixth Forms* (Windsor: NFER Publishing, 1977), pp. 86–9.

[2] Although some new administrators have reintroduced the method as part of 'toughening up' in areas of low standards.

UK system could have great advantages: because our certification device is, broadly speaking, criteria-referenced (that is the certifying board declares the candidate has reached a specified standard which is monitored across the country and over the years), the age at which a person sits the examination is irrelevant to the validity of the certificate. The test can be attempted and the candidate succeed earlier or considerably later than the most frequent age. In the US, on the other hand, because certification is, broadly speaking, based on averages in courses over final years, failure can less easily be rectified by going more slowly. This advantage of the much maligned UK examination system could be utilized to assist inner-city pupils.[1] However, the advantage is sacrificed if there is to be a break at 16+. The learning gap and the fresh start, which I described earlier, make an elongated course impossible. How can this be avoided? The problem is also related to pupil numbers in a year-group (as opposed to the almost obsessive British concern with pupil numbers in 'a school'). In depopulated inner-city areas few schools will have sufficient pupils at 15+ and 16+ to offer a full range of learning activities to suit the individual needs of the students. So few will have sufficient at 17+ and 18+ that *separate* sixth-form provision becomes inevitable – thus institutionalizing the break completely.

The question of range is not often well understood. Given the kind of students we are talking about, we want a large age-cohort to be able to offer the variety of activities and levels and combinations of those activities and levels that they need. We do not want to keep them as one 'class'. We want to offer them a range. A range always consists of three things: first, a range of activities, or subjects; secondly, a range of levels. At the moment in many schools you have to give up, for instance, modern languages after 16+ unless you happen to be good enough to go on to GCE A-level. This is a very poor kind of education provision for the students we are talking about, who might well need a modern language for city employment. Thirdly, you need a range of combinations of those levels and activities. By simple curriculum rules, if you increase any one of those three for the same size of pupil body, you decrease at least one, if not both, of the other two. I cannot, therefore, see that the small sixth forms in our inner-city schools are going to offer what the students require. This is not an economic point, but an educational one. I am not suggesting, however, that we require bizarre subjects. I am not

[1] There is a further point that is not concerned with age breaks. Because there is little or no cross-validation of high school grades in the US, and thus of high school graduation (even allowing for the effective regional assessment boards), graduation as a certification device has little regional or national standing. Thus, curiously, school reputation becomes even more important than in the UK, where the national validity of the examinations as certifying devices allows the achieving student from a low-achieving school broadly the same start as one from a more prestigious school. This is not so in the US, and the reputation of a poor school in a poor area hangs more powerfully round a student's neck than in Britain.

even saying we should offer the more remote languages. I am simply stressing that in the basic subjects we are going to need a variety of the kinds of courses and of levels: English should be offered in styles of literature and different kinds of options at different levels, as should modern languages, mathematics, and so forth.

This point about range is closely related to that of the seriousness of a break at 16+. There need to be opportunities for students to opt, in the fourth or in the fifth years, for some or all of their courses to be aimed at 17+ examinations. No school with a small age-cohort can manage to provide this crucial facility. A school that could would be offering continuity of teaching as well as continuity of curriculum across that break.

I have therefore argued on behalf of the older school student for two features, both of which begin to shape the age divisions in my mind: first, for continuity at 16+, and secondly for a large age-group. The first of these involves an institution in which years four to seven (age 15 to 18) are all taught. The large age-group suggests the need to split the school at 14+ if the over-all number of pupils on one site is not to be too great. This would lead either to junior and senior high on the Leicester model,[1] or a so-called split-site school, perhaps 'federated' on the Oxfordshire model. (Unexpectedly perhaps, rural depopulation offers many of the same problems as urban depopulation.)

It might be objected that it is strange to accept a split at 14+ when I have argued so strenuously against one at 16+. However, there are two types of differences between the two splits, both of which argue to my mind for the possibility, even advantage, of one at 14+ and against the more conventional one at 16+.

First, in terms of adolescent development, as far as one can generalize, there is a new settling down at around 15, and a focusing on the adult world. The watershed from childhood to adulthood is recognizable at around that age. Many teachers have observed a new seriousness at that stage. Conversely, the 16+ stage has only (in Britain) a legal validity: without the fact of our legal leaving age being at the point, we should see instead a continuation, as is clearly felt in America.

Secondly, given the small age-cohorts of inner-city areas, the low ability profile and the comparatively low staying-on rate, it is impossible to provide an adequate range of courses after the compulsory end of schooling with anything less than about 300 or 360 pupils of 15+ and 16+. This means that if schools are planned to hold pupils from age 11 upwards, they will virtually always have to feed a separate sixth-form centre. The only way to avoid this is to have twelve-form-entry schools, and few areas can sustain these unless they are to replace many schools, and leave whole swathes of

[1] See A. N. Fairbain, *The Leicestershire Plan* (London: Heinemann Educational Books, 1980).

the city without educational buildings. Put another way, as schools get smaller because of depopulation, they can be reduced in size vertically – that is keeping the same age-range, but with fewer pupils in a year; or horizontally – that is by having fewer years in the school, but keeping large numbers in each age-group. The first is not as feasible as it sounds, first, because it severely restricts the range of provision from 15 upwards; but secondly, also because in this country sixth-form provision would virtually never be possible, and so the very pupils who most require continuity at that age would be driven to a new, separate institution. However, a split at 14+ could be an 'internal' split (unlike the Leicestershire pattern), that is a change of site, but not of institution, curriculum or pastoral staff.

This pattern of schooling would allow smallish numbers of pupils of ages 12 to 14 (roughly the ages of an American junior high or the Leicestershire junior high) moving into a large age-group fed by a number of smaller schools for the option years. Thus continuity would be possible from 14+ to the end of schooling, whether at 16+, 17+, or 18+. It is likely that:

1. staying on rates would be higher;
2. continuity and academic success would be higher;
3. a more adult and suitable atmosphere and regime could be established for all the fourth and fifth years;
4. only those who really wanted to would go to further education at 16+, rather than, as at present, many leaving for the course and company impossible to find in the tiny sixth forms.

Such a pattern places the break at the most suitable age, and within an institution; thus its difficulties can more easily be worked at than those between institutions, even with the kind of community of schools that I have advocated. It groups pupils in a way that permits a suitable atmosphere. The American senior and junior high school has recognized this, and even in the most difficult areas of, for instance, Washington, Boston or San Francisco, the British visitor cannot help noticing that the senior high is more like our sixth-form college or further education college – the students, despite their numbers, do not have to be herded in the way that younger ones are. The centre of gravity is the 16- to 17-year-old, not the 14- to 15-year-old.

If the educational planning unit were to be as small as the one I outlined in the previous section (one senior high, two junior high, and perhaps five primary schools), I would accept that senior and junior high could be separate schools. However, in anything larger, I should want to see them as one multi-site but unitary institution. No doubt a 'house' organization would be used to give vertical continuity so that, for instance, three 'legs' would each be a house, coming side by side in the fourth year, but with the same pastoral head across the years. This pattern is shown in Figure 10:1.

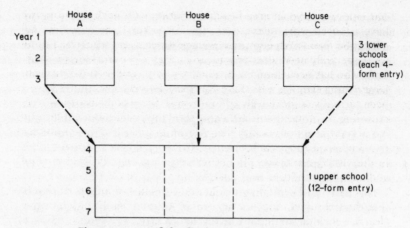

Figure 10:1   A 'federal' school with twelve-form entry

In the United Kingdom there is a small but growing use of the word 'federal' to classify such a group of schools working together. I am not sure that it is a happy or even accurate usage. The word means: 'of or pertaining to, or of the nature of that form of government in which two or more states constitute a political unity while remaining independent as to their internal affairs'.[1] However, as Michael Rutter reminds us in Chapter 8, it is precisely a large degree of unanimity in internal affairs – consistency of regime – that is required, certainly if the lower sections are to be an adequate preparation for the upper section. Still less would I wish for curriculum independence. 'Federation' may be an appropriate first stage for linking schools of declining rolls and insufficient pupils of older years, but it must be only one stage on the way towards full unification.

On the grounds then of expediency with small numbers, poor ability profiles and low educational aspiration, in hoping to keep the crucial continuity and to create the most suitable atmosphere, I recommend an 'internal' split at 14+ and then one unit with 15- to 18-year-old pupils.

Pre-school

Even accepting that school can, if it acts rightly, be very powerful at school age, and that pre-school has not determined everything, there is a great deal of truth in the argument advanced by Maurice Kogan that much urban partnership money should be devoted to a coherent, consistent, multi-disciplinary pre-school approach. While schools can do a great deal when pupils reach them, it would be so much more valuable if we worked at the pre-school age. In most of

[1] *Shorter Oxford English Dictionary*, 3rd edn.

our cities we have an area health authority, with health visitors; we have a social-work team, with social workers; and we have an education team, with education welfare officers and teachers. I think we desperately need a reciprocity and a very close working tie. Anybody who has been round with a health visitor, and seen parents with large young families will share this view. In very few homes have I been actually shocked by the physical provision, or the over-crowding, or noticed any lack of parental interest. As David Quinton has argued, it is not warmth that is lacking. I have, however, noticed that interest is physically orientated. For instance, I visited with a health visitor, a mother, Miss B, who was suckling her seventh child and had seven children under the age of 8. She was able to speak with great clarity and great certainty about problems of an eye discharge that the baby had, and yet there were all these children who quite clearly were not having any conversation with anybody except each other. They had little adult–child interaction; they were already in a 'peer-group prison'; their language was not being extended beyond their immediate needs; and their socialization was such that they would later have difficulty responding to the variety of conventions of the urban world in general, and school in particular.

There has been considerable academic debate about the precise effects of early upbringing. That language acquisition is affected is indisputable, though there has been a reaction away from describing these pupils as having a 'language deficiency'. Bernstein, whose work led perhaps to an over-simplified view of limited language, puts it thus: 'The concept [compensatory education] implies that something is lacking in the family and so in the child. As a result, the children are unable to benefit from schools.'[1] However much he and others have wished to change from 'deficiency models' to ones seeing the positive achievements of pre-school children – what they have developed rather than what they have not – any plan for inner-city education has to start with a sense of these young children and their difficulties. Eve Holmes, a principal educational psychologist at the Tavistock Clinic in London, said of one group of children: 'It was alarming. Their inability to sit still and listen guaranteed their failure to learn.' Some of the children from such homes cannot play, cannot concentrate, and are not aware of being spoken to unless called by name. As one worker described a group of pre-school children: 'They had very little sense of themselves and almost no experience of being listened to, talked to, or thought of as individuals.'

Looking at such patterns of early upbringing, one is impressed by how much we have achieved in physical care, but how little else. It is obvious that an opportunity is being missed to bring some 'educational' help through the health visitor service. What is needed

[1] B. Bernstein, 'A critique of the concept of compensatory education', in D. Rubenstein and C. Stoveman (eds), *Education for Democracy* (Harmondsworth: Penguin Books, 1970).

is what I should wish to call a new professional synthesis, in which health, education and social services are seen as different but related, and are available as co-ordinated complementary services from birth. As Eric Midwinter has written: 'Not only were distinctions between education, health, and welfare futile, they could be positively harmful.'[1]

Pre-school work designed to meet this need has been developed in a number of inner-city areas, each taking a different pattern. The Deptford Home Visiting Project was funded by the local education authority (ILEA), using professional 'educational home visitors'. The aims were those required to meet the pre-school needs as I see them:

> By visiting homes, the project hopes to teach parents who traditionally feel a child's education only starts when he enters school, and who are unaware of the importance of their own role in the early development of their children. We hope that by helping parents develop and reinforce their skills as educators, their children will be enabled to have greater opportunities to achieve their full potential.[2]

Visits lead to higher language test scores on the one hand and greater involvement by parents in their children's education on the other. EHVs were based on nursery schools, often used parents' rooms, and started a variety of parent groups, as well as visiting about thirty-five families each week throughout the year. More recently the professional expertise has been used to train and use volunteer visitors.

Other projects have seen the use of volunteers not merely as a way of making better use of professionals, but as valuable in itself. For instance 'Home Start' was funded by the Department of Health and Social Security in Leicester with Urban Aid money. Its objectives fit the needs that I have described:

1. To support and encourage mothers with their pre-school children, and show them how it is they can help their children to learn and develop their many potentials, so that ultimately they may lead fuller and happier lives.
2. To work with any families who are experiencing frustrations or difficulties with their pre-school children, or even simply where the parent is in need of support and encouragement.
3. To use volunteers for the Home-Start visits. In a 'Mum-to-Mum' relationship, one mother can share her time, concern and skills with another, thus representing a caring community, while at the same time doing useful preventive work, which social workers and health visitors, who are already over-burdened, can never hope to undertake alone. Home-Start is developmental rather than remedial.
4. To build on the parent as the 'sustaining agent' in the child's life and to build on the home as the 'sustaining background'. Thus a Home-Start volunteer can offer an individual programme to suit the needs of a

---

[1] Eric Midwinter, 'Pre-school Priorities', *Where*, vol. 135, February 1978. (London: Advisory Centre for Education.)

[2] *Deptford Educational Home Visiting Project* (London: Inner London Education Authority, 1974).

particular family, helping the parents and children to develop their skills and attitudes and to maximize the effective use of the space and materials available to them.

5. To concentrate on the use of inexpensive or expendable materials in even the poorest homes and to show the parent how she can turn everyday activities and tasks into tools of teaching.

Thus the emphasis has been on fostering self-help; and the central figure was the 'Home-Start Volunteer'. Liverpool's 'Home Link', which was run by 'Priority', similarly based its planning on the ideal that 'pre-school provision was a question of nursing the natural growth of locally orientated initiatives'.[1] However, it developed this idea further, stressing the need to educate young and old simultaneously, the former through the latter:

> We pressed the point that pre-schooling and adult education are one and the same thing, inextricably linked . . . it is essential to the education of the rising generation that the adults responsible for their upbringing should themselves be constantly involved in the education process.[2]

Still other patterns have been more school-focused, and have concentrated on the most at-risk children. In North London, for instance, a small nursery class was set up in association with the Tavistock Clinic. A small group of the most severely deprived 3-year-olds were given intensive nursery care. After a period of individual attention of half an hour a day, the children had a regular, 'inviolable' class.

Comparisons with a control group of seven similar children were dramatic. Most of the others were eventually referred for special help or to special schools. They proved to be violent and unpredictable, disruptive, and unmanageable or else very withdrawn.

I am therefore arguing that an inner-city education programme must have pre-school work as one of its components. The case has been summed up by Harriett Wilson and G. W. Herbert in their study, *Parents and Children in the Inner City:*

> In a period of low economic growth the priority should be on the creation of pre-school provisions for disadvantaged children, and this might be achieved by co-operation of the social services and education departments. In addition, there should be an attempt to concentrate existing resources of primary schools in deprived areas to achieve the following:
> 1. a sense of purpose and mastery in the children;
> 2. the social skills needed to become a member of the school community.
> Both (1) and (2) are once more part of the competence skills in which disadvantaged children are deficient.
> 3. the language and comprehension required in explaining and controlling the world, and, at a later stage, in acquiring literacy and numeracy.[3]

[1] E. Midwinter, op. cit.

[2] E. Midwinter, op. cit.

[3] Harriett Wilson and G. W. Herbert, *Parents and Children in the Inner City* (London: Routledge & Kegan Paul, 1978), pp. 196–7.

School leadership

When Michael Rutter argues that schools do have an effect, and that this effect is substantially the effect of school organization, he is inevitably making a point about school leadership. The variables that he discussed are not ones that can be 'got right' by central administration sending directives. They depend on a quality of institutional leadership. Have we, then, asked ourselves how we prepare people for such positions, train them, retain them and keep them fresh? In particular, how do we attract the best, or at least not the below average, to inner-city areas, and not give them the feeling after five, six or seven years that they have 'done their bit' and can decently get out to suburban pastures – just at the time when they have seen one generation through the school and the parents are beginning to know and trust the individual head. These are points of relevance to the whole of schooling, but of special importance in the difficult inner-city areas.

The British and American systems are diametrically opposed: the British could be called 'amateur', and be said to suffer from the faults of amateurism. Conversely, the American could be called 'professional', and be said to suffer from the appropriate faults. The American principal has left teaching, and is clearly labelled an 'administrator' not a 'teacher', belonging to a different union, contracted for different hours and operating in different ways. While the system potentially offers greater expertise, it would be true to say that the individual principal frequently sees him or herself as a mere functionary, following rules and checking procedures. Indeed, many principals speak of their task as 'regulatory'. This is symbolized by the practice of some inner-city American school districts (for example, Portland, Oregon) of moving their principals every five or so years. The arguments for this are clear, but it hardly lends itself to involved leadership. In the UK, on the other hand, there is little or no training. Head teachers have worked their way up by showing themselves reasonably good at the subordinate team-leadership posts in the school, ones which barely exist in the US (for example, the US chairman of department has only part of the leadership function of the UK head of department). Of the two systems, the first risks technical expertise without leadership (a pattern further encouraged by the immense power at district level described on pp. 167–170); whereas the second risks ill-prepared and even ill-chosen people, who virtually cannot be shifted. It is difficult to judge which is the least well suited to the inner-city needs. Certainly I felt that many American principals, while having good individual qualities, found their jobs unrewarding, felt they were acting merely as ciphers, and certainly were not seen by teachers as 'leaders' of curriculum, pedagogy or atmosphere. In Britain it is difficult to resist the generalization that inner-city leadership is so much less attractive than that offered elsewhere that the general calibre of head is lower than required.

Teacher suitability and commitment are both so important that administrators should do everything possible to give school and teacher the mutual freedom to choose each other. Some British authorities and many American districts allocate teachers. No doubt problems of contraction, expansion or reorganization will make this necessary from time to time, but the degree of working together required (see pp. 170–171) really depends on a closer involvement in teacher selection by the individual school than this mechanical process. Time after time an American principal will answer the question 'What would be the greatest help you could be given?' by saying: 'The freedom to select my own staff; only then can I be accountable; only then can we make a "school".' If schools matter, and if it is largely their organization that matters, then in a devolved system how we select, train and keep fresh our heads is a real issue.

Twinning

My last organizational point is twinning between schools and non-educational institutions. Even if my ideal school is now part of the community, and is therefore not as isolated as one feels at the moment, schools are by their nature somewhat isolated places. I do not actually believe that turning them into community centres helps solve that particular problem as far as morale is concerned, certainly not as far as responsiveness is concerned. I am not arguing against throwing a school open for adult classes and so forth; I am merely saying I do not think it breaks down this need for a school to see that it is an organization which other organizations should understand. In Boston, where the schools were still under Court ruling, it was striking that every high school was linked with an institution of higher education *and* an industrial firm. The IBM twinning, which we have been trying at Woodberry Down since 1976, with one location of IBM in Basinghall Street in the City, seems to me the kind of way in which two organizations with apparently different problems can learn from each other. Sometimes things go wrong, but that is also an opportunity for mutual learning. The kind of advantage that I have in mind is that the problems of the tension between the pastoral view of the pupil and the academic view of the pupil are not dissimilar to some of the problems in industrial terms. The question of staff career development, which we have probably thought that we are quite good at in schools, is something that industrial firms are sometimes better at than schools are. There are all kinds of unexpected learnings in such twinning enterprises, and I believe in long ongoing relationships of that kind.

There are, though, differences between twinning as I am describing it and other kinds of links between schools and other organizations.

The first is that usually individual friendship is the means of starting and maintaining the link. Of course, should that friendship deteriorate or should one of the individuals move somewhere else, then often the links are broken. In twinning as I envisage it, the two organizations have their constant fraternity. We hope that there will be some friendships coming out of that, but it really does not matter if some people do not get on well – others will. It is not dependent on individuals; individuals will benefit from it, and it will benefit from individuals. Secondly, most school–industrial links hitherto have worked on the basis that we will give industry some understanding so that they can give us some practical help. I would like to reverse that; I would like any practical help to be a vehicle for understanding. That is an important reversal.

The New York Urban Coalition is perhaps the most famous example of an extended concept of twinning. Organized in 1967, in the wake of the urban riots, the Coalition was conceived as a 'catalytic force in bringing the responses of the private sector to bear on the problems of disadvantaged minorities in New York City'. In education its primary emphasis has been in establishing mini-schools as an educational option. But in recent years the priorities have been to help improve planning in the school districts as a whole. Almost inevitably, though, it seems that the size of the enterprise has brought together funds and co-ordinated – both valuable – but has not brought schools closer to other organizations.

Pastoral care

It is a curious English phrase; no other educational system in the world uses it or understands it; however, it serves its purpose by labelling the caring focus of all teachers. It is above all useful for the reasons I gave on page 164: it brings together matters that are otherwise, and in other countries, separate. To see discipline in one person's hands, guidance in someone else's hands, and a home-room teacher being somebody else, as in an American high school, is to make one realize that the strange British phrase 'pastoral care' at least gives us a coherent relationship between all these matters.

It is generally and easily felt in Britain that whatever may be wrong with schools, pastoral care is flourishing, indeed maybe is even the cuckoo that has tipped the egg of learning out of the nest. Despite the worrying conclusion by Grace quoted by Marten Shipman on page 74, which suggests that teachers rate each other too heavily according to their perceived pastoral qualities, the most important point that has to be made about pastoral care is the striking lack of expertise. It is the aspect of professional life for which all teachers were least well trained – indeed most were not trained at all for this aspect. There are few of our HMIs who have had substantial experience in middle-management pastoral roles, and even rather few headteachers who can truly be said to have had as much pastoral responsibility in their careers as they have had leading 'academic' departments. There is very little in-service work, and what there is has been counselling orientated – not in itself harmful, but hardly a sound basis for the pastoral care of a whole school. Very few LEAs have senior advisers with pastoral-care responsibilities. The Schools Council has not considered the task; nor has the National Foundation for Educational Research in any depth. And so one could go on: the hard fact is that the inner-city emphasis on the importance of pastoral care had not been helped by any senior support.

Not only is there a lack of expertise, but it is easy for schools to develop a curious variety of misunderstandings.[1] On page 164 I spoke about one of these – the artificial polarity between caring and demanding. There is another fallacy that also worries me very much. Pastoral care is defined by some teachers as 'getting to know' the student. In itself there is no value simply in getting to know students. The object of the effort is whether having got to know them one can feed back to the pupils some kind of response which will enable those pupils in some way to master their own lives and develop. It is an extremely tricky problem because you cannot have good pastoral relationships if you do not know students, but knowing them can be a cul-de-sac, a nice cul-de-sac, a rewardingly warm cul-de-sac, but not necessarily one of value to the student.

One of the major functions of the pastoral voice is curiously one that is frequently simply never embarked upon, that is to speak for the needs of the pupil to the school as a curriculum-planning institution. There are too many schools in which the teachers in their pastoral role have no voice at all in syllabus planning. Heads of year or house are expected to counsel the pupils into choosing from a range of options over which they have no influence, and are expected to encourage or discipline students in relationship to subject teaching of a syllabus over which they have neither the duty nor the right to voice opinions. If the local curriculum planning is to be both local and planning, the pastoral organization of a school must have a cogent and influential voice in the planning mechanisms.

At the heart of pastoral care is guidance: personal, educational and vocational. The more open a school is, the more we wish for pupils to have choice, and the more we wish pupils to be freed from the accident of birth or the tyranny of the year group, the more important is guidance. In the inner city this is especially important. Neave[2] has shown from his examination analysis that success in moving to higher education depends ever more in the comprehensive

[1] For a study of these, see R. Best et al., 'Pastoral care as process', in R. Best et al. (eds), Perspectives on Pastoral Care (London: Heinemann Educational Books, 1980).
[2] Guy Neave, How They Fared: Impact of the Comprehensive School upon the University (London: Routledge & Kegan Paul, 1975).

school than in the selective school on support. Too often this has been translated by professional opinion to mean simply support from the home. In fact, of course, it also means support from the year group and from the school. Professor John Eggleston of Keele University has argued from his research that: 'as the school system ceases to label children, the more important this support becomes during decisions about staying on, course choice, and examination entries.'[1]

An important part of this support in schools with a large number of low-achieving children is the use of feedback, to help the pupils *make use* of test data. We know from a variety of studies that the expectations of immigrant families may be unreasonably high, and the expectations of locally born parents unreasonably low. Indeed Wilson and Herbert have shown 'low maternal expectation' from the youngest ages. For instance, in discussing giving young (aged 3 to 4 years) children small errands to do, one mother said: 'He can't talk very well, so I don't send him.'[2] The pastoral implications of these unduly low or unduly high expectations require great care in the feedback of response and test data, and the helping of pupils to perceive its value (and not merely regard it as punitive) and to make use of it.

A related misunderstanding is to see pastoral work as entirely concerned with working on a one-to-one basis. This is a gross confusion, and one that has been fostered by the over-emphasis on counselling in pastoral in-service training. Schools work, and always will, in groups for most of their time. Therefore most of the pastoral help given will have to be in groups. There are very few who have worked out what this means,[3] and there is a huge weight of evidence that team leadership by heads of year or house is especially weak in giving assistance with these pastoral group skills. What I am stressing here is that pastoral care is not just Leroy and I sitting in a room, or even Leroy and I stopping on the staircase having a chat; it is also I and a whole group of pupils working together, particularly through many of the aspects of social learning which are necessary for these students. Only thus will the inner-city pupils gain the social control to make use of school. As Wilson and Herbert say: 'The sharing of possessions, the fair allocation of a much desired object, patient waiting for one's turn, are behaviour patterns that need to be learnt.' And, one might add, learnt in a group and under the leadership largely of a pastoral figure.

There is also a great deal of individual case-work in any proper pastoral-care system. Indeed the social problems of very many of our

[1] *The Times Educational Supplement*, 24 January 1975.
[2] Wilson and Herbert, op. cit., p. 123.
[3] c.f. Keith Blackburn, *The Tutor* (London: Heinemann Educational Books, 1975); Leslie Button, *Developmental Group Work with Adolescents* (London: Routledge & Kegan Paul, 1974); Douglas Hamblyn, *The Teacher and Pastoral Care* (Oxford: Blackwell, 1978).

pupils will require extensive liaison work. However, what needs stressing is how much of this individual case-work is hard, practical mechanics, and how little counselling. The reception of pupils and families is one illustration, an important one in inner-city areas of high population mobility, as many are. Many schools can be boarded as simply as jumping on a bus. Mother turns up unexpectedly, the secretary places the child in a class, and the headteacher sends him round with a helpful fellow pupil. Being known is important if we are going to have the kind of care we want. With the shifting population of some inner-city schools which have a third of their roll different at the end of the year from that at the beginning, we have got to have proper provision for the reception of new pupils, both at the ordinary stage of transfer or intake and because of mobility. The obvious way is to have some kind of reception centre where a student can be prepared for ordinary classes gradually, with some preparation work on particular books and particular sequences that are being handled at that moment in class. It is a political delusion to feel that we will solve the problems of the mobile pupil by organizing the curriculum more rigorously. It may need organizing for other reasons, but not, I think, to solve the particular problems of mobility. That requires reception facilities and good internal communication processes. Indeed one of the tests of a pastoral or guidance system is how rapidly it can help the pupil make sense of her or his new experiences.

The family school

The British reaction to the comparative failure of city schools and the stubborn persistence of class differential in educational success has been to look to 'the community'. Thus much discussion of inner-city education has been in terms of how much 'community involvement' can be created. The tradition was formulated most powerfully in the Cambridgeshire village college,[1] picked up in the Leicestershire scheme, given fresh life by writers like Cyril Poster and John Sharp, and then, one could say, urbanized by Eric Midwinter.

While I see the power of the concept in rural areas, I am less certain in the true inner city. Of course those who live in an area need a range of activities. Of course educational provision is among these, and various types of formal and informal further education must be provided. And of course a school should generate a varied life of activities. However, the parents who use a secondary school for their children frequently cannot be said to be either *the* community or *a* community. Frequently they want to, and do, find their evening activities from a bewildering cross-section of providers. The very idea of attempting to focus a majority of these in one building and

[1] c.f. Harry Ree, *Educator Extraordinary* (London: Longman, 1976).

through one organization – the school – could be said to be un-urban, for towns are characterized, as earlier contributors have stressed, by variety of provision. Further, even the most energetic of school staffs have limited energies. They are not funded, paid, staffed or trained to act as a hub of adult activities. It is true that some such schools are given extra staffing to assist, but I should suggest that in most cases this in no way compensates for the time and thought that have to be contributed from the teachers at all levels. There will be areas where the community school in some form or other, with suitable staff and buildings, will flourish, as it clearly has. However, I should like to shift the emphasis, playing down a school's obligation to a single view of a community, and its resulting gains, and to offer instead what I shall call 'a family school', one which relates to each family whose pupils it serves on a direct family-to-school basis, a school of 'communities'.

In a densely populated area, with considerable criss-crossing to work, to schools, to shops and for entertainment, the importance of the school is more on a family-to-school basis than a family-to-family basis. In many areas there is no recognizable single community to serve, nor can the school create one. There are, though, the series of families who look towards the school, and to whom, individually, the school should be orientated. The school can go a considerable way to lessen the effects of the fractures of family life, for it is stable, and it offers a multi-faceted care and interest. I have the strong feeling that for many the sheer warmth, humanity, interest, and even fuss that the school offers to all who are concerned with it, are socially and emotionally important. For many it is one of the few stable and continually caring units.

The profession of teachers has long complained about the lack of interest in education by many parents. My experience is that almost all parents have a real interest in the education of their own children, but only an intermittent interest in education as a whole. There is a huge concern and care in areas such as those where I work, but it manifests itself in keenness to visit individually as a family, to hear about and talk about their own children. I therefore find what I call the social orientation of much writing about relationship with parents potentially misleading. While any school will develop some social events, I am suspicious of stressing a community school's weight of external social activities, which are not learning focused. I wish to build the contact round an interest in the individual student. I do not particularly wish to build it round evenings on how modern maths is taught. It is curious how certain of the left-wing writers about urban schools have stressed what is, in essence, a very middle-class activity – the value of demonstration evenings, of discussion evenings, of committees. I think inner-city parents want individual meetings, and that the way of approach should not be about 'schemes' and 'subjects' but about a particular pupil.

David Quinton has given a picture of one group of families which goes against some at least of the popular teachers' views of inner-city families. An important point from the picture is that families are there and are strong. Disruption does not of itself necessarily harm a child, but the lack of continuity that follows more in inner-city areas than elsewhere certainly can. The school should not in any way try to replace the family, but it can and must support the family, and its continuity is one of its main strengths. David Quinton stresses that parents 'do not lack interest': they do, though, as he describes, lack the organizational skills, and often are unhappy knowing this difficulty. The family school is organized so as to help in this respect.

The kind of contact I am advocating is really further from the practice of most schools than it sounds. Naturally, all of us in schools endeavour to make some contact with families, but because of the difficulties of time, facilities and attitude, these contacts are frequently far more limited than we care to admit to ourselves. The first step is a thorough reception interview for all pupils and with both parent figures (if there are two caring for the pupil). This is the basis of all later communication, and its importance in establishing the family and personal facts about the pupil cannot be over-emphasized. A school has the decision about whether to have this interview carried out by a senior person or the teacher closest to the daily care. At Woodberry Down the problem is resolved by having two separate interviews, one with the head and later one with the pastoral figure (head of house). Subsequently, there is a need for two kinds of meeting. There are those requested, maybe even on rather slight grounds, by parents. These must be responded to, and, indeed, there must be a ready availability of professional staff to cope with the inevitable unplanned 'crisis' visit. If possible, though, this should be avoided to ensure that the responsible teacher seen is indeed most likely to be the one who knows the pupil and can take action. The third kind of contact could be described as the routine review interview, to be held at least at the crucial stages of the pupil's progress, and to involve the parents meeting not only the central pastoral figure, but also the teachers. For this to be possible a school requires a good reception office and waiting space, good telephone system and telephonist, good secretarial help, good internal communication systems and good internal records. It needs also to have a way of making its internal organization known to those outside the school who have a professional responsibility towards any of the pupils: youth club leaders, social workers, etc. Above all, of course, the school must have a willingness to listen to individual parents, not only for the sake of the care of their son or daughter, but also so that the school hears the message of parental concern. No parent–teacher associations, elected representatives or committees can substitute for the voice of individuals; and social events, useful as they may be for helping the atmosphere of understanding, are no substitute for individual consultation with parents. The family school is more valuable than the community school for it can serve the true communities of an area.

Curriculum

Although both Britain and America set great store in the 1960s by curriculum renewal as the key way of improving schooling, there is some evidence that inner-city schools in the UK came to put extended and intensified pastoral care higher in the ranks of hopeful solutions. The thesis of this whole series is that the organization of the educational institution should be primarily focused on using 'organization' to cover the whole functioning of the institution. Michael Rutter's chapter, and the research reported fully in *Fifteen Thousand Hours*[1], support this approach. Within this, the curriculum is the main organizational focus, for it embodies the teaching aims of the school. Unfortunately, curriculum theory is one of the aspects of education which is furthest away from the realities of schools, and teachers planning their courses have as a result had too little help. As Lawrence Stenhouse puts it:

> The teaching of education as an undifferentiated field has been largely supplanted by the teaching of constituent disciplines ... This change in curriculum has increased the rigour and the intellectual tone of education courses. It has done little for their relevance to the problem of improving the practice of teaching.[2]

Yet teaching is mere chance without curriculum, and I should argue that in the troubled areas with which we are concerned curriculum planning needs to be extra rigorous and careful to ensure that those already behind do not lose further as a result of gaps or fractures in the curriculum.

Three fallacies

Before I can be positive I must pay some attention to the three most common fallacies, for they confuse curriculum planning in schools.

1. Curriculum credibility

Ian Lister talks, virtually without qualification, about 'a curriculum no one believes in',[3] and is one of many who hold that it is self-evident that the curriculum is breaking down. Although some of the similar remarks are based on evidence, most are mere expressions of

---

[1] M. Rutter, B. Maugham, P. Mortimore and J. Ouston, *Fifteen Thousand Hours: Secondary Schools and their Effects on Children* (London: Open Books, 1979).

[2] Lawrence Stenhouse, *An Introduction to Curriculum Research and Development* (London: Heinemann Educational Books, 1975), p. vii.

[3] Ian Lister, *De-schooling* (Cambridge: Cambridge University Press, 1974), cover.

prejudice, often wilfully ignoring the facts of schools – that pupils respond better to most parts of the conscious curriculum than they do to the school regime as a whole. When Paul Goodman declares 'the schools less and less represent any human values' one is amazed by the quasi-historical touch in the 'less and less', and looks at the human values represented by much of the curriculum with bewilderment. Indeed as British schools move towards what P. E. Daunt has called 'the familial model',[1] the human concern has increased. What work has been done to investigate the curriculum in support of such criticisms has been mainly directed at the humanities, indeed almost entirely the social studies. Thus Nell Keddie's influential chapter 'classroom knowledge',[2] which certainly contains valuable criticisms, is, in her words, 'focused on the humanities department . . . based on history, geography, and social science'.[3] On the other hand, successful experiences which are typical of school, but not typical of comment on school by the critics, include drama, individual reading tuition, commercial studies, the crafts, technical drawing, and instrumental tuition, to make a merely personal list.

2. Class-culture conflict

A second fallacy is that there is what is glibly called a 'class-culture' conflict. This is a further sociological attitude which bases its conclusion on the presumed alienation of 'working-class pupils' from 'middle-class culture'. Certainly the curriculum can be seen as 'political', saying some things to girls and other things to boys, for instance, and giving each models of themselves and each other; and certainly knowledge is 'politically' shifted into the curriculum. However, the evidence on the acceptability of the curriculum to working-class pupils does not support the crude notion of conflict. Those teachers who have worked in suburban areas and inner-city areas usually agree that the working-class pupil has less of a barrier to much art and literature. Similar findings are reported by investigators of the teaching of aspects of the popular mass media in classes – one way proposed by certain teachers as reducing the 'class-culture gap':

41% said that they did not want teachers to introduce mass media material into the classroom. The majority of these pupils had a very 'instrumental' attitude to education. In their view, schools exist to provide examination passes which will hopefully secure a well paid job, and that consequently time should not be wasted listening to pop records or looking at films. Others added what teachers should 'stick to teaching' and that 'what you do out of school is none of their business'. Pupils holding these opinions

---

[1] P. E. Daunt, op. cit.
[2] In Michael F. D. Young, *Knowledge and Control* (West Drayton: Collier Macmillan, 1971).
[3] ibid., p. 133.

were more likely to be working class than middle class; in fact almost half (49%) of the working-class pupils said that they did not want their teachers to talk about the mass media in lessons compared with 28% of the middle-class respondents. Clearly, then, the introduction of more mass media material into lessons is not likely to provide an immediate solution to the problem of finding a curriculum which working-class children will find relevant and interesting.[1]

Obviously this is not in itself evidence to refute the existence of any kind of school–pupil gap, but it is confirmation that the traditional aspects of teaching (labelled as 'middle-class' by observers) are what pupils both expect, and want, from school; they demand that school should be a complementary environment to their out-of-school life.

My view is that the working-class pupil takes activities more directly for what they are. Conversely the middle-class child tends to feel he ought to relate what is offered to other values, and there his responses are confused more readily by external comparisons. Thus the experiences a school has to offer are less often spoilt for the working-class pupil by association. He will take a story or poem for what it is, and be neither impressed nor alienated by the name and thus the half-known reputation of the author. I often remember a religious studies class of 14-year-olds to whom I showed a series of slides of the Christmas story in art. The few middle-class children found the experience 'churchy' and off-putting; the remainder were impressed by the technique of the needlework of embroideries, the intricacy of mosaic, and the atmosphere of the paintings.

The theory that best seems to fit the facts as I obseve them in schools is that explored in an important study by Robert Witkin.[2] He designed a study to investigate the question: 'Does the working-class child evaluate his school experience less positively than the middle-class child?' His findings were based on English lessons (interestingly an aspect of school often cited as an example of the culture gap), and showed quite firmly: 'Working-class children are more positive and middle-class children are less positive.'[3] He explains this in the following way:

> The theoretical viewpoint which I have proposed to account for (and indeed to predict) these results may be summarised as follows. The expectations constituting the roles of the middle-class child are largely generated at a superordinate level. They extend far into his social time and social space to serve to link his behaviour in different social systems. The expectations constituting the roles of the working-class child are to a greater extent generated within particular social systems which involve

[1] Graham Murdock and Guy Phelps, *Mass Media and the Secondary School* (London: Macmillan, 1973), p. 146.
[2] Robert Witkin, 'Social class influence on the amount and type of positive evaluation of school lessons', originally published in *Sociology*, vol. 5, no. 2 (May 1971), and reprinted in John Eggleston (ed.), *Contemporary Research in the Sociology of Education* (London: Methuen, 1974).
[3] ibid., p. 318.

him. These systems are not articulated for him, and his behaviour does not have to be referred to a superordinate system for evaluation. He is more free than the middle-class child to exploit those opportunities for immediate gratification that may exist and at the same time because of his lack of a superordinate reference he is less able to distance himself from the definitions of his behaviour and experience as they are generated within the school.[1]

And he concludes:

It does not appear that the social structure of schools and the experience of children within them can profitably be described in terms of the class-culture conflict model.[2]

3. 'Basics'

In the face of the undoubted attainment problems in inner cities, the public have led a cry of 'back to basics', and in America have often pulled the school district administrators with them. I suppose there is nothing inherently wrong with the phrase – no education approach can wish to avoid its true 'basics'. However, as popularized the movement rests on a dangerous semantic confusion. This is well illustrated if the use of the full stop is considered. Certainly there is a sense in which the full stop is basic; that is, it is concerned with signalling sense grouping of words to the reader – a basic function – and it is the most important of the punctuation symbols. However, it is not basic in the sense of 'primary', that is mastered early and finished with. Similarly reading is basic in the sense that most other learning is heavily dependent on it, but it is not basic in the sense that it can be mastered early with no further development necessary. I. A. Richards is tellingly quoted in the Bullock report on this: 'We are all of us learning to read all our lives.' These are neither of them matters which are easy to learn, nor that can be mastered merely by rigorous concentration on them alone: wider purposes (not properly labelled 'basic') are necessary to provide adequate contexts for the growth of the 'basic'.

Responding to public alarm many American districts (for example, Florida and Washington) have set up a series of 'minimum competency' tests. In as much as such criterion-referenced tests are a better way of monitoring achievement than internal grades, this is to be welcomed, but in as much as those state- or district-mandated tests can become ends in themselves, and drain the curriculum they are meant to service of any life or extension, they are to be regretted. It is depressing to see pupils of 12 and 13 in black schools in Portland, Oregon, for instance, having a daily run at picking out subjects from predicates, in a mistaken idea that this is 'basic' and will therefore give a firm 'base' for language growth. It is depressing in a

[1] ibid., p. 321.
[2] ibid., p. 323.

Washington junior high to be told that science classes used to be brought to the library to follow up investigations, but that there is no longer time for this as a result of the emphasis on 'basics' demanded by the testing programme.

'Basics' is a seductively tough word that masks a mushy meaning; as a way forward for areas with low attainment it is misleading. It has one valuable sense: our pupils must work in a school which has a clear set of priorities. Getting the priorities right will involve curriculum planning of much greater complexity than envisaged in 'getting back to basics'. On the other hand, I entirely accept that the specific teaching of skills is necessary. Too often in the inner city we have put down to 'difficult backgrounds' problems that have been cognitive, and which actual teaching can help pupils master. We have overstressed motivation, which is not a teaching method, at the expense of careful teaching of skills, the mastery of which is itself encouraging. 'Being able' is one of the best motivators. Thus in the curriculum mix the specific didactic teaching of certain skills must be included. A constant diet of self-initiated methods, with no opportunity to teach the ingredients, is especially dangerous with the inner-city child. But that is not the same as the too readily seized phrase 'back to basics'.

Aspects of curriculum

Planning

For too long the British curriculum-planning debate has stirred around the ingredients of 'who should control'. The means of decision-making is important only to the extent that it affects the quality of the decision, and the arguments about decision-making have largely ignored both what kinds of decisions might be made and how these could be implemented. The hard fact is that there is little curriculum planning in British schools. If those of us who work in schools look back at the agendas of the meetings we have sat through in the last two or three years, we would find very few of them were about curriculum planning. Since the Bullock report, I have been to innumerable conferences in different schools and different centres on 'language across the curriculum'. It dawned on me after three years of struggling with this that the reason for the problem was simple: most of us do not have a curriculum across which to put the language policy. We have a series of separate subjects; we do not have a planning system. When the DES talk about areas of curriculum in their recent booklet,[1] they use a metaphor which I think does not help us much further either. Language, numeracy, visual literacy –

[1] *The Curriculum 16–19* (London: Department of Education and Science, 1978).

these are not really 'areas'; 'areas' suggest that when you are in one, you are not in the other. In fact when you are in mathematics, you are in language as well. We therefore need a different metaphor.

The most common curriculum-planning failure in Britain is to take for granted that there will be a teacher team responsible for 'X', and then to discuss what that team should teach. Thus a school will discuss what should be done in 'religious studies'; what should be the content of 'English'; what kind of 'maths' should be taught. All these questions put the cart before the horse: the starting-point must surely be to draw up an over-all list of what a pupil needs from school, and from that to develop lists of what she or he requires personally by way of concepts, information, attitudes and skills. Only then is it possible to break the list down and divide it between teams, some items going to certain teams and others being handled by all.

American curriculum planning is, as I said earlier (page 170), more thorough than ours in its vertical continuity. This is clearly of especial benefit to the inner-city child. But American planning, by its distance from the classroom, and above all by its separate subject sequences, makes whole-school planning possibly even more difficut. It is rare to find one curriculum continuum showing any awareness of any of the other ones. They are planned by separate groups, and implemented by separate teaching teams, coming together only for the administrator and not for the pupil. When the separate curriculum plans are in fact made with cognisance of each other the greater strength and impact are immediately obvious. For instance, in an elementary school in Portland, Oregon, with a science class working in the library, I saw in action a language arts programme that spoke of putting the skills in context and a science programme that listed the skills of research, library usage and reading in science as part of its necessary techniques. Such interlinking is rare on both sides of the Atlantic.

Only with 'through planning' based on over-all lists of aims, and co-ordinated, can a consistent programme be devised. The kinds of starting-point that it could use can be seen in Wilson and Herbert's analysis of the needs of deprived inner-city children:

1. Because of the high incidence of learning problems (and often behaviour difficulties) in priority areas, it seems superfluous to use screening techniques to 'identify' children. It is nevertheless important to train teachers in sequential diagnosis and prescription.
2. The all-round poor performance of the disadvantaged, as illustrated by our results, should lead to all-round programmes, but *not* to the assumption that non-verbal and physical skills should be trained before literacy work is started.
3. 'Remedial' work should not be regarded as something which goes on for part of the day, but rather as integral with the whole curriculum; in

other words, the remedial teacher should be an adviser to the whole staff on methods, materials and language content.

4. Because some children will be spasmodic attenders, the curriculum should be geared to sequences for individuals rather than groups.

5. The implications of the 'chaperonage' concept should be explored in the context of the school. Children need to be watched and cared about, and chaperonage should be taken beyond mere negative restrictions to become a means of creating a base from which autonomy and competence can grow.

6. Our evidence that the absence of chaperonage at home is linked with delinquency and poor adjustment in the classroom indicates the need for the school to make informal and helpful contact with families showing this pattern before trouble starts.

7. Severely disadvantaged boys appear to have an increased prevalence of anxious or dependent behaviour in late primary school. We need to ask whether the school itself is partly responsible for this, and to take early steps to overcome it.

8. School attendance difficulties in the disadvantaged child should be recognized as a deep and continuous problem, which cannot be solved by any of the usual combinations of persuasion, pressure, and care proceedings. We need more flexible resources and placements, including some schools or units with highly individual approaches. The concept of residential 'assessment' with its implications that there are personal problems which can be assessed away from home, should be dropped for such children, and the residential facilities should be used for creative and positive purposes.[1]

Their summary is simple but compelling – and far from present achievements:

> There is the same need for individual care, experience and encouragement of mastery, and structured achievement in language, basic literacy and numeracy, together with co-ordination of approaches at the transition from one age level of schooling to the next.[2]

This approach leads to what I should call a 'whole-school programme', that is, however separate the teaching teams, one that is planned to give vertical coherence across the years and horizontal coherence across the learning activities, a coherence which can only be planned locally.[3]

Continuity

The corollary of pupil population mobility is curriculum continuity; the support for pupils who start education already behind their peers in attainment is also continuity. Such continuity will have to be more detailed than the current British pattern, and yet less cramping than

---

[1] Harriett Wilson and G. W. Herbert, *Parents and Children in the Inner City* (London: Routledge and Kegan Paul, 1978), pp. 197–8.

[2] ibid., p. 177.

[3] I expand my ideas on curriculum planning and the personal needs of the pupil in my chapter 'The pastoral curriculum', in R. Best *et al.*, *Perspectives on Pastoral Care* (London: Heinemann Educational Books, 1980).

that in the US (which is why I argued for a 'community of schools' on page 171). A key question of educational administration is how to achieve continuity, and yet in the whole of the literature on curriculum from both Britain and America there has been very little work done on it.

The most important part of this continuity is that sequencing can then become possible. Of course, proper sequencing does not usually mean that topics are dealt with and dropped. However, it does imply that all that is taught is at least done with full cognisance of the future, and probably with an eye to its later practical application. This requires a very detailed study of teaching methods, for it is not merely the topic that has to be agreed, but the explanations to be used. Such explanations should be distillations not obscurations, what Professor Skemp calls 'relationship learning' not merely 'instrumental learning'. Such distillations have the power of organic growth; whereas short-cut obscurations do nothing more than get the pupil and teacher through the next stages. For instance, it is very common to tell a pupil learning multiplication that a number can be multiplied by 10 'by adding a nought'. This is *not* in fact what is being done,[1] and the pupil is thus having his rudimentary grasp of number, which depends on place value, obscured and confused, and there is no potential for the future (try multiplying a decimal fraction such as 5·3 by ten according to that method!). Similar 'blind' explanations are given about upper-case letters (inaccurately called 'big'), full stops (often said to show 'long pauses'), subtraction ('pay back'), and the interpretation of graphs.

Those were examples in which explanations had no future. The opposite is the failure to prepare for the later use of concepts by their early introduction. This is especially true of the humanities, in which there is very little relevance in early work to the needs of later years: key concepts are not introduced.

Vocational v. general

In defining the mis-match between schooling and inner-city employment offers in Chapter 6, Pat White has re-focused the old debate about vocational versus general education. The curious point is that if we argue, as I certainly should in the light of her points, that schooling should be more satisfactorily related to employment opportunities, this does not, in my view, lead to a narrowly defined vocational series of courses. For instance, Pat White describes young people who do not have 'the confidence to travel and compete'. Such young people require more than a saleable specific skill. The service industries require qualities of personality, communication, sympathy and planning ability that are near to any definition of the *general* aims of education.

[1] More accurately, the digits are being moved one place to the left, and any resulting gap in the unit column filled by a nought.

Our concept of vocational education will have to have a wider approach than we have known on both sides of the Atlantic. Even the quasi-vocational courses will need to have a strong emphasis on personal skills, including the difficult-to-teach social skills. This obviously creates a tension: to keep the special flavour and mode of a vocational course, but without losing the opportunity to develop powers of thought and verbal abilities is difficult – the vocational education tradition has been to simplify to a form of rote learning. Washington/Munro High School in Portland, Oregon, is an example of a school where specialized vocational work includes courses in medical careers (such as dentristry), child development, food services and secretarial work. What impressed me was the way the pupils were getting a very good *general* education through the medium of a very specific, apparently *vocational*, course.

My suggestion is that quasi-vocational courses may be a perfectly good vehicle for general education, but at the same time give pupils a better understanding of the working world. It is indefensible that as educators we criticize industrialists for not being able to define more helpfully what their employment needs are, but then when we devise a work-oriented course we slip too easily into a parody of the most limited apprentice system: 'do it like this'. Work-oriented courses must be planned as part of the whole curriculum, be part of all pupils' education (not only those who consider that is the job for them after leaving), and be treated as ways of preparing pupils for the employment available. Looked at radically, there is no conflict between education for careers and education for leisure – one programme properly devised can do both.

The locality

I have argued that the curriculum should be related to the locality. The major factor will be the range of ethnic backgrounds in the area served by the school as well as in the world in which the pupils will later make their own lives.

We know that this is a tense matter. Racial attitudes are compounded by population mobility. On the whole, as Nicholas Deakin has shown,[1] those who leave are those with roots in the area, the long established. Of one area he studied (Islington in London) he wrote: 'Change in Islington and its increasing heterogeneity in terms of ethnic and social class appears to have become a "push" factor in the migration process.'[2] Further, the immigrants who move out to the new towns are on the whole those with the greater skills, leaving behind, therefore, the least skilled, fairly new migrants and the least

[1] Nicholas Deakin and Clare Ungerson, *Leaving London* (London: Heinemann Educational Books, 1977).
[2] ibid., p. 112.

successful older residents, who envy those of their old associates who have left. This clearly leaves a tension which education has to face. This is an important and complicated issue, and for the purposes of this account I want merely to point to the dual responsibility of a curriculum plan: it must in effect explain the past and prepare for the future. In attempting to meet these needs, it is easy for schools to develop two weaknesses: separatism and stereotyping.

By separatism, I mean the temptation to see education in and about a certain ethnic background as primarily for the pupils of that background. It is, of course, valuable for Hispanic pupils to have a feel for their own past, as it is for the children of West Indian or Asian parents, but equally each needs to learn about each other. Black Studies, for instance, may have a place in an option or elective system, but not if it is a substitute for the basic curriculum being such as will include the studies of black peoples.

By stereotyping I have in mind the risk of merely peppering a basically unchanged curriculum with tourist-type references to the non-indigenous ethnic cultures. It is a serious danger that the less familiar cultures will be introduced as 'colourful' and strange, and that lacking the intellectual concepts the student will come from the learning in many ways less understanding of difference than before. For instance, other religions should not be taught in terms of their 'customs', but should be taught in the context of the function of religion, how it works and how various religions have developed.

Under the pressure of the Lau case[1] in San Francisco, and Federal Court rulings, so-called 'bilingual' courses have been carefully developed in many US cities. Although some of these suffer from separatism, many approach the problem as a truly educational way by taking the concepts agreed to be necessary for the core curriculum, and teaching these through material from a variety of cultural backgrounds. For instance, grade 3 pupils (aged 8) in some New York schools study a core curriculum: 'Bilingual Cross Cultural Social Studies Objectives: comparison of cultures in ecosystems around the world'. The introduction states:

> At each sequential level, learning objectives will encourage the student to acquire skills to enable him or her to live in a expanding world of inter-dependent cultures. The school serves as the context for every child to increase awareness of himself or herself as a person, as a member of a family and a culture, and as a member of a classroom and to develop an understanding of social and political organization in their own classroom. From that base, students go on to an understanding of the differences among cultural groups based on various cultural adaptations and forms of economic and social organization which meet universal human needs. Affective as well as cognitive development is included in the

[1] Lau was the prosecuting student in a successful case against the school district.

Core Curriculum which suggests activities such as social values clarification since differences as well as similarities are explored.

Thus the inner-city school system needs to ensure that cultural variety permeates its vertical curriculum planning, starting with the key concepts and working in suitable topic material from the earliest ages. The literature, art and music of different peoples should be introduced throughout. The key biological facts and concepts should be taught in context. Preparation for a multicultural society cannot be achieved by tacking on bits to the surface of schooling: it must be fundamental.

Finally, I wonder if we are wise in our search for relevance and impact on the pupils to make our inner-city curriculum totally urban. Certainly the built environment will feature substantially, but I do not think it is merely sentimental to suggest that the urban school could benefit from featuring the growing of living things. There are few schools that have attempted this. One virtually all-black school in the Roxborough district of Boston has been created as a 'magnet school' with an emphasis on horticulture, and it seemed that the major place in the school filled by this creative activity was a softening and positive influence. Similarly Whittaker Campus in Portland has made itself 'a suburban school with an inner-city population'. Built close to the airport, but near the centre of the city, the school has a 23·5 acre site. The housing development that was expected did not come. The school is therefore fed by pupils bussed from the surrounding inner-city areas and creates an impressive inner-city education round greenhouses, arboretums, lakes and animals!

Using the services

What does it mean for the curriculum if to some extent at least city stresses are related to the difficulties of coping with a complex environment? I should argue that this involves our attempting to analyse what skills are required to handle modern society, and seeing how these can be placed in the curriculum.

It is frequently argued that ours is a scientific society, and therefore school science teaching is essential; or that it is a technological society, and therefore technology is vital. It is probably more accurate to say that ours is a bureaucratic society, one which is characterized by hierarchical organizations, one in which individuals work for large organizations, and in which service of all kinds comes to the individual through such organizations. When we talk of the middle class gaining more from the welfare state, we are making a comment on their ability to *use* these services. When we note that many inner-city areas have, for instance, high infant mortality rates, we are commenting not so much on the physical provision of inner-city housing, but the apparent inability of the population to plan, to use services, to follow up and to understand the organization of, for example, hospitals. Important as are the biological aspects of health, no mere extension of school science teaching will go far to change this lack. I therefore consider that there must be in the curriculum elements that work towards giving the pupils the abilities regarded so far as middle-class monopolies:

> an understanding of the general features of organizations, hierarchy and responsibility;
> a knowledge of the particular services available, their purposes and characteristics;
> development of the communication skills required for dealing with everyone from receptionist to doctor.

To be able to use the services in today's society is a crucial survival skill.

Language

The final curriculum aspect on which I wish to comment is language. The sad irony is that inner-city life and employment has become increasingly language demanding, but it is in language terms that inner-city school pupils are especially failing. One danger is that the response to this will be to separate the teaching of language, and reduce language education to a series of decontextualized drills – for such a move is at least 'doing something about it'. There is little hope that such an approach will help. What is required is a whole-school approach, what in the UK (following the Bullock Report)[1] has come to be called 'language across the curriculum'.[2] The arguments for this are very great in all circumstances, but are particularly so in inner-city schools.

The start for such a policy is an attitude towards language that has to be worked out by the staff of a school in the face of its own local language situation. We know intellectually that ghetto language is not deficient in logic and structure; we can accept the important claim that 'the black English vernacular is the vehicle of communication used by some of the most talented and effective speakers of the English language',[3] and yet we have to accept language difficulties in the face of reading, writing, and even speaking in certain contexts. Somehow this tension has to be resolved, and a way found of relishing and retaining the strengths of the pupil's speech while assisting its growth towards greater flexibility, its ability to modulate

---

[1] *A Language for Life* (HMSO, 1975), see Chapter 11.

[2] For a full discussion see Michael Marland, *Language Across the Curriculum* (London: Heinemann Education Books, 1977).

[3] William Labov, *Language in the Inner City: Studies in the Black English Vernacular* (Philadelphia: University of Pennsylvania Press, 1972; Oxford: Blackwell, 1977), p. 396.

from in-group to public uses without which the modern inner-city dweller is trapped. For this, language must be seen not as a 'subject' or an 'area', but a facet of all learning. This involves very careful and sensitive whole-school curriculum planning.

Conclusion

It does matter what is offered for learning, and it does matter how that is planned. The difficulties faced by the pupils whom we are considering are such that the content and approach of the curriculum need extra care: there is no time to waste and no space for failure.

Teaching and learning styles

The notion that there is a special kind of 'inner-city' teaching is clearly unacceptable, yet teachers with long experience outside the inner city speak vividly of the difficulties they had re-learning their relationship and classroom skills when they moved into an inner-city school. While it is difficult to believe that good teaching in an inner-city school would not also succeed anywhere else, it is probably true that the balance of aspects would be more critcial in the areas we are concerned with, and the level of skill would need to be high. The threshold for 'getting by' as a teacher is much higher.

The conditions described earlier in this book could be summed up in three major respects. The behaviour profile of the school population will include roughly twice as many disturbed children;[1] the ability profile will include few of high measured verbal ability, and many below average (that is the shift is from the above-average to the below, not merely to the average); thirdly, all the tensions of society will be represented in the school, with pupils embodying the country's racial, housing, social, economic and marital problems in high numbers. The question is then how should a team of teachers react? What aspects of teaching style should be emphasized?

Intensity

The first characteristic I should wish to stress is the need for intensity. It is one of the findings of Michael Rutter's team,[2] which in its turn echoes the research by Neville Bennett[3] that showed that the primary-school pupils who learned most were those whose classrooms were so organized that they had most time learning. It is not always realized

[1] c.f. M. Rutter, 'Why are London children so disturbed?', *Proceedings of the Royal Society of Medicine*, vol. 66, December 1973, pp. 1121-1222.

[2] c.f. page 143.

[3] Neville Bennett, *Teaching Styles and Pupil Progress* (London: Open Books, 1976) pp. 157-163: 'Careful and clear structuring of activities together with a curriculum which emphasizes cognitive content are the key to enhanced academic content.'

how easily the learning time in school can be frittered away with late starts to lessons, interruptions, ill discipline, and the sheer mechanics of classroom administration. In a hardworking primary-school teacher's class, Vera Southgate-Booth has shown that sheer over-work can lead to a teacher's never giving a pupil more than forty-five seconds of uninterrupted time, and that as a result pupils are never heard reading for more than a part of a minute.[1] Similarly, Lunzer and Gardner investigating top junior and lower secondary class-rooms expected to find a large amount of reading, but instead found very little, and that was frequently broken into – for example, even in fourth-year social studies, only five per cent of the time spent reading was continuous.[2] Our pupils cannot afford this wasted time; but more than that, the attitude bred by allowing or even encouraging low levels of task-orientation are particularly harmful, I should suggest, for the pupil whose problems are those of typical inner-city conditions.

It is necessary then to ensure that the time is focused on learning, and that the task in hand is given a high priority. This need not involve a distant or over-pressured teaching approach, but it does imply a relative modesty on the part of the teacher, who must see him or herself as helping an instrumental need, not merely indulging her or his own personality. This implies putting curriculum continuity before teacher continuity, even in the inner city. However, many of the classroom solutions offered by some who have been daunted by the problems depend even more than ever on a stable teaching force. For instance, a young teacher wrote in a magazine that purported to offer new approaches to inner-city problems (*Raded*): 'The subject is little more than an excuse to enter into a constructive personal relationship.' While one can understand the motives behind such a suggestion, it is very dangerous to put relationships before content, skills and activities. Such a solution would find the continued mobility of younger teachers even more of a problem. In a school that is overtly relationship-based rather than curriculum-based, you lose continuity hopelessly. You can pick up from where another left off in a scheme of activity and learning far more satisfactorily than in a personal relationship! Friendships should flourish, but not at the expense of learning.

Attitudes

Almost all teachers who chose to work in inner-city schools are generous with their personal time and humanely concerned for the

[1] Vera Southgate, Helen Arnold and Sandra Johnson, 'The use of teachers' and children's time in Extending Beginning Reading', in E. Hunter-Grundin and H. U. Grundin (eds), *Reading: Implementing the Bullock Report* (London: Ward Lock Educational, 1978).

[2] E. Lunzer and K. Gardner, *The Effective Use of Reading* (London: Heinemann Educational Books, 1979).

wellbeing of the children for whom they are responsible. However, there is an ever present possibility that good intentions mask dangerous attitudes which belittle the possibilities of educational growth for the pupils. These attitudes are often the more powerful for being unconscious and for being part of a generally generous and well-meant approach. It is possible to have racism without racists, and degrading attitudes without ostensible scorn. The three danger areas are social, intellectual and racial.

Teachers are not substantially the intellectually most able or the socially most confident sector of society. Despite the cries of 'middle-class bias' thrown at them, it is now well accepted that the profession is not securely middle class, indeed teaching is traditionally one of the ways into the lower rungs of the middle classes. Similarly, in Britain, college of education entrants have not been from the highest ability ranges, or the method of education likely to give the greatest intellectual stimulation. Even those with university degrees have usually been from the second band. In the US it has been similarly shown that education departments at universities recruit many whose standard of work is less than the average in other departments. These factors combine to make many teachers insecure in their position, a feeling which is strengthened by low public esteem, poorish pay, and a nagging sense that the job is never done. Such insecurity too easily leads in a perhaps perverse way to branding the deficiencies of pupils as greater than they are, and of ending up with low expectations of the possibilities of their learning. That this can be combined with great day-to-day optimism and charity to the pupils makes matters no better. It may lead to an emphasis on the social aspects of a teacher's role that is positively dangerous when there is so much to be learned, and it may lead to a major under-teaching justified by the pointlessness of aiming high in the face of such immense difficulties of background. This is then extended to relaxing standards for the children of deprived homes: 'How can you expect him to be on time to school, living in a house like that?'; 'How can you expect her to do any homework, when Dad's a cripple?'; 'How can you expect him to learn to read, when Mum's got so many men friends?' – and the list of justifications for low expectations grows.

Racial attitudes are even more subtle. I am not now concerned with pure hostility, nor even the hidden version of it that inevitably emerges occasionally. What is more worrying is a well-meaning low expectation. One headmistress of a junior school said that there were no racial problems at all in her school: 'They're all cuddly little darlings.' With that she embraced one of the black girls, asking 'Aren't they all dears?'! Others of us become so used to the expectation that, for instance, girls of West Indian families are noisier than others, they they are allowed (and thus virtually encouraged) to make interruptive noises in class. At its worst this approach can be summed up by the 'steel bands and basketball' approach of some teachers to their black children of West Indian origin, expecting little by way of learning, but passing such failures off as inevitable for children who 'have got so much rhythm'! This is disenabling and belittling.

There is ample evidence that American schools similarly expect low academic achievement from black pupils, and that recent moves to improve the standing of the black population have sometimes even encouraged this by giving unjustified high grades in school and college to blacks. Thomas Sowell has written bitterly of this in *Black Education: Myths and Tragedies*.[1] He describes with horror the effects of the lowering of entrance standards and the relaxing of grade standards, which he alleges a number of prestigeous USA universities deliberately allowed in the sixties in order to obtain Federal government funding. According to Sowell, this actually kept able black students out of these universities, and, perhaps even worse, reduced the value of the grades being given. He alleges that many inner-city schools have habitually done the same thing in their awarding of grades.

The story of Chicago's Leroy Lovelace, and the students who picketed his classes for an entire day to protest that he awarded so few As and Bs, illustrates what surprise the opposite approach causes.[2] Lovelace declared: 'You have to be dedicated and make demands on the kids. You can't be any more kind to the kids than society is going to be to them. And the standards for an inner-city school must be no different than any other school... I'm not going to lower the standards... because it's not fair to the kids.'[3]

Generalizations are inevitable, even though they are literally the vehicle of prejudice. Teachers, like other professionals, are bound to develop their generalizations, and these will include racial generalizations. Indeed many such generalizations *do* have considerable truth in them. To deny that is to make the problem even harder to tackle. However, the generalizations apply only at certain times and in certain places. They are the results of selection processes, as is illustrated by the completely different stereotype of the West Indian in British and American schools: in the former he is likely to be seen as a low achiever; in the latter as, in the phrases of informal prejudice, 'the jew of the blacks'.

An East London 15-year-old said of a reading teacher who he alleged let the white children read aloud for long periods, but when it came to the blacks' turn stopped after a short time:

That woman never knew she was doing it, man. You would have asked her, maybe she'd tell you she treats us all the same but for some reason the

---

[1] New York: McKay, 1972.

[2] Sylvester Munroe, 'Leroy Lovelace', *Newsweek*, 12 September 1977.

[3] Quotation taken direct from Sylvester Munroe's original text to *Newsweek*, but not printed in the published magazine.

white kids do better than the black kids. Can't tell you why that is, but they do. Maybe it's their home life, you know. That woman never once saw what she was doing, and I'm not sure the white kids did either. But the black kids did.[1]

Whether or not that particular accusation is true, it is certain that unhelpful stereotypes are hard to fight, and are more powerful when unacknowledged – or created in well-meaning warmth, for then the very kindness is denying the teaching style required.

Individual strength

John Dickinson speaks about 'the prison of the peer group'. It is this 'prison' that John Bazalgette finds is the real prison when pupils say 'school is just like a prison'.[2] Michael Rutter speculates that what effect social mix has is probably mediated via the peer group. On the other hand, many British inner-city teachers have deliberately tried to compensate for the presumed deficiencies of pupils' out-of-school lives by elaborating group work as the major classroom style. I wish to suggest that one of the prime aims in seeking for a teaching style is to find ways of ameliorating the power of the peer group.

It could be said that a prior condition of learning is the willingness to be alone, and the unsuccessful student is frequently one who cannot be alone without being lonely. Many inner-city families make this difficult to achieve, as my analysis in the following section suggests. There are pupils thrown on the peer group, and dependent on it for much of the emotional sustenance and socialization that in easier areas come from interaction with adults. This suggests that peer groups should not dominate in the classroom. When there is individual work, it should indeed be individual, and not the old group working together again. Carefully supervised time should be found in lessons for the quiet activities that require working alone, and which at first will therefore be painful, even torture, to many children: reading, writing, drawing, calculating. The aim will be to help the pupil gain satisfaction from the individual work, and gradually feel able to leave the warmth of the peer group when he or she needs to for individual purposes. Without this, learning is impossible, and an important part of growing up is denied the child.

Supervision

A constant function of any society is to supervise its young, yet the supervisory function of schools is not frequently discussed. Michael Rutter and Paul Widlake agree in their different ways on the need for

---

[1] Thomas L. Cottle, *Black Testimony: Voices of Britain's West Indians* (London: Wildwood House, 1978).

[2] In a talk 'The Pupil, the Tutor and the School', given to an Organization in Schools Courses conference on Pastoral Care, Churchill College, Cambridge, August 1978.

a consistency of supervision approaches in schools. The question that has to be answered is – 'What kind of supervision style is likely to be most effective?'

One starting-point is to note the varieties of parental supervision which pupils have experienced. Careful research on this confirms what informal school observation suggest. Harriett Wilson and G. W. Herbert have looked at 'chaperonage' by parents of inner-city children. They devised a 'chaperonage' index, which measures the parents' supervision. These figures show the likelihood that 'chaperonage exercised when the boys were aged 10–11 affects their behaviour when they are three years older.'[1] The table reproduced below shows the relationship in terms of delinquency at 13.

Figure 10:2   Chaperonage and delinquency: boys aged 13

| | CHAPERONAGE | | | |
	Much	Some	None	Total
Delinquent	1	2	7	10
Non-delinquent	6	12	1	19
Total	7	14	8	29

The authors go on to study the results of variations in 'strictness' and 'permissiveness' in parents. By the time boys are aged 10 to 11 classroom behaviour can be seen to correlate with delinquent behaviour. As the authors say: 'at this age [10 to 11] boys with little guidance or structure in their lives are becoming more prone to signs of stress or antagonism in facing the demands of school.'[2]

Wilson and Herbert found in their analysis of 'achievement, self-reliance, and responsibility' something similar. Of pre-school children they wrote:

The children's experience of independence is a paradoxical combination of independence from their mothers at an age when children are considered too young by most Nottingham families, and restricted movement in situations considered normal by other families.[3]

Many an inner-city teacher would recognize some of their verbatim quotations from mothers:

When anything doesn't go right for him, he shouts and bangs and Father clouts him.

Sometimes he gets like that. I don't know what makes him like it. I shove him out the bloody door, and he gets himself back to normal.

[1] Harriett Wilson and G. W. Herbert, *Parents and Children in the Inner City* (London: Routledge & Kegan Paul, 1978), p. 173.
[2] ibid., p. 179.
[3] ibid., p. 144.

Wilson and Herbert comment:

> It appears that hardly ever is an attempt made to make the child or children understand the issues involved in a conflict and to help them sort these issues out.[1]

In their sub-sample of children of West Indian parents, Rutter and his associates[2] have shown that the strongest correlation between children's misbehaviour in the classroom and any environmental index is with non-communication with fathers. As they say:

> Few associations were found with the quality of the child's relationship with his mother but disorder or deviance in the child was associated with the mother's report that the father rarely or never conversed with the child and with her report that he did not confide in his father.[3]

No doubt these are fathers whose regime would be as 'strict' as many others, but it lacks a relationship. It is like the families of younger children just described in that there is little 'talking through' of difficulties, and little scope for learning the multitude of social signals and the adjustments required by them.

The Rutter team went on to say:

> It was possible only to examine a few of the major variables associated with disorder with the West Indian group. In many respects the facts were similar to those found in studies of non-immigrant families. Thus, children not living with their two natural parents, who had had at least a week in the care of the local authority, whose mothers showed little warmth to their husbands, and whose fathers failed to communicate with them were especially at risk. It seems that disruption and disturbance of family relationships renders the child in a West Indian family more at risk of disorder, just as it does in a non-immigrant family.[4]

It is worth trying to convert these qualified generalizations into pictures of actual families. From my experience, I think of one, for instance, in which PH is a boy among six others, with no father. The family meal is served regularly in the evening, and during that the mother insists on a very strict regime, with no getting up and no calling out. Yet after the meal, the mother goes away from the family room and the children scatter until bedtime, the point about which is not so much that it is rather late as that at that time there is a further strict imposition of a rule. Between the imposition of supper regulations and bedtime regulations, however, there is rarely or never any adult–child contact. This is 'unmoderated control', in which there is no modulation between vigorous rule (reinforced if

---

[1] ibid.

[2] M. Rutter, W. Yule, Michael Berger, Bridget Yule, Janis Morton and Christopher Bagley, 'Children of West Indian Immigrants – I. Rates of Behavioural Deviance and of Psychiatric Disorder', *Journal of Psychology and Psychiatry*, vol. 15, 1974.

[3] ibid., p. 256.

[4] ibid., p. 260.

necessary by violence) and a non-relationship. Young people from
such families are rarely likely to respond easily to the subtle social
controls (looks, expressions, slight remarks), on which we all depend
to gauge the reactions of others.

From this kind of analysis it is possible to construct a pattern of
school regime that might work. It is likely to have clear and
uncomplex rules of acceptable behaviour, which should be consistently required by all the adults. It is likely to have developed a
graduated series of occasions for freedom. These should grow in
length and extent, but only slowly; for many years there will be a
need for closer 'chaperonage' than might otherwise be expected. For
instance, classes should not be left unsupervised; the contrast
between supervised classes and virtually unsupervised breaks should
be softened; assignments or projects should not be too long,
ambitious, or open-ended, until experience on more modest tasks
has been consolidated. In other words, teachers should seek to avoid
matters getting out of control, with the resultant chaos, for that
replicates the strict alternating with un-chaperoned regime. Further,
the ending of chaos requires abrupt shouts and the imposition of
strict controls, whereas in an already orderly situation, minor signs
can be used to modify behaviour. Among all this must be the
opportunity to talk with adults. This is difficult to manage in large-
group situations without the others misbehaving. Large-group work
directed to considering behaviour and making social controls more
explicit and better understood will be valuable. Residential experience, with its need for social control, will help. Over all there
needs to be a greater 'chaperonage' to give an experience of good
order, and prohibitions need to be as few as possible, but carefully
talked through. It would be good if the school site was as protected
from trouble spots as architecture, fittings and supervision can make
it. These pupils cannot cope with the vacillation between full strict
control and the confused turmoil that so easily builds up in school
buildings or on a school site.

Support

If the schools are to meet the challenge, they require adequate
support. I do not consider that the mechanics of running the
complex institution of a school have been properly considered. For
instance, I consider that for the most economical return on the
investment in teachers and buildings an elaborate clerical back-up is
required. There is a cheap, effective way to send hard-pressed heads
of year/house and heads of departments home from school feeling
they are on top of their jobs – give them more helpers.

We are all conditioned to think of education predominantly in
terms of teachers. Through the years of the bulge we strained to

produce enough 'teachers'; the introduction of comprehensive schools, innovation, and inner-city emigration produced 'teacher turnover'; now we have 'teacher unemployment', and pressures to find ways of keeping teachers in jobs. The unions continue the emphasis. There is not an 'educational' union, only 'teacher unions', and they, quite naturally, stress the position of the teacher. Certainly the teacher is the key figure in schooling, but just as her or his task is to make it easier for her or his pupils to learn, so there must be others whose task is to make it easier for the teacher to teach. My belief is that by undervaluing these others, 'para-professionals', we have in fact undervalued the teacher. Perhaps worse, by under-investing in para-professionals we have wasted part of the massive investment in teachers. The ILEA have been notably ahead of most of the result of the country in realizing this, as is shown by their use of school secretaries (nearer to bursars), housecraft and other subject ancillaries, media resources officers, audio-visual aid assistants, and librarians. Even the Alternative Use of Resources scheme, by which schools are financed, highlights the fact that there are choices in spending to be made – and a school can buy extra ancillaries.

At a time of economic toughness it appears likely that teachers' unions and elected members might well agree to cut ancillaries first. Many people have a tendency to lump all non-teaching staff under the phrase 'office staff'. The British dislike of offices, and the notion that you are not helping children unless you are among them in the classroom, combine to confuse the issue of what exactly is required of a support team to help a teacher help her or his pupils. Part of that requirement is most effectively and economically carried out by staff who are not qualified teachers and who are not paid as much.

Let us take a few widely accepted education policies and assess the demands they make on the system: education for the whole community – community relations need a receptionist, clerical facilities and time for communication; close relationships with parents – means letters, phone calls, filing and a receptionist; individual care of pupils – needs records and filing; consultation with governors, parents, staff and pupils – requires discussion papers, minutes and preparation for meetings. Individualized teaching needs worksheets and special planning; curricular scrutiny needs meetings, discussion papers, questionnaires and syllabuses; the range of learning resources means selecting, ordering, storing, issuing, checking and maintaining – all clerical tasks which are often badly done by teachers. Add to those the recent Health and Safety, Employment, Racial Discrimination, and Equal Opportunities legislation, which all contrive to make administration more complicated, and the burden on a school's staff becomes immense. Yet, in spite of the fact that reports from committees at all levels urge schools into additional activities, only the Bullock report made a convincing attempt to look at the logistics of the ideas in terms of non-teaching support.

I see the crucial failure of curriculum planning in schools in our decentralized system as a direct result of our emphasis on teachers in a total educational system. Since our British system throws the major burden of planning onto the schools themselves, it would seem sensible to facilitate that planning, partly by refocusing the role of the Schools Council and HM Inspectorate so that they assist institutional decision-making, and partly by giving better training for this aspect of senior- and middle-management roles. But an important part simply means looking at the servicing needs of teachers. School-based planning rests on proper, and properly used, clerical and other ancillary staff. Otherwise teachers waste time and energy making a bad job of work better done by others.

Take, for example, pastoral care. Its highest ideals are dependent on mundane paperwork and basic communications. In London we have special reasons for extremely efficient pastoral care because of the high number of problem families and the tripartite split of Education, Area Health, and Social Services. Such care requires a partnership between teaching and clerical staff; it requires efficient records, appointment-making, collection of information and first-rate filing. I would hazard that, quite apart from a school's general administrative needs, one full-time secretarial, clerical helper to every 300 pupils, plus a full-time receptionist, is needed for a properly organized system of pastoral care.

There is a prevalent notion that the younger the child, the less ancillary help is required. Further education colleges are much better off than schools. I have compared the teaching staff at an FE college in London with that of Woodberry Down Comprehensive School. Woodberry Down has 85 full-time teachers to 1300 pupils; a similar ratio to that of the college with 170 full-time teaching staff to 2500 students. But the non-educational needs of students at the FE college are met by one administrative officer, five executives, twenty-five clerical staff, a machine operator, and typists. Woodberry Down has one executive, two clerical staff, plus thirty-seven and a half hours clerical and thirty hours general assistant a week in term-time only. Obviously the needs are not precisely comparable. Part-time students involve more clerical work, particularly at enrolment time when special overtime arrangements are made, but FE students are not traditionally offered as much pastoral attention.

The load thrown onto office staff in schools in verging on the impossible. Here is the job specification for a small London secondary school:

The secretary is responsible for organizing and running a busy office with the help of two part-time staff, one working 25 hours weekly and the other twelve hours weekly. He/she must work in close liaison with the head-mistress at all times. An understanding of pupils and their problems is needed and the secretary must be able to deal with difficult situations tactfully and effectively.

The school office handles admission procedures, medical inspection arrangements, internal reports, the maintenance of pupils' records and the checking of attendance records as well as statistical work; in liaison with the Media Resources Officer, the office also produces a considerable volume of informative work.

The school secretary is also accounting officer, responsible for the disbursement account, banking of monies, collection and banking dinner money and keeping of school meals accounts and records, school journey funds, payment and accounting for weekly wages of non-teaching staff.

Although a real job, this reads like a parody of an April Fool's issue of a staffing circular!

Such a situation would not be tolerated in cash-conscious industries like publishing, where one finds that value for money is insisted upon: that means supporting the highly paid with numerous, suitable ancillaries. In education heads of year or house are paid between £6000 and £7000 a year, and yet often have to two-finger type their own letters. Their job satisfaction is low because they cannot properly handle the paperwork even for urgent cases. There is a need for perhaps LEAs and the Schools Council to carry out some form of O and M research into the ancillary staff requirements in schools.

I find the problem similar to that of a GP who said in a letter to the *British Medical Journal*: 'There is no recognition of the secretarial work in keeping the records straight.' In spite of his difficulties he remained a GP, but decided to invest in four full-time staff – a relatively high number for his single-handed practice – and built a satisfactory professional life around them. He was the doctor, not the secretary and not the filing clerk, and could operate as a professional.

Things are pretty desperate for middle management. You cannot raise their salaries or turn back the tide of inner-city depopulation; nor can you resolve the social and behavioural problems of the huge bulk of inner-city children. However, you can support fully-stretched heads of department and heads of year/house by giving them help – and I do not mean support from central, difficult-to-use, existing facilities. The efficient, economic way to do it is to increase the number of helpers. I freely admit that our profession is bad at using ancillaries, and we need training at the time of promotion to middle management. As the GP who is now working hard, doing a good job and enjoying it, says: 'I'm not saying you become a good GP by having lots of ancillary staff, but there is no way you can be a good doctor without them.' Of course, similar arguments apply to other forms of support – librarians and media resources personnel.

Conclusion

Just as the inner-city child is not different from other children, the inner-city school must not be seen as an entirely different kind of school. However, it does need to be related in organization, pastoral care, curriculum, and teaching style to the special density of inter-locking features of the inner city. Falling rolls, while they produce acute administration problems, do also produce possibilities: if there is planned contraction there is an opportunity for getting the team-work close.

Decisions have to be made coherently at governmental, system, group of schools, school, section of school, class, and individual student levels to ensure that schooling is an experience which is, and is felt to be, part of life by pupils and families. This depends on how best we can increase the number of profitable meetings between teacher and taught and what Michael Rutter calls the availability of ordinary teachers for talks. Such institution 'climates' do not just happen: they are created by the organizational decisions and the leadership style.

A Reading List

Compiled by Eleanor Yates

This is a wide-ranging, though obviously not necessarily complete, list of further reading designed to be valuable for teachers and administrators concerned with inner-city education. It includes references cited in footnotes only if the book as a whole is judged to be worth recommending to readers of this volume.

Bantock, G. H., *Culture, Industrialization and Education*. London: Routledge & Kegan Paul, 1968; *Education in an Industrial Society*. London: Faber, 1973.

Barnes, J. and Raynor, J., *The Urban Setting*. Open University course, 'Education and the urban environment'. Milton Keynes: Open University, 1978.

Bazalgette, J., *School Life and Work Life: Study of Transition in the Inner City*. London: Hutchinson Educational, 1978.

Bellaby, P., *Sociology of Comprehensive Schooling*. London: Methuen, 1978.

Berg, L., *Risinghill: Death of a Comprehensive School*. Harmondsworth: Penguin Books, 1969.

Birley, D. and Dufton, A., *Equal Chance: Equalities and Inequalities of Educational Opportunity*. London: Routledge & Kegan Paul, 1971.

Birley, D., *Planning and Education*. London: Routledge & Kegan Paul, 1972.

Blackstone, T., *Education and Day Care for Young Children in Need: The American Experience*. London: National Council of Social Service, 1973; *First Schools of the Future*. London: Fabian Society, 1972; (ed.), *Social Policy and Administration in Britain: A Bibliography*. London: Pinter, 1975.

Blishen, E., *Roaring Boys*. Bath: Chivers, 1974.

Boyd, J., *Community Education and Urban Schools*. London: Longman, 1977.

Braithwaite, E. R., *To Sir with Love*. London: Bodley Head, 1959.

Byrne, D. *et al.*, *Poverty of Education: A Study in the Politics of Opportunity*. London: Martin Robertson, 1975.

Byrne, E. M., *Planning and Educational Inequality: A Study of the Rationale of Resource Allocation*. Windsor: NFER Publishing, 1974.

Claydon, L. F., *Renewing Urban Teaching*. Cambridge: Cambridge University Press, 1974; *The Urban School*. London: Allen & Unwin, 1975.

Davies, H., *The Creighton Report: Year in the Life of a Comprehensive*. London: Hamish Hamilton, 1976.

Deakin, N. and Ungerson, C., *Leaving London: Planned Mobility and the Inner City*. London: Heinemann Educational Books, 1977.

Department of Education and Science, *Educational Priority*. Research Project Reports, Vols 1–4. London: HMSO, 1972–75.

Easthope, G., *Community, Hierarchy and Open Education*. London: Routledge & Kegan Paul, 1975.

Edwards, A. D. and Furlong, V. J., *The Language of Teaching*. London: Heinemann Educational Books, 1978.

Eggleston, J., *Ecology of the School*. London: Methuen, 1977.

Eggleston, S. J., *Adolescence and Community: Youth Service in Britain*. London: Edward Arnold, 1976.

Evans, M. and Fleming, A., *Tower Hamlets: An Educational Case Study*. Open University course, 'Education and the urban environment'. Milton Keynes: Open University, 1978.

Field, F. (ed.), *Education and the Urban Crisis*. London: Routledge & Kegan Paul, 1977.

Fink, L. A. and Ducharme, R. A. (eds), *Crisis in Urban Education*. New York: John Wiley, 1975.

Flude, M. and Ahier, J. (eds), *Educability, Schools and Ideology*. London: Croom Helm, 1976.

Fowler, G. and Raggett, P., *Participation and Accountability*. Open University course, 'Education and the urban environment'. Milton Keynes: Open University, 1978.

Francis, H., *Language in Childhood: Form and Function in Language Learning*. London: Elek Books, 1975; *Language in Teaching and Learning*. London: Allen & Unwin, 1978.

Garner, N., *Teaching in the Urban Community School*. London: Ward Lock Educational, 1973.

Gentry, A. *et al.*, *Urban education: The Hope Factor*. Philadelphia: Saunders, 1972.

Giles, K. and Woolfe, R., *Deprivation, Disadvantage and Compensation*. Milton Keynes: Open University, 1977.

Giles, Raymond, *The West Indian Experience in British Schools, Multi-racial Education and Social Disadvantage in London*. London: Heinemann Educational Books, 1977.

Ginsburg, H., *The Myth of the Deprived Child: Poor Children's Intellect and Education*. Englewood Cliffs, N.J.: Prentice-Hall, 1972.

Golby, M. and Fleming, A., *Urban Schooling*. Open University course, 'Education and the urban environment'. Milton Keynes: Open University, 1978.

Grace, G. R., *Teachers, Ideology and Control: Study in Urban Education*. London: Routledge & Kegan Paul, 1978; *Role Conflict and the Teacher*. London: Routledge & Kegan Paul, 1972.

Hall, S. and Jefferson, T. (eds), *Resistance Through Rituals. Youth Subcultures in Post-war Britain*. London: Hutchinson Educational, 1976.

Hamnet, C. and Braham, P. *Inequality in the City*. Open University course, 'Education and the urban environment'. Milton Keynes: Open University, 1978.

Harris, E. and Vaudin, S., Open University course, 'Urban education', Folder 2: *Urban Childhood*. Milton Keynes: Open University, 1974.

Harrison, B., *Education, Training and the Urban Ghetto*. Baltimore: Johns Hopkins University Press, 1973.

Heidenreich, R., *Urban Education*. Clifton, Virginia: College Readings, 1972.

Herndon, J., *The Way It's Spozed to Be. A Year in the Ghetto School*. London: Pitman, 1974.

Hummel, R. C. and Nagle, J. M., *Urban Education in America: Problems and Prospects*. New York: Oxford University Press, 1973.

Hymes, D. (ed.), *Language in Culture and Society*. New York: Harper & Row, 1964.

Janowitz, M., *Institution Building in Urban Education*. Chicago: University of Chicago Press, 1972.

Jencks, C., Smith, M., Acland, H., Bane, M. J., Cohen, D., Gintis, H., Heyns, B. and Michelson, S., *Inequality: A Reassessment of the Effects of Family and Schooling in America*. New York: Basic Books, 1972; Harmondsworth: Penguin Books, 1975.

Jenkins, D. and Raggatt, P., *Alternatives for Urban Schools*. Open University course, 'Urban education'. Milton Keynes: Open University, 1974.

Keddie, N. (ed.), *Tinker, Tailor: The Myth of Cultural Deprivation*. Harmondsworth: Penguin Books, 1975.

King, E. J., *Education and Social Change*. Oxford: Pergamon, 1966.

Kogan, M., *Educational Policy Making: A Study of Interest Groups and Parliament*. London: Allen & Unwin, 1975; *The Politics of Educational Change*. London: Fontana, 1978.

Kogan, M. and Packwood, T., *The Advisory Councils and Committees in Education*. London: Routledge & Kegan Paul, 1974.

Kogan, M. and Pope, M., *Challenge of Change*. Windsor: NFER Publishing, 1973.

Labov, W., *Language in the Inner City: Studies in the Black English Vernacular*. Philadelphia: University of Pennsylvania Press, 1973; *Social Stratification of English in New York City*. Arlington, Virginia: Centre for Applied Linguistics, 1966.

Leinwand, G. (ed.), *Governing the City*. New York: Pocket Books, 1971.

Lightfoot, A., *Urban Education in Social Perspective*. Chicago: Rand McNally, 1978.

Lowenstein, L. F., *Violence in Schools and its Treatment*. Hemel Hempstead: National Association of Schoolmasters, 1972.

Lutz, F. W. (ed.), *Toward Improved Urban Education*. Belmont: Jones, 1970.

Marcus, S. and Vairo, P. D., *Urban Education: Crisis or Opportunity*. Metuchen, N.J.: Scarecrow Press, 1972.

Marland, M., *The Craft of the Classroom: A Survival Guide*. London: Heinemann Educational Books, 1975; *Head of Department*. London: Heinemann Educational Books, 1971; *Language Across the Curriculum*. London: Heinemann Educational Books, 1977; *Pastoral Care: Organizing the Care and Guidance of the Individual Pupil in a Comprehensive School*. London: Heinemann Educational Books, 1974.

Mays, J. B., *Education and the Urban Child*. Liverpool: Liverpool University Press, 1962.

Moss, M. H., *Deprivation and Disadvantage?* Open University course, 'Language and learning'. Milton Keynes: Open University, 1973.

National Commission on the Reform of Secondary Education, *The Reform of Secondary Education*. New York and London: McGraw-Hill, 1973.

Newson, J. and Newson, E., *Four Years Old in an Urban Community*. Harmondsworth: Penguin Books, 1970; *Patterns of Infant Care in an Urban Community*. Harmondsworth: Penguin Books, 1971; *Perspectives on*

School at Seven Years Old. London: Allen & Unwin, 1977; *Seven Years Old in the Home Environment*. London: Allen & Unwin, 1976.

Oates, J., *People in Cities: An Ecological Approach*. Open University course, 'Urban education'. Milton Keynes: Open University, 1974.

Ogbu, J., *Next Generation: An Ethnography of Education in an Urban Neighbourhood*. New York: Academic Press, 1973.

Passow, A. H. (ed.), *Urban Education in the 1970s: Reflections and a Look Ahead*. New York: Teachers College Press, 1971.

Raggatt, P. C. M. (ed.), *Education in the Cities of England*. London: Sage Publications, 1974.

Raggatt, P. C. M. and Evans, M., *Urban Education*, Vol. 3. The Political Context. London: Ward Lock Educational, 1977.

Raggatt, P. C. M., Byrne, D., Fletcher, B., Williamson, B. and Zeldin, D., *Whose School?* Open University course, 'Urban education'. Milton Keynes: Open University, 1974.

Raynor, J., *Issues in Urban Education*. Open University course, 'Urban education'. Milton Keynes: Open University, 1974.

Raynor, J., and Harden, J., *Readings in Urban Education*, Vol. 1. Cities, Communities and the Young. London: Routledge & Kegan Paul, 1973; *Readings in Urban Education*, Vol. 2. Equality and City Schools. London: Routledge & Kegan Paul, 1973.

Raynor, J., Harden, J., Harris, E., Craft, M., Byrne, D., Williamson, B. and Fletcher, B., *Urban Context*. Open University course, 'Urban education'. Milton Keynes: Open University, 1974.

Raynor, J. and Harris, E. (eds), *Urban Education*, Vol. 1. The City Experience. London: Ward Lock Educational, 1977; *Urban Education*, Vol. 2. Schooling in the City. London: Ward Lock Educational, 1977.

Reeder, D. A. (ed.), *Urban Education in the Nineteenth Century*. London: Taylor & Francis, 1977.

Robins, D. and Cohen, P., *Knuckle Sandwich: Growing Up in the Working-class City*. Harmondsworth: Penguin Books, 1978.

Robinson, M., *Schools and Social Work*. London: Routledge & Kegan Paul, 1978.

Robinson, P., *Education and Poverty*. London: Methuen, 1976.

Ruffin, S. C. Jr, *Urban Education as Practitioners View it*. Reston, Virginia: National Association of Secondary School Principals, 1976.

Rutter, M., *Helping Troubled Children*. Harmondsworth: Penguin Books, 1975.

Rutter, M. and Madge, N., *Cycles of Disadvantage*. London: Heinemann Educational Books, 1976,

Rutter, M., Maughan, B., Mortimore, P., Ouston, J. and Smith, A. *Fifteen Thousand Hours: Secondary Schools and their Effects on Children*. London: Open Books, 1979.

Sanches, M. and Blount, B. (eds), *Sociocultural Dimensions of Language Change*. New York: Academic Press, 1977; *Sociocultural Dimensions of Language Use*. New York: Academic Press, 1975.

Schools Council, *'Cross'd with Adversity': The Education of Socially Disadvantaged Children in Secondary Schools*. Schools Council Working Paper 27. London: Evans/Methuen Educational, 1970.

Sharp, R. and Green, A., *Education and Social Control: A Study of Progressive Primary Education*. London: Routledge & Kegan Paul, 1975.

Shipman, M. D., *Childhood: A Sociological Perspective*. Windsor: NFER Publishing, 1972; *Limitations of Social Research*. London: Longman, 1973;

Organization and Impact of Social Research: Six Original Case Studies in Education and Behavioural Research. London: Routledge & Kegan Paul, 1976; *The Sociology of the School.* London: Longman, 1975.

Shipman, M. D. *et al., Inside a Curriculum Project: A Case Study in the Process of Curriculum Change.* London: Methuen Educational, 1974.

Silberman, C. E., *Crisis in the Classroom.* New York: Random House, 1971.

Smith, G., Gray, J. and Barnes, J., *Policy and Priority.* Open University course, 'Education and the urban environment'. Milton Keynes: Open University, 1978.

Smith, M., *Urban Education: The Black Child and You.* Morristown, N.J.: General Learning Press, 1976.

Snow, C. E. and Ferguson, C. A. (eds), *Talking to Children: Language Input and Acquisition.* Cambridge: Cambridge University Press, 1977.

Street-Porter, R., *Race, Children and Cities.* Open Univeristy course, 'Education and the urban environment'. Milton Keynes: Open University, 1978.

Stubbs, M., *Language, Schools and Classrooms.* London: Methuen, 1976.

Sumner, R., *Looking at School Achievement.* Windsor: NFER Publishing, 1974; *Monitoring National Standards of Attainment in Schools.* Windsor: NFER Publishing, 1977.

Sumner, R. and Bradley, K., *Assessment for Transition.* Windsor: NFER Publishing, 1977.

Sumner, R. and Warburton, F. W., *Achievement in Secondary School: Attitudes, Personality and School Success.* Windsor: NFER Publishing, 1972.

Thornbury, R., *The Changing Urban School.* London: Methuen, 1978.

Tyack, D. B., *The One Best System: A History of American Urban Education.* Cambridge, Mass.: Harvard University Press, 1974.

Tyler, W., *Sociology of Educational Inequality.* London: Methuen, 1977.

Waterson, N. and Snow, C. E., *Development of Communication.* New York: Wiley, 1978.

West, D. J. and Farrington, D. P., *Who Becomes Delinquent?* Cambridge Studies in Criminology. London: Heinemann Educational Books, 1973.

Whiteside, T., *Sociology of Educational Innovation.* London: Methuen, 1978.

Widlake, P., *Successful Teaching in the Urban School.* London: Ward Lock, 1976.

Widlake, P. (ed.), *Remedial Education: Programmes and Progress.* London: Longman, 1977.

Wilson, H. and Herbert, G. W., *Parents and Children in the Inner City.* London: Routledge & Kegan Paul, 1978.

Wright, B. A., *Urban Education Studies,* 8 vols, and teacher's guides. New York: John Day, 1967.

Zeldin, D., *Education in Urban Communities.* Open University course, 'Urban education'. Milton Keynes: Open University, 1974.

The Contributors

TESSA BLACKSTONE

Taught in the Department of Social Administration at the London School of Economics for twelve years. Was a Fellow of the Centre for Studies in Social Policy in London between 1972 and 1974. From 1975 to 1978 she was an adviser in the Central Policy Review Staff, Cabinet Office. She is now Professor of Educational Administration at the Institute of Education, London. Tessa Blackstone has done research in various educational areas, including pre-school education and the universities. She is the author of *A Fair Start* and *Education and Day Care for Young Children in Need: the American Experience*.

NICHOLAS DEAKIN

Began his working life as a civil servant, working in the Home Office (where he spent some time in the Children's Department). He subsequently left Whitehall to work as Assistant Director of the Survey of Race Relations in Britain – a five-year study of race relations funded by the Nuffield Foundation. He was co-author, with Jim Rose, of the final report of the Survey, *Colour and Citizenship*.

After teaching and research at the University of Sussex, he joined the Greater London Council at the end of 1971 as Head of Social Studies in the Planning and Transportation Department, with responsibility for studies on housing policy, deprivation, and leisure and recreation. Since 1977 he has been Assistant head of the Policy Studies and Intelligence Branch, Director General's Department, and represents the Greater London Council at officer level on a number of the inner-city Partnerships recently established by the Department of the Environment. He is the author of *Leaving London*.

MAURICE KOGAN

Is Professor of Government and Social Administration at Brunel University. After some years in the Department of Education and Science, where his work included acting as Secretary to the Plowden Committee on Primary Education, he joined Brunel University as Director of the Hospital Organization Research Unit. Since then he has concentrated on the government and policies of the welfare state with particular concentration on education, health and social services.

His work outside Brunel has included membership of the Social Science Research Council, of the University Grants Committee Sub-committee on Education, the Davies Committee on Hospital Complaints Procedure and the Houghton Committee on Teachers' Pay. He was one of the specialist advisers to the Parliamentary Sub-committee that studied policy-making in the Department of Education and Science.

His research studies have included acting as a Statutory Assessor to the Race Relations Board on the Ealing bussing issue, and a study of decision-making in the National Health Service undertaken on behalf of the Royal Commission. He is currently engaged in directing a project on the roles of schools, parents, and social services and a follow-up project on disaffected pupils. He is also studying the role of research management in the Department of Health and Social Security.

Maurice Kogan's publications include *The Organization of a Social Services Department*, *The Politics of Education*, *The Government of Education*, *County Hall*, *Challenge of Change*, *Advisory Councils and Committees in Education*, *Educational Policy Making* and *The Politics of Educational Change*.

MICHAEL MARLAND

Read English and History at Cambridge. After appointments as Head of English Department, and then Director of Studies, in other comprehensive schools, he was Headmaster of Woodberry Down School from 1971 until 1979. He is now Headmaster of North Westminster Area Community School. He was a member of the Bullock Committee on the Teaching of Reading and Uses of English, and is currently Chairman of the Schools Council's English Committee, and of the National Book League's Use of Books in Schools Working Party. He is a frequent lecturer and broadcaster.

He is general editor of the Heinemann Organization in Schools Series, and Longman Imprint Books. He has published a large number of books for teachers (including *Pastoral Care* and *Head of Department*). Recent publications include: *The Craft of the Classroom*, and a guide for young teachers; *The Pressure of Life*, an anthology of television plays for class reading; *The Minority Experience*, an anthology. He is a member of the National Book League Executive. In 1977 Michael Marland was made a CBE.

DAVID QUINTON

Is a lecturer in the Department of Child and Adolescent Psychiatry at the Institute of Psychiatry, London. He read social anthropology at Cambridge and then, as a Commonwealth Scholar, at the University of Ibadan, Nigeria. Since 1964 he has worked at the Institute of Psychiatry with Professor Rutter and others on a number of epidemiological studies concerned with the family and social factors associated with the development of children's problems. He has been particularly concerned with the development of techniques of family interviewing and is currently advising a number of projects in Britain and Europe on these.

A major focus of his research has been concerned with area differences in the rates of child disorders, and the relationship between these and family patterns and environmental circumstances. He is currently editing a book with Professor Rutter on a comparative study of an Inner London Borough and the Isle of Wight, data from which has been published in several scientific papers. His current research is concerned with the present circumstances and parenting skills of young adults who spent part of their childhood in care.

MICHAEL RUTTER

Is Professor of Child Psychiatry at the University of London, and Honorary Consultant Psychiatrist in the Children's Department of the Maudsley Hospital. He was previously a member of the scientific staff of the Medical Research Council Social Psychiatry Unit. He has undertaken teaching both in this country and abroad, particularly in the USA. He is currently Visiting Professor in the Department of Psychology, University of Surrey, and is the Rock Carling Fellow of the Nuffield Provincial Hospitals Trust for 1979. He is the author of a number of books including *Helping Troubled Children*; he is co-author of *Cycles of Disadvantage*, and *Fifteen Thousand Hours*, and co-editor of *Child Psychiatry: Modern Approaches*. His many research interests include protective factors in children's response to stress, schools as social institutions, and ecological influence on development.

MARTEN SHIPMAN

Studied at the London School of Economics after working in industry and serving in the Royal Navy and the Police.

After professional training he taught in a London secondary modern school. From 1961 to 1969 he lectured at Worcester College of Education, becoming principal lecturer and Head of the Sociology Department. From 1969 to 1972 he was senior lecturer in Education at the University of Keele. Until 1978 he was Director of Research and Statistics for the Inner London Education Authority. He is now Professor of Education at the University of Warwick. Dr Shipman is also Visiting Professor of Sociology in the University of Surrey. He is the author of books and articles on sociology, education and social research methods, including *In-School Evaluation*.

PAT WHITE

Read geography at Cambridge (Girton). Graduate entrant to the London County Council as an Administrative Officer. Entered LCC Youth Employment Service (later to become the Inner London Education Authority Careers Service) in 1961. Worked throughout South London; her particular specialities were the less able, the handicapped, ethnic minorities, and the disadvantaged generally.

Pat White has had two periods out of the Careers Service: eighteen months secondment to the Greater London Council research unit to work on a survey of handicapped young workers through the ILEA, and six months in Nigeria working basically for the IMF on a transport and communications validity study. Pat White is now Senior Careers Officer for the ILEA.

PAUL WIDLAKE

Took a degree in English and History and a PGCE at the University of Wales, and taught in schools in South Wales, Warwickshire and Walsall before becoming Head of the Remedial Service, and lately Inspector for Special Education, at Wolverhampton. His postgraduate studies have included a Diploma in the Psychology of Childhood and a Master of Education degree at Birmingham University. He was research officer to the Birmingham Educational Priority Area project and contributed to the Halsey Report (1972).

He was joint author (with Professor Ronald Guilliford) of a report for the Schools Council project, Teaching Materials for Disadvantaged Pupils. Since then he has been Head of the Centre for Studies in Educational Handicap at Didsbury School of Education, Manchester Polytechnic, where he is in charge, inter alia, of in-service courses on educational handicap. He has published six books and numerous articles and papers on aspects of learning and disadvantage; most recently *Successful Teaching in the Urban School* and *The Education of the Socially Handicapped Child*.

Index

Brunel University, 149–50
Bullock Report (*A Language for Life*),
   169, 191, 192, 199, 208
bureaucracy, 198–9
Burnham Committee, 84

Calcutta, 113–15, 123
Callaghan, James, 108
Caloustie Gulbenkian Foundation,
   45
Cambridgeshire village colleges,
   158, 185
'Camembert colonialists', 33
careers: education, 21, 107–108;
   guidance, 26, 151; officers, 100;
   service, 18
Central Policy Review Staff, 23
Centre for Studies in Educational
   Handicap (CSEH), 112, 115, 116,
   123, 124
chaperonage, 205, 207
Chicago, 2, 11–12, 13, 164n, 170,
   203
child-centred education, 79, 80
child development, 80, 133
child guidance clinics, 154, 155, 157,
   158
children in care, 48, 51, 53, 55
city, earlier views of the, 11–12
class size, 23, 126, 136
classroom management, 144
Clegg, A., 139–40, 143
Cleveland, 4, 166
Clydeside, 15
Cockcroft, David, 101
cognitive skills, 76, 77
Coleman, Alice, 35, 40
Coleman, James, 127, 128
Community Development Projects
   (CDPs), 16, 17, 37, 86
Community Industry Scheme, 16
community participation in education, 25–6; *see also* family school
community school, 26, 158–9, 185–
   6, 208
community of schools, 7, 169, 171,
   194
compensatory education, 126, 127,
   177
comprehensive community programmes (CCPs), 16

comprehensive education, 73,
   165–6, 183–4
Compulsory Miseducation (Goodman),
   125
conflict in schools, 122–3, 124
continuity, 164, 170–1, 172, 174,
   175, 180, 194–5, 201
control of education, 167–70
Cook Taylor, 45
Craft of the Classroom, The (Marland),
   140
crime, 3–4, 32, 45, 47, 53, 62, 63
Crisis in the Classroom (Silberman), 126
curriculum: class-culture conflict in,
   189–91; core, 100, *see also* basic
   skills; credibility, 188–9; diluted,
   72–3, 80–1, 91; fallacies about,
   188–92; innovation, 72, 73, 74,
   79, 80–1, 87; planning, 143, 150–
   1, 164, 168–9, 170–1, 175, 183,
   188, 192–4, 208, 209; related to
   locality, 196–8; relevant, 189–90;
   variety of, 111
'Curriculum for inequality' (Shipman), 72

Daunt, Pat, 165, 189
Deakin, Nicholas, 2, 4, 196
Death at an Early Age (Kozol), 126
delinquency, 45, 46, 53, 128–9, 132,
   134, 137, 139–40, 194, 205
Denmark, 122
Department of Education and
   Science, 18, 20, 123, 193
Department of Employment, 16
Department of the Environment, 13,
   16, 17, 19, 20, 39
Department of Health and Social
   Security, 20, 157, 178
deprivation, 15, 22, 52, 126–7
Deptford Home Visiting Project,
   178
Dickinson, John, 204
Didsbury, 112, 115, 123, 124
disadvantage, 46, 47–8, 51, 61–4,
   83–4, 98–9, 136, 145–6; cycle of,
   48
discipline, 72, 73, 79, 82, 88, 89, 91,
   119, 122, 134, 139, 140, 144–5,
   150, 151, 164, 182

discrimination, positive, 15, 21, 69–
92; *see also* educational priority
areas
disturbed children, 2, 61–4, 200
Docklands, 17
Donnison, David, 44
Douglas, M., 18
drugs, 3
Dunn, Lloyd, 77n

East Anglia, 22
Eating the Indian Air (Morris), 113
economy, national, 20, 41, 85, 88,
96, 98, 102–103, 127, 208
education finance, 18, 69, 70, 82–3,
135–6, 166–7; *see also* resource
allocation
education welfare officer (EWO),
151, 154–5, 177
education welfare service, 154–5,
178
educational home visitors, 178
educational priority areas, 15, 21,
53, 70, 77, 83, 84, 86, 126
Eggleston, John, 184
elderly, 19, 30, 32, 36, 43, 44, 105,
197
employee, 103
employers, 71, 88, 97, 100, 103, 108
employment, 18, 20, 21, 29, 30, 31,
32, 34, 39, 42, 43, 44, 47, 87, 90,
95–109, 129, 151, 157–8, 159, 195,
199, 208
Employment Protection Act, 83, 85
Employment Services Agency, 18
Engelmann, S., 76, 77, 79
English, 72, 169, 174
environment, 17, 18, 19, 20, 31, 32,
33, 39, 52, 59–61, 91, 98, 158, 159
equality in education, 70–1, 73, 127,
165
ethnic minorities, 14–15, 21, 27, 33,
36, 37, 43, 44, 47, 72, 79, 99, 197;
see also black children, West Indians
Europe, 46
European Economic Community,
109
evaluation, 85, 89, 90
Evanston High School, 164n
Evertson, C. M., 140

examinations, 73, 75, 129, 130–1,
132, 134, 139, 141, 143, 172–3,
183, 184, 189
extracurricular activities, 118–19,
121

failure, 137, 139
family: life, 45–67, 158, 206; pre-
school influence of, 133; problems, 51, 58, 61, 64, 65, 66–7, 206;
school, 185–8; –school relationship, 186, 187; size, 45, 47, 48, 52,
53, 57, 61, 62, 63, 67, 84; *see also*
parents
federal schools, 170, 174, 176
*Fifteen Thousand Hours: Secondary
Schools and their Effects on Children*
(Rutter *et al.*), 188
Financial Times, 39
Florida, 191
Follow Through, 74, 76, 77, 79
formal/informal teaching methods,
78–9, 80
Forster, E. M., 166
fourteen-plus break, 174, 175, 176
free schools, 25
Freire, R., 126n
further education, 19, 24, 91, 157,
158, 159, 175, 185, 209

Gans, Herbert J., 6
Gardner, K., 201
Garth, Dennis, 129
Gateshead, 16, 17
geography, 73
Giles, R., 91
Glasgow, 13, 19, 69, 115
Goodman, Paul, 125n, 189
government, inner-city policy, 15–
16, 17–20, 33, 37–41, 70, 84,
88–9; expenditure, 16, 17, 18, 33;
see also educational finance, re-
source allocation
Grace, G., 88, 91, 111
grammar schools, 5, 172
Gray, Grace, 129
Gray, J., 87
Greater London Council, 39, 97
Green, A., 112
Green Belt, 34, 147
Greer, Colin, 5, 6, 182